THE JAPANESE

WRITTEN

WORD

A Unique Reader

Glenn Melchinger and **Helene Kasha**

with a Special Contribution by

Eitetsu Yamaguchi

KODANSHA INTERNATIONAL
Tokyo • New York • London

A NOTE ON ROMANIZATION

In the background material in this book, and in the English translations as well, the romanization of Japanese follows the Hepburn system (with the exception that *n,* rather than *m,* precedes *m, b,* and *p*). Throughout the book, Japanese names are given in the Japanese order, with surname preceding given name.

In the romanized version of the Japanese text, however, another system is used in order to help the student to correlate the two scripts with greater ease and understanding. Below are given the main features of this system.

1. Kanji are romanized in upper case. If the kanji is a compound, the parts of the compound are separated by hyphens in romanization (e.g., 食事 become SHOKU-KI).

2. Hiragana are romanized in lower case (e.g., いま becomes "ima").

3. If a word in Japanese script is a combination of kanji and hiragana (such as 食べる), the romanization is a combination of upper and lower case (e.g., TAberu).

4. Katakana is romanized as lower-case italics (e.g., ニワトリ becomes *niwatori*).

5. Long vowels in the romanized version of the Japanese text follow the Japanese script (e.g., おお = oo; おう = ou); macrons are not used.

6. Kanji with *ateji* (i.e., variant readings supplied by the author in the form of *rubi,* or superior hiragana over the kanji) are italicized. For example, 在宅 is generally read "zaitaku," but Shiga Naoya gives the character a variant reading—在宅. This kanji compound appears in the romanization as *UCHI.*

7. When the Japanese script has superior dots (e.g., うわあ), which are used for emphasis, the romanization makes use of underlining (e.g., <u>uwaa</u>).

8. Notwithstanding the above, each romanized sentence begins with a capital letter.

9. When a romanized quotation appears within a sentence, the first word of the quotation is in lower case.

10. When sentences in the Japanese script do not end in a period, which often happens with quotations, the romanized version also does not end in a period.

11. "San," as in "Suzuki-san," is preceded by a hyphen.

12. Also note that the *rubi* in the Japanese texts (that is, the hiragana that appears over kanji and indicates readings) appears here as it appeared in the originals.

Distributed in the United States by Kodansha America, Inc., 114 Fifth Avenue, New York, N.Y. 10011, and in the United Kingdom and continental Europe by Kodansha Europe Ltd., 95 Aldwych, London WC2B 4JF. Published by Kodansha International Ltd., 17-14 Otowa 1-chome, Bunkyo-ku, Tokyo 112-8652, and Kodansha America, Inc.

Copyright © 1998 by Helene Kasha
All rights reserved. Printed in Japan
First edition, 1998
98 99 00 10 9 8 7 6 5 4 3 2 1
ISBN 4-7700-2126-7

The IN-FOLIO layered technique is protected by U.S. Patent No. 4,734,036

CIP Data Available

Contents

Preface

*T*he Japanese Written Word: A Unique Reader is a sampler and not a literary anthol-
ogy. Its aim is primarily to present original Japanese texts that are accessible to
the student of the Japanese language and to offer some insight into several facets
of Japanese culture, as seen through literary and other texts. A more ambitious aim of the
The Japanese Written Word is to encourage the student to do additional reading and further research on various topics, which we hope to assist by occasionally citing books and
authors in the "background" sections. We took care not to be dogmatic concerning the
background information and cultural notes, for we live, after all, in a rapidly changing
world. Indeed, students might ask themselves how the shopping patterns or the ecological
situation has evolved since the year this book was published.

We have included a conversation between the internationally known conductor Ozawa
Seiji and the famous mathematician Hironaka Heisuke. Also included are portions of
Honda Sōichirō's personal remarks on his management philosophy. The ecology unit dis-
cusses Japanese concerns and attempts to alleviate certain problems, which, in the end, are
not unlike those encountered in other industrialized nations.

The literary pieces were selected from the early modern period as well as from contemporary writings. In the latter we have included examples of the light genre favored by
today's younger generation. No such sampler would be complete without the inclusion of
an A-bomb literary piece and poem. This immense tragedy is deeply rooted in the Japanese subconscious, even though today's forward-looking younger generation may not be
fully aware of it. We have also included a unit on poems with much background information.

How to present such disparate material was somewhat of a challenge, which was over-
come by grouping related topics into pairs or juxtaposing them for comparison.

As to the language-pedagogical aspects, several support levels are included. One level
is provided by the "Phrases and Usage" notes, which assist the student in gaining a better
understanding of the language and its mechanics. Another level consists of exercises on
content, idiomatic expressions, and other matters in multiple-choice form, challenging the
student to learn the Japanese language in greater depth.

As a departure from the typical reader, we are using the IN-FOLIO layered system (U.S. Patent No 4,734,036), which allows the student to read and comprehend a full page of Japanese text with the discrete help of the romanization and literal translation that are available on separate pages in same-line registry. The IN-FOLIO system encourages self-study and allows the student to better locate a kanji through its same-registry romanization.

It should be pointed out that the literal translations are meant to serve as a tool for the comprehension of the Japanese texts and not as their literary equivalents.

I take this opportunity to thank Prof. Miryam Sas of U. C. Berkeley for her guidance and encouragement. I also would like to thank Masaaki Kinugasa for his help in the poetry section; Karen Thornber for sharing her knowledge on Tōge Sankichi; Dr. Timothy S. George presently at the Edwin O. Reischauer Institute for his contribution to the background information on ecology; and Prof. Graham Parkes for contributing the early Buddhist period item. I also would like to thank Ted Mack and especially Miho Nonaka for the research work each has provided.

And mostly, I would like to express my gratitude to Prof. Eitetsu Yamaguchi of Yale University for formulating the comprehension questions as well as the idiomatic phrase and multiple-choice exercises with each piece, and for providing guidance as to the suitability of the pieces from a language-pedagogical point of view, which is one of the most important components of a reader.

Finally, our team would like to thank Messrs. Michael Brase and Shigeyoshi Suzuki of Kodansha International for their meticulous care during the editing stages and throughout the publishing process.

It is hoped that the richness of the content and the unique presentation will be helpful to the student for the comprehension of genuine Japanese texts.

Helene Kasha
New Haven, 1998

How to Use This Reader

The IN-FOLIO layered technique (U.S. Patent No. 4,734,036) allows you to read, comprehend, and fully appreciate the original Japanese text, regardless of your level of proficiency. The Japanese, its phonetization, and English translation appear on consecutive odd-numbered pages. First read the Japanese page and then, if necessary, briefly consult the phonetization and/or translation of a word or expression which appears on the following pages in same-line registry, and immediately revert to the Japanese text. In this way, your eyes remain focused on the spot where you left off, enabling a smooth and uninterrupted reading of the original.

The IN-FOLIO layered technique allows instant access to the pronunciation and meaning of kanji and is far less cumbersome than having to leave the text to look up the kanji in another field of vision. The Japanese text continues on odd-numbered pages, past the phonetization and translation pages.

Additional support is provided by "Phrases and Usage," which face the Japanese text. The even-numbered pages contain various types of background information and exercises. The book also contains a number of illustrations that are directly related to the text. In addition to their illustrative value, they can serve as vehicles to stimulate class discussion in Japanese. Note, also, that in order to further challenge the student, a key to the multiple-choice questions has not been provided.

H. K.

To the Student

This reader has been designed to give the ambitious student as many advantages as possible. We assume the student already possesses a certain degree of knowledge, but wherever possible this book is designed to provide as many keys as possible to the unlocking of the many styles of Japanese writing.

My motivation for participating in this project was to do for students of Japanese what one of my teachers did for me when I was fortunate enough to study at Doshisha University in Kyoto. I hoped to save the student from excessive dictionary work, which, while admittedly a necessary skill, robs the student of valuable learning time. Thus, redundancy has been built into the format of the text so as to give the student information when and where it is weeded. Nothing would give me greater pleasure than having this reader be profitably used by those seeking to speed up their language acquisition.

The translations herein are literal. Some will seem awkward. The goal of the translation is not to be artful, but to try to reveal the literal meaning of the Japanese, and to be as faithful to the Japanese sentence structure as possible. Where this approach would produce nonsense or inaccurate translations unhelpful to the reader's understanding, a slightly more idiomatic approach has been used. In either case, the student is deliberately left room to improve and play on the rendering of the Japanese into English.

Good luck in your study of Japanese. May it bring you all the rewards it has brought me.

Glenn T. Melchinger
Honolulu, 1998

語句と語法: Phrases and Usage

- 暗夜・あんや: (literary) a dark night
- 行路・こうろ: a path; a passage; a passing
- 序詞・じょし: a prologue
- 主人公・しゅじんこう: the main character; protagonist
- 追憶・ついおく: recollection; memories
- 自分に・じぶんに: (exists to) oneself [に with ある indicates a certain state exists in regard to someone; here, の＝が]
- 祖父・そふ: grandfather
- 母・はは: mother
- 産後・さんご: after birth; postpartum
- 病気・びょうき: sickness; illness
- 死ぬ・しぬ: to die [cf. なくなる, a polite euphemism, like "pass away" in English]
- 二月・ふたつき: two months
- 不意に・ふいに: unexpectedly; suddenly; abruptly
- 現われる・あらわれる: to appear; turn up
- 時・とき: time
- ある・或る: a certain; one (evening)
- 夕方・ゆうがた: evening; dusk
- 門・もん: gate [most older style, traditional houses have gates]
- 遊ぶ・あそぶ: to play
- 見知らぬ・みしらぬ: unknown (by sight) [ぬ＝ない]
- 老人・ろうじん: an old man (person)
- 立つ・たつ: to stand
- 目の落ち窪んだ・めのおちくぼんだ: with sunken eyes [in this modifying phrase の works like が, as a subject marker; 落ち窪む・おちくぼむ: sink in; cave in]
- 猫背・ねこぜ: stoop; stoop-shouldered
- 何(なん)となく: somehow; in some undefinable way [cf. どことなく]
- 見すぼらしい・みすぼらしい: shabby; seedy looking
- 何(なん)ということなく: here, "for no particular reason," "for some unknown reason"
- 反感・はんかん: antipathy; ill feeling
- 笑顔・えがお: a smiling face
- 作る・つくる: to make; construct
- 話しかける・はなしかける: to start/begin to talk to someone; strike up a conversation
- (volitional verb form) 〜うとする: to try to do 〜; make an effort to 〜
- 一種・いっしゅ: a kind of; a type of
- 悪意・あくい: malicious intent; ill will
- はぐらかす: to give the slip; dodge (a question)
- 下(した)を向く(むく): to face downwards
- 釣上る・つりあがる: to be pulled up; slant upwards
- 口元・くちもと: corners of the mouth
- 囲む・かこむ: to enclose; surround; encircle
- 深い・ふかい: deep
- 皺・しわ: wrinkles (in skin, cloth)
- 変に・へんに: strangely
- 下品・げひん: low class; vulgar
- 印象・いんしょう: an impression
- 受ける・うける: to receive; get
- 早く・はやく: quickly [cf. 速く: speedily (of rate/pace)]
- 行く・いく: to go
- 腹・はら: "belly"; in one's heart; in one's mind
- 〜ながら: while (doing 〜)
- なお: (what's) more; further
- 意固地に・いこじに: stubbornly
- なかなか: describes something which doesn't happen easily or quickly; followed by a negative in this sense
- 場・ば: a place
- 〜を立去る・たちさる: to leave a place [を marks the place one leaves]
- 妙に・みょうに: curiously; strangely; oddly
- いたたまらない: to find something unbearable
- 気持・きもち: feeling
- 立上がる・たちあがる: to stand up
- 門内・もんない: inside the gate
- 駆け込む・かけこむ: to run inside (the gate)
- オイオイ: おい ("hey") informal [can be rude; note that here it is used towards a child]
- お前・おまえ: you [informal, or to one younger or of lower or equal status]
- 〜かネ: an informal question; "I wonder if…"
- 背後・うしろ: from behind [usually read はいご]
- 言葉・ことば: words
- 突きのめす・つきのめす: to knock over
- のめす: added to a limited number of other verbs: "to do thoroughly/completely"
- 感じる・かんじる: to feel
- 立止る・たちどまる: to stop in one's tracks
- 振返る・ふりかえる: to look back (over one's shoulder)
- 心では: in my heart; in one's inner thoughts
- 首・くび: "neck" [here, "head"; くびを振る(ふる): to shake one's head (to mean "no")]
- おとなしい・大人しい: gentle; meek
- うなずく・肯く: to nod (in the affirmative)

暗夜行路（抄）

志賀直哉

序詞 （主人公の追憶）

　私が自分に祖父のあることを知ったのは、私の母が産後の病気で死に、その後二月ほど経って、不意に祖父が私の前に現われて来た、その時であった。私の六歳の時であった。

　ある夕方、私は一人、門の前で遊んでいると、見知らぬ老人がそこへ来て立った。目の落ち窪んだ、猫背の何となく見すぼらしい老人だった。私は何ということなくそれに反感を持った。

　老人は笑顔を作って何か私に話しかけようとした。しかし私は一種の悪意から、それをはぐらかして下を向いてしまった。釣上った口元、それを囲んだ深い皺、変に下品な印象を受けた。「早く行け」私は腹でそう思いながら、なお意固地に下を向いていた。

　しかし老人はなかなかその場を立去ろうとはしなかった。私は妙にいたたまらない気持になって来た。私は不意に立上がって門内へ駆け込んだ。その時、

　「オイオイお前は謙作かネ」と老人が背後から言った。

　私はその言葉で突きのめされたように感じた。そして立止った。振返った私は心では用心していたが、首はいつかおとなしくうなずいてしまった。

Shiga Naoya

Shiga Naoya (1883–1971) was born in northern Japan but brought up in Tokyo. He was raised by his grandparents, who held Shiga's parents responsible for the untimely death of the family's oldest son. His family were of former samurai status and wealthy bourgeoisie. In 1900 Shiga met Uchimura Kanzō, a Christian proselytizer. Although he did not convert to Christianity, he was strongly influenced by Kanzō. He became interested in Western art and literature, some elements of which, such as the autobiographical style, can be found in his writings. Shiga's relationship with his father became strained in 1910 when he dropped out of the University of Tokyo. His father disapproved of Shiga's bohemian lifestyle and involvements in social issues, as well as opposing Shiga's desire to marry a housemaid. In 1914 Shiga married Kadenokōji Sadako of aristocratic background, but still against his father's wishes. They had seven children, two of whom died at a young age. It should be noted that Shiga Naoya's mother died when he was twelve.

Shiga began his writing career with short stories in the 1910s. Although he virtually stopped writing in 1937, at the time of his death in 1971 he was considered one of the most important Japanese writers. *Anya Kōro*, Shiga's only full-length novel, and its English version *A Dark Night's Passing*—superbly translated by Edwin McClellan—are still widely read today.

Anya Kōro is part autobiography and part fiction. Shiga's social background is similar to that of Kensaku, the novel's protagonist, but Shiga stems from a relatively stable family, unlike Kensaku's dysfunctional one. Kensaku's grandfather, for example, is the antithesis of Shiga's grandfather, and there are no direct parallels between Naoko, Kensaku's wife, and Shiga's wife, Sadako.

Anya Kōro was written between 1921 and 1937. From 1921 to 1928 it appeared serially in a well-known newspaper and reached completion only after a hiatus of nine years. The novel is considered by many readers to belong to the genre known as "I novel" (*watakushi shōsetsu*), in which the narrator lays bare his every action and inner thought. Shiga's celebrated style has influenced a number of Japanese authors. On the other hand, some critics have criticized *Anya Kōro* for its lack of a plot. Lengthy and seemingly superfluous passages, written perhaps to accommodate the newspaper's daily serialization format, alternate with others that brilliantly describe the inner self, as well as urban, natural, and village landscapes. *The Prologue* is an example of Shiga's fine craftsmanship.

Additional Reading:

    Keene, Donald. *Dawn to the West.* Vol. 2. New York: Holt, Rinehart and Winston, 1984.

    Shiga, Naoya. *A Dark Night's Passing.* Translated by Edwin McClellan. Tokyo, New York, London: Kodansha International, 1976.

AN-YA KOU-RO (SHOU)

SHI-GA NAO-YA

JO-SHI (SHU-JIN-KOU no TSUI-OKU)

WATASHI ga JI-BUN ni SO-FU no aru koto o SHItta no wa, WATASHI no HAHA ga SAN-GO no BYOU-KI de SHIni, sono GO FUTA-TSUKI hodo TAtte, FU-I ni SO-FU ga WATASHI no MAE ni ARAwarete KIta, sono TOKI de atta. WATASHI no MUTTSU no TOKI de atta.

Aru YUU-GATA, WATASHI wa HITO-RI, MON no MAE de ASOnde iru to, MI-SHIranu ROU-JIN ga soko e KIte TAtta. ME no OchiKUBOnda, NEKO-ZE no NAN to naku MIsuborashi-i ROU-JIN datta. WATASHI wa NAN to iu koto naku sore ni HAN-KAN o MOtta.

ROU-JIN wa E-GAO o TSUKUtte NANI ka WATASHI ni HANAshikakeyou to shita. Shikashi WATASHI wa IS-SHU no AKU-I kara, sore o hagurakashite SHITA o MUite shimatta. TSURI-AGA-tta KUCHI-MOTO, sore o KAKOnda FUKAi SHIWA, HEN ni GE-HIN na IN-SHOU o Uketa. "HAYAku Ike" WATASHI wa HARA de sou OMOinagara, nao I-KO-JI ni SHITA o MUite ita.

Shikashi ROU-JIN wa nakanaka sono BA o TACHI-SArou to wa shinakatta. WATASHI wa MYOU ni itatamaranai KI-MOCHI ni natte KIta. WATASHI wa FU-I ni TACHI-Agatte MON-NAI e KAkeKOnda. Sono TOKI,

"*oioi* oMAE wa KEN-SAKU ka *ne*" to ROU-JIN ga *USHIRO* kara Itta.

WATASHI wa sono KOTO-BA de TSUkinomesareta you ni KANjita. Soshite TACHI-DOMAtta. FURI-KAEtta WATASHI wa KOKORO de wa YOU-JIN shite ita ga, KUBI wa itsuka otonashiku una-zuite shimatta.

House with traditional gate; recently a rare sight in the city.

A Dark Night's Passing (An Excerpt)

Shiga Naoya

Prologue (The Hero's Memories)

I learned I had a grandfather at that time, when about two months had passed after
my Mother had died after giving birth, and grandfather unexpectedly appeared before
me. It was when I was six years old.

One evening, when I was alone, playing before our gate, an old man I did not know came
and stood there. He was a somehow shabby old man, with sunken eyes and a stooped back. I,
for no particular reason, held a feeling of antipathy for that.

The old man put on a smiling face and tried to speak to me. But, from a kind of ill will,
I evaded that and looked down. [From] the upwardly slanted corners of his mouth, the deep
wrinkles that surrounded it, I received a strangely vulgar impression. "Get out of here
quickly," I thought in my gut, as I faced downward more stubbornly [trying to ignore him].

But the old man didn't come close to leaving that easily. I began to feel, strangely,
that I couldn't stand it anymore. I stood up abruptly and ran inside the gate.
Just then,

"Hey, hey! Are you Kensaku, I wonder?" the old man called from behind.

I felt as if I had been struck down by those words. And so I stopped.
I was cautious when I looked back but, without thinking my [head]
obediently nodded.

- 在宅・うち: "at home" [usually read ざいたく, which would sound strangely formal here]
- 訊く・きく: to ask
- うわ手(て)・上手: "high handed"; imperious
- 物言い・ものいい: way of speaking
- 圧迫(あっぱく)する: to put pressure on; oppress
- 近寄る・ちかよる: to draw close to; approach near to
- 頭・あたま: head
- 手(て)をやる: to put a hand on; touch
- 解る・わかる: to understand/know [also written 分かる]
- 不思議な・ふしぎな: strange; mysterious
- 本能・ほんのう: instinct
- 近い・ちかい: near; close
- 肉親・にくしん: relative; one of the same blood
- すでに・既に: already; previously
- 息苦しい・いきぐるしい: have difficulty breathing; feel suffocated
- やって来(く)る: to come; approach
- 初めて・はじめて: for the first time
- ～として: as ～ (my grandfather)
- 父・ちち: father
- 紹介(しょうかい)する: to introduce
- さらに・更に: still more; further
- ～ほど: to ～ extent; about
- ～すると: when (about 10 days had) passed/gone by
- 引き取る・ひきとる: to take care of; look after (a child)
- 根岸・ねぎし: a place name
- お行の松・おぎょう の まつ: place name
- 松・まつ: pine
- 横町・よこちょう: a side/back street
- 奥・おく: the depths of
- 小さい・ちいさい: small; tiny
- 古家・ふるいえ: an old house
- ～の他に・のほかに: other than ～
- 周囲・しゅうい: surroundings
- 空気・くうき: air; atmosphere
- 全く・まったく: completely; totally
- 今(いま)まで: up until now
- 変わっている・かわっている: to be changed; be different
- すべて・全て: everything
- 貧乏臭い・びんぼうくさい: to "stink" of poverty; squalid [貧乏 = poor]
- 同胞・きょうだい: brothers; siblings in general (including sisters) [usually read どうほう]
- 皆・みな: everyone
- 自家・うち: one's own house; (usually read じか)
- 残る・のこる: to remain; to stay behind

- 子供(こども)ながらに: even though I was a child (who was too young to make judgments about such things)
- 面白い・おもしろい: amusing; interesting [as here, often used in the negative to express discontent]
- 不公平・ふこうへい: unfair; unjust
- 幼児・ようじ: infant; a small child
- (～ に)慣(な)らされる: to be used/accustomed (to ～)
- 今(いま)にはじ(始)まったこと: something which started (just) now
- なぜかを…訊(き)く: to ask why…
- ～気(き)が起(お)こる: (an idea) occurs (to someone) to ～
- 生涯・しょうがい: one's life; one's lifetime
- たびたび: frequently; repeatedly
- 起こる・おこる: to occur; happen
- 漠然(ばくぜん)とした: vague; nebulous
- 予感・よかん: premonition; a feeling (something will happen)
- 淋しい・さびしい: lonely; desolate; lonesome
- それにつけても: "about that"; which reminded me of …
- 憶う・おもう: to recall; think of
- 悲しい・かなしい: sad; sorrowful; melancholy
- 積極的・せっきょくてき: "active"; positive
- つらい: tough; hard; trying [つらく: hard; forcefully]
- 当る・あたる: here, to treat [also, to hit; strike]
- 常に・つねに: always; at all times
- 冷たい・つめたい: cold (to the touch or in temperament); removed; inhospitable
- が: but
- あまりに: too much; excessively
- 父子・ふし: father-child (relationship) [cf. 親子・おやこ: parent-child]
- 関係・かんけい: relationship [人間(にんげん)関係; "human relations"]
- 経験・けいけん: experience
- 全体・ぜんたい: the whole; the totality
- 同じ・おなじ: same
- ～に比較(ひかく)する: to compare to ～/contrast with ～
- ～さえしらない: don't know even ～
- それゆえ: because of/due to that
- そう悲(かな)しくは感(かん)じなかった: didn't feel all that sad
- どちらかと言(い)えば: if I were to say which
- 邪慳・じゃけん: nasty; hardhearted; cruel
- ことごとに: at every instance
- 叱る・しかる: to scold
- 実際・じっさい: (in) actuality
- きかん坊・きかんほう: naughty/unruly/unmanageable child
- わがまま: selfish; doing exactly as one wishes
- (verb) ～ず: ＝ ～ないで

Family Matters, Then and Now

「お父さんは在宅かネ？」と老人が訊いた。

私は首を振った。しかしこのうわ手な物言いが変に私を圧迫した。

老人は近寄って来て、私の頭へ手をやり、

「大きくなった」と言った。

この老人が何者であるか、私には解らなかった。しかしある不思議な本能で、それが近い肉親であることをすでに感じていた。私は息苦しくなって来た。

老人はそのまま帰って行った。

二三日するとその老人はまたやって来た。その時私は初めてそれを祖父として父から紹介された。

さらに十日ほどすると、なぜか私だけがその祖父の家に引きとられることになった。そして私は根岸のお行の松に近いある横町の奥の小さい古家に引きとられて行った。

そこには祖父の他にお栄という二十三四の女がいた。

私の周囲の空気は全く今までとは変っていた。すべてが貧乏臭く下品だった。

他の同胞が皆自家に残っているのに、自分だけがこの下品な祖父に引きとられたことは、子供ながらに面白くなかった。しかし不公平には幼児から慣らされていた。今に始まったことでないだけ、なぜかを他人に訊く気も私には起らなかった。しかしこういう風にして、こんなことが、これからの生涯にもたびたび起るだろうという漠然とした予感が、私の気持を淋しくした。それにつけても私は二ヶ月前に死んだ母を憶い、悲しい気持になった。

父は私に積極的につらく当ることはなかったが、常に常に冷たかった。が、このことには私はあまりに慣らされていた。それが私にとって父子関係の経験としての全体だった。私は他の同胞の同じ経験をそれに比較するさえ知らなかった。それゆえ、私はそのことをそう悲しくは感じなかった。

母は何方かと言えば私には邪慳だった。私はことごとに叱られた。実際私はきかん坊でわがままでもあった。が、同じことが他の同胞では叱られず、私の場合だけでは叱られるようなことがよ

ANYA KŌRO

*T*he *Prologue* of *Anya Kōro* has much bearing on the latter parts of the novel. Here, Kensaku, the novel's hero, recalls a number of incidents that marked him as a small boy. After a lapse of several years, we meet him again as a handsome young man. The first-person narrative then changes to the third person, although the tone remains intensely personal, as if the author had identified himself with Kensaku.

Through fine observation, the novel becomes a chronicle of time and place. Rainy evenings in Tokyo, encounters with geishas, buying a present in the Ginza or at a village potter, or a family traveling in a train compartment—all are depicted in vivid detail. The calm and beauty of a seascape draw us in. There is richness of texture, with depictions of the fuss surrounding a marriage proposal or the excitement of a fire festival, and the narrative is at times engrossing. Kensaku is shown to be helpless when his firstborn is stricken with a fatal illness. Other passages are lengthy and seemingly unrelated to the plot.

One may disapprove of Kensaku's profligate life and judge him harshly for his irritability, lack of moral courage, tormented self, or self-imposed loneliness. In self-deprecation, he likens himself to a "spoiled child." He is not an antihero, however, for we recognize in him a sensitive individual with a highly intuitive intelligence, honest with himself and willing to reveal his inner self in all circumstances.

Kensaku is obsessed by adulteresses, to the point of losing control of himself when he learns of his wife's transgression. He is also a writer who fails to deliver, a man beset by doubts and preoccupied by dilemmas: when a transgression is openly confessed, has it any value? When writing is a form of confession, can it ever be sincere?

The key to Kensaku's inner being is the revelation of how he was conceived. Central to the novel is a tormented longing for his mother, who died when he was six. The plot is not dense, but seemingly disparate events eventually tie in with each other, especially in parts 3 and 4. At the end of part 1, we get an early inkling of Kensaku's need to escape from dissipation and city life into nature. Tired of an overly complex life and of the difficult relationship with his wife, Naoko, he leaves his home for the mountains (part 4). There, he finds solace at Daisen Temple, a Zen-Buddhist retreat, where he is reconciled with Naoko.

"OTOU-san wa *UCHI* ka *ne?*" to ROU-JIN ga KIita.

WATASHI wa KUBI o FUtta. Shikashi kono uwaTE na MONO-Ii ga HEN ni WATASHI o AP-PAKU shita.

ROU-JIN wa CHIKA-YOtte KIte, WATASHI no ATAMA e TE o yari,

"OOkiku natta" to Itta.

Kono ROU-JIN ga NANI-MONO de aru ka, WATASHI ni wa WAKAranakatta. Shikashi aru FU-SHI-GI na HON-NOU de, sore ga CHIKAi NIKU-SHIN de aru koto o sude ni KANjite ita. WATASHI wa IKI-GURUshiku natte KIta.

ROU-JIN wa sono mama KAEtte Itta.

NI-SAN-NICHI suru to sono ROU-JIN wa mata yatte KIta. Sono TOKI WATASHI wa HAJImete so-re o SO-FU toshite CHICHI kara SHOU-KAI sareta.

Sara ni TOO-KA hodo suru to, naze ka WATASHI dake ga sono SO-FU no UCHI ni HIkito-rareru koto ni natta. Soshite WATASHI wa NE-GISHI no oGYOU no MATSU ni CHIKAi aru YOKO-CHOU no OKU no CHIIsai FURU-IE ni HIkitorarete Itta.

Soko ni wa SO-FU no HOKA ni oEI to iu NI-JUU-SAN-SHI no ONNA ga ita.

WATASHI no SHUU-I no KUU-KI wa MATTAku IMA made to wa KAWAtte ita. Subete ga BIN-BOU-KUSA-ku GE-HIN datta.

HOKA no *KYOUDAI* ga MINA *UCHI* ni NOKOtte iru no ni, JI-BUN dake ga kono GE-HIN na SO-FU ni HIkitorareta koto wa, KODOMOnagara ni OMO-SHIROku nakatta. Shikashi FU-KOU-HEI ni wa YOU-JI kara NArasarete ita. IMA ni HAJImatta koto de nai da-ke, naze ka o *HITO* ni KIku KI mo WATASHI ni wa OKOranakatta. Shikashi kou i-u FUU ni shite, konna koto ga, kore kara no SHOU-GAI ni mo tabitabi OKOru da-rou to iu BAKU-ZEN to shita YO-KAN ga, WATASHI no KI-MOCHI o SABIshiku shita. Sore ni tsu-kete mo WATASHI wa NI-KA-GETSU MAE ni SHInda HAHA o OMOi, KANAshii KI-MOCHI ni natta.

CHICHI wa WATASHI ni SEK-KYOKU-TEKI ni tsuraku ATAru koto wa nakatta ga, TSUNE ni TSUNE ni TSUMEta-katta. Ga, kono koto ni wa WATASHI wa amari ni NArasarete ita. Sore ga WATASHI ni totte FU-SHI KAN-KEI no KEI-KEN toshite no ZEN-TAI datta. WATASHI wa HOKA no *KYOUDAI* no ONAji KEI-KEN o sore ni HI-KAKU suru sae SHIranakatta. Sore yue, WATASHI wa so-no koto o sou KANAshiku wa KANjinakatta.

HAHA wa *DOCHIRA* ka to Ieba WATASHI ni wa JA-KEN datta. WATASHI wa kotogoto ni SHIKArare-ta. JIS-SAI WATASHI wa kikanBOU de wagamama de mo atta. Ga, ONAji koto ga TA no *KYOUDAI* de wa SHIKArarezu, WATASHI no BA-AI dake de wa SHIKArareru you na koto ga yo-

The roots of the original Ogyō no Matsu (Ogyō Pine). The tree was estimated to be 350 years old when it died in 1928. It had been a landmark since the Edo period, when it was depicted in Ukiyo-e.

A wood-framed house near Ogyō no Matsu in Negishi. This type of house is rapidly disappearing from Tokyo.

"Is your father home?" the old man asked.

I shook my head. But this highhanded way of speaking pressed strangely on me.

The old man approached and, putting his hand on my head, said

"You've gotten big."

As to who exactly this old man was, I had no understanding. But, due to some mysterious instinct, I felt I already knew that he was some close relation. It grew difficult for me to breathe.

The old man left without another word.

That old man came again in another two or three days. Then I was introduced to him by my father for the first time as my grandfather.

When another ten days or so had passed, for some reason it turned out that I alone would be taken [to live] in that grandfather's house. So I went and was taken into a small old house in the inner part of a certain back alley close to the Ogyō Pine in Negishi.

There, other than Grandpa, was a woman of twenty-three or -four called Oei.

The atmosphere of my surroundings was completely changed from that up till now. Everything stunk of poverty and was vulgar.

Although my other siblings all remained at my house, the fact that I alone had been taken in by this vulgar Grandpa was, though I was a child, not very amusing. But I had been accustomed to unfairness from my infancy. If only because [this treatment] was something which had not just started, for some reason it never occurred to me to ask someone about it. But the vague feeling that from now on this sort of thing would probably occasionally happen in this way, made me feel very sad. More than before I thought of my mother who died two months ago, and became very sad.

My father never actively treated me harshly, but he was always, always cold [to me]. But, I was abundantly used to this. For me, that was the whole of my experience of the father-child relationship. I didn't even know to compare that with the same experiences of my other siblings. Because of that, I did not feel so sad about those matters.

My mother, if I were to say [how she treated me], was nasty to me. I was scolded in everything [I did]. Actually, I was an unruly child, and was even selfish. But, on many occasions, the same [behavior], went unscolded in my siblings, and was only

- ～にもかかわらず: regardless of
- 心(こころ)から～を愛(あい)する: to love ～ from (the bottom of one's) heart
- 慕う・したう: to love; hate to part from; think fondly, lovingly of
- 四つ(よっつ) 五つ(いつつ): four or five (years old) [ages one to nine may be read in *kun-yomi* as here, or *on-yomi* plus 歳(さい)]
- 忘れる・わすれる: to forget
- とにかく: in any case; anyhow
- 秋・あき: fall; autumn
- 人々・ひとびと: people (his family and the servants)
- 夕餉・ゆうげ: the evening meal (archaic)
- 支度・したく: preparations
- 忙しい・せわしい: busy
- 働く・はたらく: to work
- 隙・すき: an opening; a lapse (in someone's guard)
- しも・下: lower; secondary
- 手洗場・ちょうずば: a "hand washing place," a euphemism for a room with a toilet; strictly speaking, not a "bathroom"; baths are separate from toilets in traditional Japanese houses
- 屋根・やね: roof
- 掛(か)け捨(す)ててある: to be left leaning against
- 梯子・はしご: ladder
- 誰(だれ)にも: by anybody
- 気づく・きづく: notice; become aware of
- 母屋・おもや: the main house
- 登る・のぼる: to climb; ascend
- 棟伝い・むねづたい: along the ridge of a roof
- 鬼瓦・おにがわら: a tile on the end of a roof ridge in the shape of a devil's face
- ところ: a place [also 所]
- 馬乗り(うまのり)になる: to straddle (as if riding a horse with a leg on each side [cf. またがる: ride, mount])
- 快活・かいかつ: cheerful; lively; lighthearted
- 気分・きぶん: feeling; mood
- 大きな・おおきな: big; large
- 声・こえ: voice
- 唱歌・しょうか: song; singing
- 唄う・うたう: to sing [also 歌う]
- 普段・ふだん: normally; usually
- ～ばかり: only; just (from below)
- 見上げる・みあげる: to look up at
- 柿の木・かきのき: a persimmon tree
- 足の下・あしのした: below one's feet
- 西・にし: west
- 空・そら: sky
- 美しい・うつくしい: beautiful; pretty
- 夕映える・ゆうばえる: to glow in the evening sun
- 烏・からす: crow 鳥
- 飛ぶ・とぶ: to fly
- 間(ま)もなく: very soon; before long
- 呼ぶ・よぶ: to call (out to)
- 気(き)がつく: to notice
- 気味の(が)悪い・きみのわるい: creepy; spooky; eerie
- 優しい・やさしい: kind; gentle
- 調子・ちょうし: tone; manner
- 「あのね」: used to get someone's attention; informal

- じっとする: to stay where one is; not move
- 動く・うごく: to move
- V ～のじゃありません: "Don't (move)"
- おとなしい・大人しい: quiet; well-behaved
- のよ: indicates an indirect comand [e.g., you stay there quietly now]
- 眼・め: eye [also 目]
- ～て見(み)えた: seemed to (slant upwards)
- ひどい: terrible; awful; dreadful
- ただごと: an ordinary matter
- 降りる・おりる: to get down; descend
- verb ～てしまう: to do something completely [here, implies perhaps: to get down "by myself"]
- ～のまま: without change; as (it/one) is
- 後じさる・あとじさる: to move backward
- 恐怖・きょうふ: fear; fright
- 泣く・なく: to cry (shed tears)
- verb ～そうな: seemingly about to ～
- 表情・ひょうじょう: expression; an expression; a look
- こと: here, indicates a statement of fact [e.g., you are such a quiet child]
- 言うことを……きく(聞く): to listen to what (do as) someone says
- のネ: indicates a statementp of fact [e.g., you always listen to what Mother says]
- (～から)眼(め)を放す(はなす): to look away from; be distracted from
- verb ～ずにいる: "to be (there) without doing ～ [～ずに＝～ないで]
- 変に・へんに: strangely
- 鋭い・するどい: sharp; piercing
- 視線・しせん: gaze; look
- 縛る・しばる: to bind; tie up
- ～ようになる: to become as if
- 身動き・みうごき: moving one's body; movement
- 書生・しょせい: an apprentice; live-in student (who helps around the house in exchange for rent)
- 車夫・しゃふ: a live-in employee who pulls a rickshaw [this is a rich family]
- 用心深い・ようじんぶかい: careful; cautious
- 下ろす・おろす: to lower; take down
- 案の定・あんのじょう: just as expected; exactly as one thought
- 烈しい・はげしい: fierce; violent
- 打つ・うつ: to slap; hit
- 亢奮・こうふん: excitement; commotion [usually written 興奮]
- 死なれる・しなれる: "to be died on by" [the passive case occasionally is used to express events that affect one personally in an adverse way]
- verb ～てから: after ～ing
- 記憶・きおく: memories; recollection
- 急に・きゅうに: suddenly
- 明瞭(はっきり)する: to become clear [usually read めいりょう]
- 後年・こうねん: (in) later years
- verb ～たび(に): every time one ～s
- 涙・なみだ: tears
- 誘う・さそう: "to ask/invite"; induce/bring on
- 何(なん)といっても: no matter what is said
- 本統に・ほんとうに: truly (usually written 本当)

くあった。しかし、それにもかかわらず、私は心から母を慕い愛していた。

　四つか五つか忘れた。とにかく、秋の夕方のことだった。私は人々が夕餉の支度で忙しく働いている隙に、しも手洗場の屋根へ懸け捨ててあった梯子から誰にも気づかれずに一人、母屋の屋根へ登って行ったことがある。棟伝いに鬼瓦のところまで行って馬乗りになると、変に快活な気分になって、私は大きな声で唱歌を唄っていた。私としてはこんな高いところへ登ったのは初めてだった。普段下からばかり見上げていた柿の木が、今は足の下にある。
　西の空が美しく夕映えている。烏が忙しく飛んでいる……
　間もなく私は、
　「謙作。──謙作」と下で母の呼んでいるのに気がついた。それは気味の悪いほど優しい調子だった。
　「あのネ、そこにじっとしているのよ。動くのじゃ、ありませんよ。今山本が行きますからネ。そこにおとなしくしているのよ」
　母の眼は少し釣上って見えた。ひどく優しいだけただごとでないことが知れた。私は山本の来るまでに降りてしまおうと思った。そして馬乗りのまま少し後じさった。「ああっ！」母は恐怖から泣きそうな表情をした。「謙作はおとなしいこと。お母さんの言うことをよくきくのネ」
　私はじっと眼を放さずにいる、変に鋭い母の視線から縛られたようになって、身動きが出来なくなった。
　間もなく書生と車夫との手で私は用心深く下された。
　案の定、私は母から烈しく打たれた。母は亢奮から泣き出した。
　母に死なれてからこの記憶は急に明瞭して来た。後年もこれを憶うたび、いつも私は涙を誘われた。何といっても母だけは本統に自分を愛していてくれた、わたしはそう思う。

──∿──

慣用句: Idiomatic Expressions

Translate the following into idiomatic English

1. 何ということなく

自分だけが、下品で貧乏臭い祖父に引きとられていくということが、私には<u>何ということなく</u>おもしろくなかった。

2. 子供ながらに

「母だけはほんとうに自分を愛していてくれた」と私は<u>子供ながらに</u>いつも思うのだった。

3. 今に始まったことではない

小さいころからきかん坊だったらしく、私のわがままは<u>今に始まったことではない</u>。

4. それにつけても

祖父に引きとられてからも私はこれからの生涯に不公平なことがたびたび起きるだろうという予感がしていた。<u>それにつけても</u>私に対してはいつもいつも冷たかった父のことが後年もよく思い出されるのだった。

5. ことごとに

「なぜ自分だけが<u>ことごとに</u>不公平な経験をしなければならないのだろうか」と私は悲しい気持になった。

6. ただごとでない

「オイオイ、お前は謙作かネ」とその見知らぬ老人に背後から言われ、これは<u>ただごととでない</u>という気がした。

ku atta. Shikashi, sore ni mo kakawarazu, WATASHI wa KOKORO kara HAHA o SHITAi AI-
shite ita.

YOTtsu ka ITSUtsu ka WASUreta. Tonikaku, AKI no YUU-GATA no koto datta. WATASHI wa
HITO-BITO ga YUU-GE no SHI-TAKU de SEWAshiku HATARAite iru SUKI ni, shimo CHOU-ZU-BA no YANE e
KAkeSUtete atta HASHI-GO kara DARE ni mo KIzukarezu ni HITO-RI, OMO-YA no YA-NE
e NOBOtte Itta koto ga aru. MUNE-ZUTAi ni ONI-GAWARA no tokoro made Itte UMA-
NOri ni naru to, HEN ni KAI-KATSU na KI-BUN ni natte, WATASHI wa OOkina KOE de SHOU-KA o
UTAtte ita. WATASHI toshite wa konna TAKAi tokoro e NOBOtta no wa HAJImete da-
tta. FU-DAN SHITA kara bakari MI-Agete ita KAKI no KI ga, IMA wa ASHI no SHITA ni aru.
NISHI no SORA ga UTSUKUshiku YUU-BAete iru. KARASU ga SEWAshiku TOnde iru …
MAmonaku WATASHI wa,
"KEN-SAKU. — KEN-SAKU" to SHITA de HAHA no YOnde iru no ni KI ga tsuita. Sore
wa KI-MI no WARUi hodo YASAshii CHOU-SHI datta.
"Ano *ne*, soko ni jitto shite iru no yo. UGOku no ja, arimase-
n yo. IMA YAMA-MOTO ga Ikimasu kara *ne*. Soko ni otonashiku shite iru no yo"
HAHA no ME wa SUKOshi TSURI-AGAtte MIeta. Hidoku YASAshii dake tadagoto de na-
i koto ga SHIreta. WATASHI wa YAMA-MOTO no KUru made ni Orite shimaou to OMOtta.
Soshite UMA-NOri no mama SUKOshi ATOjisatta. "Aatt!" HAHA wa KYOU-FU kara NA-
kisou na HYOU-JOU o shita. "KEN-SAKU wa otonashii koto. OKAA-san no Iu ko-
to o yoku kiku no *ne*"
WATASHI wa jitto ME o HANAsazu ni iru, HEN ni SURUDOi HAHA no SHI-SEN kara SHIBArareta
you ni natte, MI-UGOki ga DEKInaku natta.
MAmonaku SHO-SEI to SHA-FU to no TE de WATASHI wa YOU-JIN-BUKAku OROsareta.
AN no JOU, WATASHI wa HAHA kara HAGEshiku Utareta. HAHA wa KOU-FUN kara NAkiDAshita.
HAHA ni SHInarete kara kono KI-OKU wa KYUU ni *HAKKIRI* shite KIta. KOU-NEN mo kore o
OMOu tabi, itsumo WATASHI wa NAMIDA o SASOwareta. NAN to itte mo HAHA dake wa HON-TOU
ni JI-BUN o AIshite ite kureta, watashi wa sou OMOu.

内容理解: Comprehension Exercises

Answer in Japanese

1. 「私」はどのようにして自分に祖父のあることを知ったのでしょうか。
2. 「私」は「見知らぬ」老人からどのような印象を受けましたか。
3. 「私」はこの老人が何者であるかすぐわかりましたか。
4. 「私」はどんなところへ引きとられて行きましたか。
5. 子供ながらに「おもしろくない」と思ったのはどうしてでしょうか。
6. どのような予感が「私」の気持を淋しくしましたか。
7. 「私」の母に対する気持は？
8. 屋根に登っている「私」は母親の声を聞いてどうしてただごとでないと思いましたか。
9. 後年この屋根登りのことを憶うたびに「私」がいつも涙を誘われるのはどうしてでしょうか。

練習問題: Exercises

True or False?

1. 門の前で「私」に話しかけようとした見すぼらしい老人が「私」にはある不思議な本能で、祖父だと感じられた。
2. 自分だけが祖父の家に引きとられるような不公平には慣らされていたし、なぜ自分だけ不公平な経験をしなければいけないかも幼児のころからよくわかっていた。
3. 「私」は心から母を慕い愛していたので、常に冷たかった父との関係をそう悲しくは感じなかった。
4. 屋根へ登った時のことを後年もよく憶い、涙を誘われるのは、母に対して自分がきかん坊でわがままだったからだ。

scolded in the cases where I did it. But, regardless of that, I loved my mother
from the heart.

I forgot if I was [when I was] four or five. Anyway, it happened on an autumn
evening. In the chance moment when people were busily working on preparations for the evening
meal, I once, without being noticed by anyone, climbed alone up to the roof of the main
house from the ladder left leaning against the roof of the outhouse. When I had gone to
the spot with the ridge's end tile and sat astride on the roof, I felt oddly cheerful
and I sang a song in a loud voice. The persimmon tree, which I ordinarily only looked
up at from below, was now below my feet.

The western sky glowed beautifully. Crows were flying about busily…

Momentarily, I [heard]

"Kensaku!…Kensaku!" and noticed my mother calling from below. It was in a
tone so kind it was eerie.

"Now, just you stay right there, OK? Don't move anywhere
now. Yamamoto is on his way now. Be a good boy and [sit] there."

The corners of Mom's eyes seemed to slant upward [as if angry]. I knew merely from [her
being] extremely kind that this was nothing ordinary. I thought I would get down by the time
Yamamoto got there. So, still straddling the roof, I backed up a little.

"Aaah!" Mother wore an expression which seemed about to cry from fear. "Be good, Kensaku!
Listen carefully to what your mother says, OK?"

I was seemingly trapped by my Mother's oddly sharp gaze, which stayed stopped upon me, and
I became unable to move.

Soon, I was carefully lowered by the hands of the live-in student and the rickshaw man.

As expected, I was fiercely hit by my mother. Mother started to cry from the excitement.

This memory suddenly became vivid to me after my mother had died. In later years, whenever
I recalled this, I was always led to tears. No matter what is said, my Mother alone really
loved me; that is what I think.

語句と語法: Phrases and Usage

NOTE: Much of the language here is the informal spoken language of schoolgirls.

- メロン: melon [here, a muskmelon]
- お弁当・おべんとう: a Japanese "box lunch" [typically, rice, meat, vegetables, pickles, etc.]
- 時間・じかん: time [here, lunchtime]
- 玉子・たまご: egg [these are 当て字・あてじ (characters assigned a random meaning or pronunciation); here the pronunciation matches with the characters' meanings well, a "ball" + "child"; a popular rendering of 卵]
- ～焼き・やき: here, fried [also, baked, grilled]
- フォーク: fork
- つきさす・突き刺す: to stick into
- 泊(とま)りにおいで: come and stay over(night) [おいで can be used formally or informally]
- みほ: Miho [a girl's name]
- 言う・いう: to say
- 中学・ちゅうがく: junior high school, equivalent to grades 7–9 [cf. 高校・こうこう high school has three grades, 10–12; 小学校・しょうがっこう: grades 1–6]
- できる: to make; form
- 友達・ともだち: friend [the first character also appears in the somewhat more formal 友人 (ゆうじん) friend; acquaintance]
- すごく・凄く: incredibly [as adv. modifying noun, not unlike "cool!"]
- 美人・びじん: a beautiful woman; a beauty
- 白くって・しろくって: white; fair (in complexion) [usually しろくて; っ is a schoolgirl affectation]
- 細くって・ほそくって: thin; narrow; slender [cf. above]
- 天然(てんねん)パーマ: "natural perm"; naturally curly hair
- 茶色い・ちゃいろい: "tea colored"; reddish brown
- 髪・かみ: hair
- 肩・かた: shoulder
- くるくるっと: describes a curling, circular motion [modifies 揺れる]
- 揺れる・ゆれる: to sway; swing
- 何(なん)だか: somehow; sort of
- お人形(にんぎょう)っぽい: doll-like [っぽい = -like, -ish, -ful]
- ごめん: sorry [little formal than ごめんなさい]
- なんだ: = なのだ with の shortened to ん [used to stress a point]
- 誕生日・たんじょうび: a birthday
- じゃ: well (if that is the case) … [shortened form of では]
- しかた(が)ない・仕方(が)ない: it can't be helped
- きれい: pretty
- 菜めし・なめし: greens mixed with rice
- にんじん・人参: here, carrots
- オレンジ: the color orange
- きいろ・黄色: yellow
- 弁当箱・べんとうばこ: "a lunch box" [はこ: box]

- 私(わたし)だったら: if it were me [i.e., my lunch]
- たりない・足りない: insufficient [cf. 足りる: to be enough; be sufficient]
- また: again
- 夫婦・ふうふ: a married couple
- おでかけなの: are (they) going out? [a mix of politeness (おー) and informality (～なの)]
- きく・聞く: to ask
- あっさり: simply; matter of factly; candidly
- うなずく・肯く: to nod (yes)
- 両親・りょうしん: "both parents"; one's parents
- 仲(なか)がいい: "a relationship is good"; be close
- しょっちゅう: all the time; constantly
- 二人で・ふたりで: as a pair; together
- コンサート: concert [probably a concert of Western classical music]
- 食事・しょくじ: meals [cf. 外食・がいしょく: eating out]
- 温泉・おんせん: hot springs
- とか…とか: indicates a non-inclusive listing
- だから: so; that's why
- もう: already
- ～回・かい: a counter for cardinal numbers
- 遊びに行く・あそびに いく: to go to visit [あそぶ is often translated as "play"]
- そのうち: among those
- 泊り・とまり: staying overnight at someone's house
- ママ: mother [here used for Miho's "chic" parents; お母さん (おかあさん) is more common]
- 写真・しゃしん: photographs
- いっぱい・一杯: lots
- みる・見る: to see; watch
- そっくり: (look) exactly alike
- やっぱり: as one expected; sure enough [cf. やはり]
- だんな・旦那: originally used by servants in reference to their master; here, "husband" with さま showing respect
- 愛する: to love
- 奥さん・おくさん: respectful term for wife; another's wife
- どうしても: no matter what
- 甘い・あまい: sweet
- たれのかかったミートボール: meatballs (topped) with sauce [の = が]
- 口・くち: mouth
- 入れる・いれる: to insert in; put in
- 結婚(けっこん)する: to marry
- なんて: or anything (like that)

メロン

江國香織

お弁当の時間に、玉子焼きにフォークをつきさして、
「きょう、うちに泊りにおいでよ」
とみほが言った。みほは、中学に入ってからできた友達で、すごく美人。白くって、細くって、天然パーマの茶色い髪が、肩のところでくるくるっと揺れる。何だかお人形っぽい感じ。
「ごめん。きょうはダメなんだ。お母さんの誕生日だから」
じゃ、しかたないね、とみほは言った。みほの弁当はいつもすごくきれい。菜めしの青、にんじんサラダのオレンジ、玉子焼きのきいろ。でもとても小さなお弁当箱だから、私だったらちょっとたりないなと思う。
「また夫婦でおでかけなの」
私がきくと、みほはあっさりうなずいた。
みほの両親は仲がいい。しょっちゅう、二人ででかけてゆく。コンサートだとか、食事だとか、温泉だとか。だから、私はみほの家に、もう三回も遊びに行った。(そのうち一回は、泊りだった。)
みほのママとは会ったことがないけれど、写真はいっぱいみた。みほのママはみほにそっくり。白くって、細くって、茶色い髪。やっぱり、すごく美人。だんなさまに愛される奥さんになるには、どうしても美人じゃなくちゃいけないのだ。
甘いたれのかかったミートボールを一つ口に入れ、私は、結婚な

Ekuni Kaori

Born in 1964 in Tokyo, Ekuni Kaori is the elder daughter of the famous essayist Ekuni Shigeru. Her career began as a children story writer. At the age of 23, she won a grand prize for children stories given by the Mainichi Shinbun with her "Story of Sanojo." In this story, a little boy named Kazetarō who was raised by a single mother accidentally meets Sanojo, a man who claims to be his father. It turns out, however, that Sanojo is the ghost image of an ancient samurai. In another vein, at age 25, she won a prize for her work "409 Radcliffe," in which she describes her experiences as a student at the University of Delaware.

Ekuni's work is known for its freshness of style, which might be likened to the feeling one derives from appreciating water-color painting. She is very popular with the younger generation. Her main themes are mythical elements, ghosts, transformation, and reincarnation. In addition to these motifs, she often describes with tenderness how the elderly, who are about to depart society, interact with the young, who about to enter it. The feeling of warm poetic essence and of *mujōkan* (or tranquility), derived from Buddhism, is expressed in her writings. Ekuni's work mirrors what a person in urbanized Japan, or anywhere else in a modern society, can hope for—removing oneself, however temporarily, from the pressures of society and trying to achieve some peace of mind. She subtly blends illusion and imagination with elements from everyday life, which is the key to her success as an author.

Meron

E-KUNI KA-ORI

OBEN-TOU no JI-KAN ni, TAMA-GO-YAki ni *fooku* o tsukisashite,

"kyou, uchi ni TOMAri ni oide yo"

to Miho ga Itta. Miho wa, CHUU-GAKU ni HAItte kara dekita TOMO-DACHI de, sugoku

BI-JIN. SHIROkutte, HOSOkutte, TEN-NEN *paama* no CHA-IROi KAMI ga, KATA no tokoro

de kurukuru tto YUreru. NAN da ka oNIN-GYOUppoi KANji.

"Gomen. Kyou wa *dame* nan da. OKAA-san no TAN-JOU-BI da kara"

Ja, shikata nai ne, to Miho wa Itta. Miho no BEN-TOU wa itsumo sugo-

ku kirei. NAmeshi no AO, ninjin *sarada* no *orenji*, TAMA-GO-YAki no ki-

iro. Demo totemo CHIIsana oBEN-TOU-BAKO da kara, WATASHI dattara chotto tari-

nai na to OMOu.

"Mata FUU-FU de odekake na no"

WATASHI ga kiku to, Miho wa assari unazuita.

Miho no RYOU-SHIN wa NAKA ga ii. Shotchuu, FUTA-RI de dekakete yuku. *Ko-*

nsaato da toka, SHOKU-JI da toka, ON-SEN da toka. Dakara, WATASHI wa Miho no IE

ni, mou SAN-KAI mo ASObi ni Itta. (Sono uchi IK-KAI wa, TOMAri datta.)

Miho no *mama* to wa Atta koto ga nai keredo, SHA-SHIN wa ippai mita.

Miho no *mama* wa Miho ni sokkuri. SHIROkutte, HOSOkutte, CHA-IROi KAMI. Ya-

ppari, sugoku BI-JIN. Danna-sama ni AIsareru OKU-san ni naru ni wa, do-

ushite mo BI-JIN ja nakucha ikenai no da.

AMAi tare no kakatta *miitobooru* o HITOtsu KUCHI ni Ire, WATASHI wa, KEK-KON na-

Box lunches with rice, meat, vegetables, and pickles.

Melon

Ekuni Kaori

At lunchtime, sticking her fork into a fried egg, Miho said,

"Today, come stay over at my house."

Miho was a friend I had made since entering junior high,

and she was incredibly beautiful. White [skin] and slim, her brown hair swung in curls

around her shoulders. [She had] somewhat of a doll-like air [to her].

"Sorry, today is no good. Because it's my mom's birthday."

"Well, too bad," Miho said. Miho's box lunch was always extremely

pretty. The green of the vegetable rice, the orange of her carrot salad, the yellow of the fried

egg. But it was such a small lunch box that, if it were for me, I think it would not be

quite enough.

"Your mom and dad are going out again?"

When I asked, Miho nodded easily.

Miho's parents had a good relationship. They were always going out as a couple.

Concerts, dining, hot springs. So I had already been to Miho's house

three times. (Of those, once was to stay the night.)

I had never met Miho's mom, but I had seen lots of photos.

Miho's mom looked just like Miho. White [skin] and slim, with brown hair.

And as expected, very beautiful. In order to become a wife loved by her husband,

it seemed one absolutely must be beautiful.

Putting one meatball with sweet sauce into my mouth, I thought, I don't want to

- 下駄箱・げたばこ: shoe locker (most schools require students to switch from outdoor shoes to indoor shoes or slippers]
- 〜通目・つうめ: 通 is a "counter" for letters; 〜目 indicates an ordinal number
- 入学(にゅうがく)する: to enter a school
- たった: only
- 男の子・おとこのこ: a boy
- ということだ: such is the way it is (are the facts of the matter)
- 封筒・ふうとう: an envelope
- 裏返す・うらがえす: to turn over
- 差出す・さしだす: to send; mail
- 名前・なまえ: name
- たしかめる・確める: to make certain/sure of; to confirm
- 興味・きょうみ: interest; curiosity
- 興味なさそうに: seemingly without interest
- カバン・鞄: a (book) bag
- しまう: to put away
- 好きな人・すきなひと: a person/someone (you) like
- 〜の: used for informal questions
- 校庭・こうてい: a schoolyard; school grounds
- 〜を歩く・あるく: to walk on (the school grounds) [を marks where they walk]
- むし暑い・む(蒸)しあつい: humid, sticky, and hot
- いない: here, means "there is no one (I like)"
- ふうん: uh-huh; I see [elongation of *fun*; used casually to express understanding or approral to someone of equal or lower status]
- こたえる・答える: to answer (a question)
- 横を・よこを: side [を again used to mark an area where someone walks or runs]
- サッカー部員(ぶいん): members of the soccer club [〜部 is used for a school club or "circle"; club activities, even sports, usually continue year round and are important for making friends and forming ties
- どやどやと: in a noisy throng/crowd
- 駆ける・かける: to run
- 「やだーっ」: here, perhaps "Yuck" is best; a shortened form of 嫌・いや, which indicates one finds something unpleasant
- 土(つち)けむり(煙): cloud of dust
- スカート: skirt (dress)
- 両手・りょうて: both hands
- ばんばん: a light hitting or beating sound
- たたく・叩く: to hit, strike, beat
- 平気・へいき: indifferent; as if nothing were happening
- 顔・かお: face
- verb stem -つづける: to continue (doing 〜)
- みのりはいいね: "How good for you, Minori," indicating envy of Minori's situation
- 横顔・よこがお: "side face"; profile
- びっくりする: to be surprised/startled

- 大人びる・おとなびる: to look grown up/mature
- きれい・奇麗: pretty
- どきっとする: to be taken aback; be startled
- 別に・べつに: with the negative, "not especially"
- ちっとも〜 ない: not in the least bit 〜
- なんか: or anything [here, emphasizes the negative meaning]
- 〜いたって: even if 〜 were
- むこうは: here, indicates "the other person" (who she likes)
- こっち: me [informal for こちら ("this side"), but indicates the speaker]
- 〜だし: used to list reasons and here indicates there may be other reasons
- 大学生・だいがくせい: a college student
- わかんない: informal for わからない [don't know]
- くん・君: a courtesy title like さん, くん is used generally in addressing young men or boys, or by older men indicating social inferiors (younger men); also a friendly form of address used by young women toward young men of the same age or younger
- 去年の今ごろ・きょねんのいまごろ: about this time last year
- 普通(ふつう)なら: "if (he/the situation) was normal"; normally
- もう〜じゃない: is no longer a 〜; もう can also mean "soon" (もうくる); "already" (もうきた); its meaning depends on the verb
- すでに・既に: already
- 自信(じしん)たっぷり: full of confidence [with superior dots to emphasize the irony]
- 俺・おれ: I [rough first-person pronoun used by men with other men of equal or lower social status]
- 留年・りゅうねん be held back; repeat a year
- 〜だわ: わ is usually used by women but a male version exists, usually used with falling or low intonation
- もしかして: perhaps; maybe, just maybe
- 夜・よる: night; evening
- 祝い(いわい)をやる: to have a celebration
- お姉(ねえ)ちゃん: Sis [〜ちゃん, a diminutive, is used like さん, but implies intimacy]
- ケーキ: cake
- 自分で: by oneself
- 焼く・やく: here, to bake
- 自慢(じまん)する: to brag/boast
- おばあちゃん: Grandmother
- ブラウス: blouse
- プレゼントする: to give a present
- それぞれ: respectively; each
- だしあう・出し合う: to share (expenses)
- 買(か)う: to buy
- にこにこする: to smile; beam
- 嬉しい・うれしい: happy; glad
- adj. stem 〜そうに: looked 〜 [used to describe 3rd persons]

んてしたくない、と思った。

　みほの下駄箱に、またラブレターが入っていた。四通目だ。入学して、たった二ヵ月で、四人の男の子がみほを好きになった、ということだ。みほは、封筒を裏返して差出した人の名前をたしかめると、興味なさそうに、それをカバンにしまった。

「好きな人、いないの」

　校庭を歩きながら、私はきいた。きょうは少しむし暑い。

「いない」

　ふうん、とこたえたとき、横をサッカー部員がどやどやと駆けていった。

「やだーっ。土けむり」

　私はスカートを両手でぱんぱんたたいたけれど、みほは平気な顔で歩きつづけた。

「みのりはいいね、好きな人がいて」

　そう言ったみほの横顔が、びっくりするほど大人びてきれいだったので、私はどきっとしてしまった。

「よくないよ、別に」

　ちっともよくなんかない。好きな人がいたって、むこうはこっちが好きじゃないんだし。

「大学生なんでしょ、その人」

「……わかんない」

　次郎くんは、去年の今ごろ大学四年生だったから、普通ならもう大学じゃない。でも、そのころすでに自信たっぷりに、俺、留年だわ、と言っていたから、もしかして、まだ大学生かもしれない。そうだといいなと思う。

「ふうん」

　興味なさそうに、みほは言った。

　その夜は、お母さんの誕生祝いをやった。去年結婚したお姉ちゃんも来た。大きなケーキを持ってきて、自分で焼いたのだと自慢した。私とおばあちゃんがブラウスをプレゼントしたら（私が二千円、おばあちゃんが五千九百円、それぞれだしあって買ったのだ）、お母さんはにこにこして、嬉しそうに、ありがとう、と言った。

FAMILY, THEN AND NOW I

The pre-war Japanese family was different from today. Three generations would live under one roof. Parents had a larger number of children. The newly-wed wife would usually move into the house of her husband and his parents. The husband was, more often than not, the uncontested head of the family, and the wife was expected to take care of the children, her husband, and his aging parents. She rarely worked outside of her home. Each person's role within the family was usually well defined.

After World War II, Japan underwent major changes. The emperor was no longer considered to be of divine origin. In a ripple effect, the head of the household, the father, also lost some of his authority. In addition, the Japanese became gradually acquainted with family structure in the United States. Moreover, rapid industrialization and increased demand for labor prompted many women to seek work outside of the home. Many women had grown accustomed to the idea during the war, when they were required to work at ammunition factories or hold down other jobs.

nte shitaku nai, to OMOtta.

Miho no GE-TA-BAKO ni, mata *raburetaa* ga HAItte ita. YON-TSUU-ME da. NYUU-GAKU

shite, tatta NI-KA-GETSU de, YO-NIN no OTOKO no KO ga Miho o SUki ni natta, to i-

u koto da. Miho wa, FUU-TOU o URA-GAEshite SASHI-DAshita HITO no NA-MAE o tashikameru

to, KYOU-MI nasasou ni, sore o *kaban* ni shimatta.

"SUki na HITO, inai no"

KOU-TEI o ARUkinagara, WATASHI wa kiita. Kyou wa SUKOshi mushiATSUi.

"Inai"

Fuun, to kotaeta toki, YOKO o *sakkaa*BU-IN ga doyadoya to KAkete

itta.

"Yadaatt. TSUCHIkemuri"

WATASHI wa *sukaato* o RYOU-TE de panpan tataita keredo, Miho wa HEI-KI na KAO

de ARUkitsuzuketa.

"Minori wa ii ne, SUki na HITO ga ite"

Sou Itta Miho no YOKO-GAO ga, bikkuri suru hodo OTO-NAbite kirei dat-

ta no de, WATASHI wa dokitto shite shimatta.

"Yoku nai yo, BETSU ni"

Chittomo yoku nanka nai. SUki na HITO ga ita tte, mukou wa kotchi

ga SUki ja nai n da shi.

"DAI-GAKU-SEI nan desho, sono HITO"

"… wakannai"

JI-ROU-kun wa, KYO-NEN no IMA goro DAI-GAKU YO-NEN-SEI datta kara, FU-TSUU nara mou

DAI-GAKU ja nai. Demo, sono koro sude ni JI-SHIN tappuri ni, ORE, RYUU-NEN da

wa, to Itte ita kara, moshikashite, mada DAI-GAKU-SEI ka mo shirenai. So-

u da to ii na to OMOu.

"Fuun"

KYOU-MI nasasou ni, Miho wa Itta.

Sono YORU wa, oKAA-san no TAN-JOU-IWAi o yatta. KYO-NEN KEK-KON shita oNEE-cha-

n mo KIta. OOkina *keeki* o MOtte kite, JI-BUN de YAita no da to JI-MAN shi-

ta. WATASHI to obaa-chan ga *burausu* o *purezento* shitara (WATASHI ga NI-SEN-EN,

obaa-chan ga GO-SEN-KYUU-HYAKU-EN, sorezore dashiatte KAtta no da), o-

KAA-san wa nikoniko shite, UREshisou ni, arigatou, to Itta.

FAMILY, THEN AND NOW II

Today, the typical Japanese family is nuclear, with one or two children. The nuclear family lives in a very small apartment in the city or a suburb, while the older generation continues to live in the family home, whether in city or country. Often a remaining parent will move in with the oldest son's family. As in most industrialized nations, household appliances facilitate the task of the wife and allow her to work outside of the home or to have more leisure time. The husband works long hours as salary man and returns late in the evening after a long ride on the trains. In these conditions, only the wife has time to take care of the children and to manage the household. For practical reasons, it is she who controls the purse strings. Over fifty percent of women now work outside of the home.

It should be noted that Japan is fortunate enough to have the highest longevity rate of all industrialized nations. On the other hand, the government is not satisfied with the 1.4 birth rate (in 1997), for who will take professional care of the aging population? Who will fill the jobs required by Japan's modern economy and its scientific research facilities.* There are signs that women will increasingly seek a scientific education.

However, respect for the older generation and emphasis on the parent-child relationship—as opposed to that between husband and wife—are still the tenets of modern Japanese society. In the case of an absentee or near-absentee father, such as depicted in "Melon," it is the mother-child bond that becomes all important. The question may be asked: How has the role of women evolved since 1998?

* In 1996, the Council for Science and Technology, chaired by Prime Minister Ryutaro Hashimoto, submitted to the government a proposal to spend 17 trillion yen on science and technology research over the next five years, a 50 percent increase over the preceding five-year budget. The money would mostly go toward research at universities and national laboratories.

Additional Reading:

Condon, Jane. *A Half Step Behind*, Revised Edition. Tokyo: Charles E. Tuttle Co., 1993.

Kodansha Encyclopedia of Japan. 9 vols. Tokyo, New York, London: Kodansha International, 1983.

Japan: An Illustrated Encyclopedia. 2 vols. Tokyo, New York, London: Kodansha International, 1993.

The Kodansha Bilingual Encyclopedia of Japan. Tokyo, New York, London: Kodansha International, 1998.

get married or anything.

There was a love letter in Miho's shoe locker again. It's the fourth one. It meant that in just two months since she came to this school, four boys had fallen for Miho. Miho, turning over the envelope and checking the sender's name, put it into her bag with seeming disinterest.

"Isn't there someone you like?"

I asked while walking through the school grounds. Today was a little muggy.

"No"

As I replied, umm, the soccer club members went running [past] in a throng.

"Yuck! Dust!"

I beat my skirt with both hands, but Miho walked on with an uncaring expression.

"You're lucky, having someone you like."

Miho's profile as she said this was so surprisingly grown-up, it startled me.

"It's not so great especially."

It's not great or anything at all. Even if [I have] someone I like, he doesn't like me.

"He's a college student, isn't he … that guy?"

"… I don't know."

Jiro was a fourth-year student at this time last year, so ordinarily he would no longer be a college student. But at that point he was already saying, full of confidence, that "I'm staying back a year," so just maybe he was still a college student. I wouldn't mind if he were.

"Humm,"

Miho said without interest.

That night we held a celebration for mom's birthday. My older sister who got married last year also came. She brought a big cake and boasted she had baked it herself. When Grandma and I gave mom a blouse (I contributed 2,000 yen and grandma 5,900 yen and we bought it) Mom smiled and said, thanks, looking happy.

- 今年・ことし: this year
- お父さん・おとうさん: Father
- なにも・何にも: nothing
- あげる・上げる: to give
- 乾杯・かんぱい: a toast
- だって: even [colloquial; = でも]
- みんな・皆: everyone [colloquial; = みな]
- のに: even though
- だけ: only
- 黙る・だまる: to fall silent; be silent
- まま: indicates an unchanged condition [e.g., 黙(だま)ったまま: remainded silent]
- もう: by now; already
- あたりまえ・当たり前: the norm; (exactly as) expected
- 誰(だれ)も: no one
- もちろん: of course
- 不思議(ふしぎ)におもう: to think strange
- パパ: like the use of ママ, reserved for Miho's stylish parents
- こういうとき(時): at a time like this
- きっと: surely
- 何(なに)か: something
- お花(はな): flowers [with honorific お]
- アクセサリー: accessories
- ほっとく: to leave alone; ignore
- からだ・体: body
- ほーっとする: to be absentminded; be "spaced out"
- めがね(眼鏡)をかける: to wear glasses
- どうせ: anyway; in any case [implies strong (negative) sentiment, in this case that her husband is always late coming home from work]
- 遅い・おそい: be late
- ほおばる: to stuff one's mouth ("cheeks")
- 誕生祝い・たんじょういわい: a birthday present
- 海外旅行・かいがいりょこう: a trip abroad
- ねだっちゃえば？: = ねだってしまえば？; ねだる: to importune [～えば used to make a suggestion: "What if you were to plead for a …"]

- ふふふと笑(わら)う: to laugh quietly to oneself
- むっつりした: sullen; sour; glum
- 聞(き)こえる: to hear
- ～ふりをする: to pretend to ～
- お茶・おちゃ: (green) tea
- のむ・飲む: to drink
- ダイヤモンドの指輪(ゆびわ): a diamond ring
- もう一度(いちど): one more time
- あたし: I [used largely by women]
- ピンクハウス: "Pink House" [a fashion house]
- ワンピース: a "one piece" dress
- 買(か)ってもらう: to have (someone) buy for one
- 今度・こんど: next [can also mean "this time"; distinguishable by context]
- 一週間違い・いっしゅうかんちがい: one week's difference; one week apart
- はいはい: yes, yes [according to tone of voice, can indicate wholehearted or reluctant (as here) affirmation]
- ごちそうさま・ご馳走様: usually said in thanks after meals, but here refers ironically to daughter's satisfaction over her expected present
- こういう人(ひと): this kind of person [with emphasis via superior dots]
- 最初(さいしょ)から: from the beginning
- 期待(きたい)する: to expect
- おしまい: the end; finished
- 一体・いったい: what on earth
- どういう人(ひと): what kind of person
- 少し・すこし: little
- あと: later
- いつものとおり(通り): exactly as always
- ハンカチ: handkerchief
- ひろげる・広げる: "widen"; to spread out
- 二学期・にがっき: second semester
- 転校(てんこう)する: to transfer to a new school
- おんなじ・同じ: same [= おなじ・同じ]
- 口調・くちょう: tone (of voice)

Family Matters, Then and Now

　今年も、お父さんはなにもあげなかった。乾杯のときだって、みんな「おめでとう」と言ったのに、お父さんだけ黙ったままだった。でも、それはもうあたりまえのことになっていて、誰も（もちろん私も）不思議には思わない。みほのパパなら、こういうとき、きっと何か（お花とかアクセサリーとか）、ママにプレゼントするんだろうなと思う。
「島木さん、ほっといていいの」
　お母さんがお姉ちゃんにきいた。島木さんというのはお姉ちゃんのだんなさま。からだが大きくて、ぼーっとしていて、めがねをかけている。
「いいの、いいの。どうせ遅いんだし」
　自分で焼いたケーキをほおばって、お姉ちゃんは言った。
「お母さん、誕生祝いに、海外旅行でもねだっちゃえば？」
　ふふふ、と、お母さんは笑った。
「そうねぇ、それもいいわねぇ」
　お父さんはむっつりしたまま、聞こえないふりでお茶をのんでいる。
「ダイヤモンドの指輪とか」
　お姉ちゃんが言い、お母さんはもう一度、ふふふ、と笑った。
「あたしね、島木さんにピンクハウスのワンピース買ってもらうんだ。今度の誕生日」
　お姉ちゃんとお母さんの誕生日は一週間違いなのだ。
「はいはい、ごちそうさま。でもね、お父さんはこういう人ですからね、プレゼントなんて、最初から期待していませんよ」
　お母さんが言い、この話はそれでおしまいになった。でも、こういう人って、一体どういう人のことだろう。

　びっくりすることがあったのは、それから少しあとだった。お弁当の時間で、みほはいつものとおり、きれいなハンカチの上にきれいなお弁当をひろげていた。
「私、二学期から転校するの」
　きょう、泊りにおいでよ、と言うのとおんなじ、普通の口調でみほが言った。

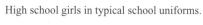
High school girls in typical school uniforms.

KO-TOSHI mo, oTOU-san wa nani mo agenakatta. KAN-PAI no toki datte, mi-nna "omedetou" to Itta no ni, oTOUsan dake DAMAtta mama datta. Demo, sore wa mou atarimae no koto ni natte ite, DARE mo (mochiron WATASHI mo) FU-SHI-GI ni wa OMOwanai. Miho no *papa* nara, kou iu toki, kit-to NANI ka (oHANA toka *akusesarii* toka), *mama* ni *purezento* suru n da-rou na to OMOu.

"SHIMA-KI-san, hottoite ii no"

oKAA-san ga oNEE-chan ni kiita. SHIMA-KI-san to iu no wa, oNEE-chan no danna-sama. Karada ga OOkikute, bootto shite ite, megane o ka-kete iru.

"Ii no, ii no. Douse OSOi n da shi"

JI-BUN de YAita *keeki* o hoobatte, oNEE-chan wa Itta.

"OKAA-san, TAN-JOU-IWAi ni, KAI-GAI RYO-KOU de mo nedatchaeba?"

Fufufu, to, oKAA-san wa WARAtta.

"Sou nee, sore mo ii wa nee"

OTOU-san wa muttsuri shita mama, KIkoenai furi de oCHA o nonde i-ru.

"*Daiyamondo* no YUBI-WA toka"

oNEE-chan ga Ii, oKAA-san wa mou ICHI-DO, fufufu, to WARAtta.

"Atashi ne, SHIMA-KI-san ni *pinkuhausu* no *wanpiisu* KAtte morau n da. KON-DO no TAN-JOU-BI"

ONEE-chan to oKAA-san no TAN-JOU-BI wa IS-SHUU-KAN CHIGAi na no da.

"Hai hai, gochisousama. Demo ne, oTOU-san wa kou iu HITO desu kara ne, *purezento* nante, SAI-SHO kara KI-TAI shite imasen yo"

oKAA-san ga Ii, kono HANASHI wa sore de oshimai ni natta. Demo, <u>kou iu HITO</u> tte, IT-TAI dou iu HITO no koto darou.

Bikkuri suru koto ga atta no wa, sore kara SUKOshi ato datta. OBEN-TOU no JI-KAN de, Miho wa itsumo no toori, kirei na *hankachi* no UE ni kire-i na oBEN-TOU o hirogete ita.

"WATASHI, NI-GAK-KI kara TEN-KOU suru no"

kyou, TOMAri ni oide yo, to Iu no to onnaji, FU-TSUU no KU-CHOU de Mi-ho ga Itta.

A typical *geta-bako*, or shoe locker, in a typical high school.

This year, too, Dad didn't give her anything. Even during the toast, although everyone said "congratulations," only Dad remained silent. But that had already become the normal [state of things], and nobody (including me, of course) thought it was strange. At times like this, if it were Miho's dad, I thought he would certainly give Mom something (flowers or accessories) as a present.

"Is it OK to forget about Mr. Shimaki?"

Mom asked my big sister. Mr. Shimaki was my sister's husband. He had a large body, was a bit slow in the head, and wore glasses.

"It's OK. It's OK. He's always [stays] late [at the office] anyway,"

Sis said, stuffing her cheeks with the cake she had baked herself.

"Mom, as a celebration of your birthday, why not press for a trip abroad?"

Hee, hee, hee, giggled Mom.

"You're right. That would be nice, wouldn't it?"

Dad, still looking sullen, drank his tea pretending he couldn't hear.

"Or a diamond ring?"

said Sis, and mom laughed once again, hee, hee, hee.

"You know, I [think I'm] going to have my husband buy me [one of those] one-piece [dresses] from Pink House, this next birthday"

Sis and Mom's birthdays are one week apart.

"OK, OK. Enough of that sweet talk. But, your father is this sort of person, [you know], so from the start I don't expect a present or any such thing,"

said Mom, and this conversation ended with that. But what on earth is "this sort of person"?

What [really] surprised me came a little after that. At lunch time, Miho spread out her pretty lunch on a clean handkerchief as always.

"From next semester I'm transferring to another school."

Miho said this in a normal tone, the same as if she had said, today come stay over at my house.

- ええっ: expresses surprise [a variation of the standard ええ]
- コーヒー牛乳(ぎゅうにゅう): coffee-flavored milk
- のみこむ・飲み込む: to drink down; swallow
- 思わず・おもわず: "without thinking"; unconsciously; in spite of oneself; involuntarily
- 声(こえ)をだ(出)す: to say aloud
- おちつく・落ち着く: to be calm/composed
- 離婚(りこん)する: to divorce
- 一緒に・いっしょに: together
- 実家・じっか: the house where one was born and raised; one's parents' home
- ながいまつ毛(げ)をしている: to have long eye lashes
- 嘘・うそ: a lie
- 裁判所・さいばんしょ: court [here, probably a family court]
- ～とか(に行っていた): lists examples of places her parents went; not an exhaustive list
- 思い出す・おもいだす: to recall; remember
- 女の人・おんなのひと: a woman
- ばかみたい: stupid; ridiculous
- うつむく: to look down; hang one's head down
- ～ひょうしに・拍子に: "on the beat"; exactly at the moment
- ぽたっと: with a plop [describes a small and soft object (a raindrop, a tear) dropping]
- 涙・なみだ: tear
- おちる・落ちる: to fall
- 手紙・てがみ: a letter
- 女・おんな: a woman; women in general
- 哀しい・かなしい: "sad"; pitiful; sorrowful

- 包む・つつむ: to wrap
- きゅっと: tightly
- しばる・縛る: to bind; tie up
- 小(ちい)さい: small
- 気(き)の強い(つよい): strong-willed [の＝が]
- うん: an informal affirmative
- 一杯・いっぱい: full
- すっと: with a quick, light movement
- 期末試験・きまつしけん: an end of the semester exam [期末＝学期末・がっきまつ]
- さばさば: composed; unruffled [essentially the same as さっぱり]
- 考(かんが)えながら: while thinking
- テレビ: television
- 帰る・かえる: to return (home)
- みやげ・土産: a gift for those waiting at home (from someone who has been traveling or gone out)
- テーブル: table
- おく・置く: to put; place
- ちょっと: a little
- あきれる・呆れる: to be astonished; shocked; disgusted
- おやばか: "doting parent" [refers to her "stupid dad," bringing a melon though her sister is not living there any more]
- 毎年・まいとし: every year
- 決まって・きまって(～する): regularly (do ～); without fail (do ～)
- V～たら: why don't you… [used to make a suggestion]
- 台所・だいどころ: the kitchen

「ええっ」
　私はコーヒー牛乳をのみこむと、思わず大きな声をだして言った。
　みほはおちついていた。
「両親が離婚するの。私はママと一緒にママの実家に行くから」
　どこ、ときいたら、横浜、とみほはこたえた。すごくながいまつ毛をしている。
　コンサートとか食事とかっていうのは嘘^{うそ}で、ほんとうは裁判所とか、両親の実家とかに行っていたのだ、とみほは言った。
　私は、写真の中のみほのママを思い出す。白くって、細くって、茶色い髪の、笑っている女の人。
「夫婦なんて、ばかみたい」
　みほが言った。うつむいたひょうしに、ぽたっと涙がおちた。
「手紙、書くね」
　私は言い、みほは黙っていた。
　女は哀^{かな}しい。美人でも、やっぱり哀しい。
　みほは、お弁当箱をハンカチで包み、きゅっとしばった。髪が、肩のところでくるくるっと揺れる。
「横浜にも、泊りに来ていいよ」
　小さくて白い、気の強そうな、みほの顔。うん、と私は言った。
　横浜の学校でも、みほの下駄箱はきっと手紙で一杯になる。でも、みほは興味なさそうに、それをすっとカバンにしまうだろう。
「その前に期末試験かぁ」
　みほが、さばさばと言った。

　夜、みほのことを考えながら、ぼーっとテレビをみていたら、お父さんが帰ってきて、「みやげだ」と言ってテーブルにメロンをおいた。私は、ちょっとあきれて、
「親ばかぁ」
　と言った。お父さんは毎年、お姉ちゃんの誕生日には決まってメロンを買ってくる。でも、今年はもう、ここにお姉ちゃんはいないのだ。
「島木さんのとこに持ってったら？」
　私が言うと、お母さんが台所から、

Melons in boxes on display at a department store.

Expensive melons being sold by catalogue.

"Eett!"

WATASHI wa *koohii*GYUU-NYUU o nomikomu to, OMOwazu OOkina KOE o dashite Itta.

Miho wa ochitsuite ita.

"RYOU-SHIN ga RI-KON suru no. WATASHI wa *mama* to IS-SHO ni *mama* no JIK-KA ni Iku kara"

Doko, to kiitara, YOKO-HAMA, to Miho wa kotaeta. Sugoku nagai matsu-
GE o shite iru.

Konsaato toka SHOKU-JI toka tte iu no wa USO de, hontou wa SAI-BAN-SHO toka, RYOU-SHIN no JIK-KA toka ni Itte ita no da, to Miho wa Itta.

WATASHI wa, SHA-SHIN no NAKA no Miho no *mama* o OMOiDAsu. SHIROkutte, HOSOkutte,
CHA-IROi KAMI no, WARAtte iru ONNA no HITO.

"FUU-FU nante, baka mitai"

Miho ga Itta. Utsumuita hyoushi ni, potatto NAMIDA ga ochita.

"TE-GAMI, KAku ne"

WATASHI wa Ii, Miho wa DAMAtte ita.

ONNA wa KANAshii. BI-JIN de mo, yappari KANAshii.

Miho wa, oBEN-TOU-BAKO o *hankachi* de TSUTSUmi, kyutto shibatta. KAMI ga,
KATA no tokoro de kurukuru tto YUreru.

"YOKO-HAMA ni mo, TOMAri ni KIte ii yo"

CHIIsakute SHIROi, KI no TSUYOsou na, Miho no KAO. Un, to WATASHI wa Itta.

YOKO-HAMA no GAK-KOU de mo, Miho no GE-TA-BAKO wa kitto TE-GAMI de IP-PAI ni naru. Demo,
Miho wa KYOU-MI nasasou ni, sore o sutto *kaban* ni shimau darou.

"Sono MAE ni KI-MATSU SHI-KEN kaa"

Miho ga, sabasaba to Itta.

YORU, Miho no koto o KANGAenagara, bootto *terebi* o mite itara, o-
TOU-san ga KAEtte kite, "miyage da" to Itte *teeburu* ni *meron* o o-
ita. WATASHI wa, chotto akirete,

"OYAbakaa"

to Itta. OTOU-san wa MAI-TOSHI, oNEE-chan no TAN-JOU-BI ni wa KImatte *meron* o KAtte kuru. Demo, KO-TOSHI wa mou, koko ni oNEE-chan wa inai
no da.

"SHIMA-KI-san no toko ni MOtte ttara?"

WATASHI ga Iu to, oKAA-san ga DAI-DOKORO kara,

慣用句: Idiomatic Expressions I

Translate the following into idiomatic English

1. あっさり～する

みほは四通目のラブレターの封筒を裏返して差出した男の子の名前を
たしかめると興味なさそうに<u>あっさり</u>とそれをカバンに<u>しまった</u>。

2. どうしても～でなくちゃいけない

お姉ちゃんは「今度の誕生日祝いは<u>どうしても</u>ピンクハウスのワンピ
ース<u>でなくちゃいけない</u>」とだんなさんにねだっているようだ。

3. どやどやと駆けていく

弁当の時間が終わるとすぐ男の子たちはサッカーボールを持って校庭の方へ<u>どやど
やと駆けていった</u>。

4. 自信たっぷりに

「今度の期末試験はぜったいだいじょうぶ」と気の強いみほは<u>自信たっぷりに</u>言
った。

5. （～を）ほおばる

弁当の時間に甘いたれのかかったミートボールを<u>ほおばり</u>ながら「みほの両親はと
ても仲がいいんだな」と私は思った。

"What?!"

I said spontaneously in a loud voice when I had swallowed my coffee milk.

Miho was calm.

"My parents are getting divorced. I'm going with mom to mom's parents' house."

When I asked where, Miho replied, Yokohama. She had very long
eyelashes.

The concerts and dining out were lies, and in reality they
spent most of the time in court or their parents' homes, said Miho.

I recall Miho's mom in the photos. A white, slim,
brown-haired, smiling woman.

"Married couples are so stupid,"

Miho said. As she cast down her head a tear plopped down.

"I'll write you letters,"

I said, but Miho was silent.

[Being a] woman is [an] unhappy [existence]. Even for beautiful women.

Miho wrapped her lunch box in her handkerchief, and tied it up tightly. Her hair
swung in circles at her shoulders.

"You can come to stay at Yokohama, too."

Miho's small, white, strong face. Yes, I said.

Even at the school in Yokohama Miho's shoe locker would certainly grow full of letters. But
Miho would probably quietly slip those into her bag disinterestedly.

"But before that, it's finals, huh,"

Miho said, clearing the air.

That night, while thinking about Miho, I was half-mindedly watching TV
when Dad came back, said "Here's a present," and placed a melon on the
table. I said, a little astonished,

"Parents [are so] stupid."

Every year Dad regularly bought a melon and brought
it [home] on Sis's birthday. But this year she wasn't even
here.

"Why don't you take it to Shimaki's place?"

When I said this, from the kitchen,

- せっかくだから: since [he's] gone to all the trouble [implies someone went to a special or deliberate effort to do something, which should be appreciated]
- うち・家: "home"; here [not at brother-in-law's]
- いただく・頂く: to eat; have [formal for 食べる・たべる "to eat"]
- お風呂・おふろ: a deep, cubical bath [one washes outside the bath and soaks inside; useful in winter for survival in drafty houses]
- 入る・はいる: to enter; take (a bath)
- と、…と、…私(わたし)で…食(た)べた: eaten by me and…and…and [grammatically, で could also be preceded by と]
- 食(た)べる: to eat
- 〜くせに: although; even though [like 〜のに、implies someone is not behaving the way one would expect or thinks natural]
- 茶の間・ちゃのま: living room; parlor
- すわる・座る: to sit
- スポーツニュース: TV program giving sports highlights of the day
- ビール: beer
- とっても: very [a more emphatic and colloquial version of とても]
- うれる・熟れる: to ripen
- かよこ: name of narrator's older sister
- 生む・うむ: to give birth
- 難産・なんざん: difficult birth
- しばらく: for a while
- 入院(にゅういん)する: to be hospitalized
- 病院・びょういん: hospital
- 陰気・いんき: gloomy; dismal
- 毎日・まいにち: everyday
- 憂鬱・ゆううつ: depressing; disheartening
- 緑色・みどりいろ: green

- 果肉・かにく: meat of the fruit
- スプーン: spoon
- すくう: to scoop up
- さぁっと: quickly [cf. さっと "instantaneously"]
- 冷気・れいき: coolness
- 食(た)べたいって: って is the colloquial equivalent of と
- すぐ: at once
- そこまで: to that extent; that much
- みあわせる・見合わせる: to look at one another
- くくくと笑(わら)う: to giggle; titter
- 声(こえ)をひそめる: to lower (one's) voice
- 死(し)ぬまで: until one dies
- 買ってやる: to buy for (someone) [やる is the informal equivalent of 上(あ)げる used toward those of equal or inferior status]
- 元気・げんき: healthy; energetic
- 真剣・しんけん: serious, grave
- 何とも・なんとも: anything; anything at all
- 返事・へんじ: reply
- ほんとに: really [shortened colloquial version of ほんとう・本当]
- おどろく・驚く: be surprised/startled
- 後ろ姿・うしろすがた: the form (appearance) from the rear
- いつもどおり・いつも通り: as always; as usual
- 無愛想・ぶあいそう: unfriendly; unsociable; dour
- せっせと: diligently; busily
- 人形・にんぎょう: doll
- みたい: like; resembling [= のよう]; seemingly; seems to [= よう]
- つめたい・冷たい: cold
- しみる: to sting; smart
- 味(あじ)がする: to have a (certain) taste

「せっかくだからうちでいただきましょう」
と言った。

　お風呂に入ってから、お母さんと、おばあちゃんと、私でメロンを食べた。（自分で買ってきたくせに、お父さんは食べなかった。茶の間に一人ですわって、スポーツニュースをみながらビールをのんでいる。）メロンは、とってもよくうれていた。

「かよこを生むときね」
　お母さんが言った。

「難産でね、産んだあともしばらく入院していたの。病院は陰気だし、毎日むし暑くて、憂鬱だったわ」

　ふうん。私は、きれいな緑色の果肉をスプーンですくって口に入れる。さぁっと冷気がひろがる。

「メロンが食べたいって言ったら、お父さんがすぐ買ってきてくれてね」

　そこまで言って、お母さんは黙った。そして、おばあちゃんとお母さんと顔をみあわせてくくくっと笑った。

「なに？」
「お父さんね」
　声をひそめて、お母さんが言う。

「これから毎年、死ぬまでメロンを買ってやるから、だから元気になってくれ、って」

　くくくっとおばあちゃんが笑い、お母さんも笑いそうな顔になって、
「真剣な顔でいうのよ。死ぬまで、なんて」
と、もう一度言った。

　私は、何とも返事ができなかった。それで毎年毎年、ほんとにメロンを買い続けているのだと思うと、笑うよりもおどろいてしまう。

　茶の間をみると、お父さんの後ろ姿はいつもどおり無愛想だった。私は、メロンをせっせとすくいながら、
「夫婦なんて、ばかみたい」
　と言ったみほの、お人形みたいな横顔を思い出していた。メロンは、甘くて、つめたくて、しみるみたいな味がした。

———◦∢∢◦———

慣用句: Idiomatic Expressions II

Translate the following into idiomatic English

6. むっつりしたまま

お弁当の時間にめずらしくむっつりしたままだったみほは、弁当箱をハンカチで包み、きゅっとしばると「両親が離婚するの」と言った。

7. (〜した) ひょうしに

「私、二学期から転校するの」とみほが言ったひょうしに、私は「ええっ」と大きな声をだしてしまった。

8. せっかくだから

私たちがお金をだしあって買って上げたブラウスを見ながら母は「お花か何かでいいと言ったのに……。でもせっかくだからいただくわ。ありがとう」と嬉しそうに言った。

9. (〜する) くせに

今日は母の誕生日だと知っているくせに父はいつもどおり無愛想で、茶の間で一人でビールを飲んでいる。

10. くくくと笑う

母は「それじゃ今度の誕生日にはダイヤモンドの指輪でもおねだりしょうかな……」と言うと、聞こえないふりでスポーツニュースを読んでいる父を見ながらくくくと笑った。

11. 声をひそめる

「夫婦なんてばかみたい」とみほは声をひそめ、うつむいたまま言った。

"Sekkaku da kara uchi de itadakimashou"

to Itta.

OFU-RO ni HAItte kara, oKAA-san to, obaa-chan to, WATASHI de *meron*

o TAbeta. (JI-BUN de KAtte kita kuse ni, oTOU-san wa TAbenakatta.

CHAnoMA ni HITO-RI de suwatte, *supootsu nyuusu* o minagara *biiru* o no-

nde iru.) *Meron* wa, tottemo yoku urete ita.

"Kayoko o Umu toki ne"

oKAA-san ga Itta.

"NAN-ZAN de ne, Unda ato mo shibaraku NYUU-IN shite ita no. BYOU-IN wa IN-KI da

shi, MAI-NICHI mushiATSUkute, YUU-UTSU datta wa"

Fuun. Watashi wa, kirei na MIDORI-IRO no KA-NIKU o *supuun* de sukutte KUCHI ni I-

reru. Saatto REI-KI ga hirogaru.

"*Meron* ga TAbetai tte Ittara, oTOU-san ga sugu KAtte kite kure-

te ne"

Soko made Itte, oKAA-san wa DAMAtta. Soshite, obaa-chan to o-

KAA-san to KAO o miawasete kukukutto WARAtta.

"Nani?"

"OTOU-san ne"

KOE o hisomete, oKAA-san ga Iu.

"Kore kara MAI-TOSHI, SHInu made *meron* o KAtte yaru kara, dakara GEN-KI ni

natte kure, tte"

Kukukutto obaa-chan ga WARAi, oKAA-san mo WARAisou na KAO ni natte,

"SHIN-KEN na KAO de iu no yo. SHInu made, nante"

to, mou ICHI-DO Itta.

WATASHI wa, NAN to mo HEN-JI ga dekinakatta. Sore de MAI-TOSHI MAI-TOSHI, honto ni *me-*

ron o KAiTSUZUkete iru no da to OMOu to, WARAu yori mo odoroite shimau.

CHAnoMA o miru to, oTOU-san no USHIroSUGATA wa itsumodoori BU-AI-SOU datta.

WATASHI wa, *meron* o sesse to sukuinagara,

"FUU-FU nante, baka mitai"

to Itta Miho no, oNIN-GYOU mitai na YOKO-GAO o OMOiDAshite ita. *Meron*

wa, AMAkute, tsumetakute, shimiru mitai na AJI ga shita.

内容理解: Comprehension Exercises

Answer in Japanese

1. みほは誰に、そしてどのようなところが「そっくり」なのでしょうか。
2. みほは男の子に興味がありそうですか。
3. みのりの好きな人とはどんな人でしょう？
4. みのりのお母さんの誕生日には毎年お父さんはプレゼントをしたり「おめでとう」と言ったりしますか。みほのパパならこういう時どんなことをするのでしょう。
5. お母さんがみのりのお姉さんに「はい、はい、ごちそうさま」と言ったのはどうしてでしょう。
6. みほは弁当の時間にどんな「びっくりすること」をみのりに言いましたか。
7. みほの両親は仲がよくて、よくコンサートとか温泉にいっていたのでしょうか。
8. みほのお父さんが「おみやげだ」と言ってメロンを持って来た時、どうしてみのりは「親ばかぁ」と言ったのでしょう。
9. お父さんはどうして毎年みのりのお姉さんの誕生日にきまってメロンを買ってくるのでしょうか。
10. みほの両親とみのりの両親との違いについてどう思いますか。みんなで話し合いましょう。

Mom said

"He went to the trouble to get it, so let's enjoy it."

After taking a bath, Mom, Grandma and I ate
the melon. (Even though he bought it himself, Dad didn't eat any.
He sat by himself in the parlor drinking beer while watching
the sports news.) The melon was very ripe.

"When I gave birth to Kayoko, you know,"

Mom said.

"It was a difficult birth and I stayed in the hospital for a while after I gave birth. The hospital
was gloomy, it was hot and humid everyday, and I was depressed."

Humm. I scooped the pretty green meat of the fruit with my spoon and put it in my
mouth. A cool sensation quickly spread.

"When I said I wanted some melon, Dad immediately went and got
one."

Saying that much, Mom was silent. Then Mom and
Grandma looked at each other and giggled.

"What?"

"Well, your Dad …"

Mom said, lowering her voice,

"… said, from now on, every year until I die, I'll buy you a melon, so
will you just get well again."

Grandma giggled, and Mom's face seemed about to laugh.

"He says this with an earnest expression. 'Until I die,' he says,"
she said once more.

I had no way I could respond. When I thought that he was really continuing
to buy melons year after year, rather than laughing [at it], I was amazed.

When I looked into the parlor, Father's back was, as always, unfriendly.
I, while assiduously scooping up melon, recalled Miho's saying,

"Married couples are so stupid,"
[and recalled] her profile, like a doll's. The melon
was sweet, cold, and had a taste that seemed to sink [into me].

語句と語法: Phrases and Usage

- 得手・えて: one's forte; what one is good at [= 得意・とくい]
- やる: to do
- 好(す)きこそ: It is exactly because one likes it (that…) [proverb: 好きこそものの上手(じょうず)なれ: "what one likes, one will do well"]
- 上手・じょうず: good; proficient
- 私・わたし: I
- 会社・かいしゃ: company; firm
- 〜以外・いがい: other than 〜
- 絶対(ぜったい)に: absolutely
- 口(くち)をだす: to speak out in an untimely manner; interfere
- わが社 (しゃ): our company (Honda)
- 組織・そしき: organization; system
- したがって: therefore; consequently
- 能率・のうりつ: efficiency
- 非常(ひじょう)に: very much; extremely
- 上(あ)がる: to rise; go up
- 社・しゃ: abbreviated form of *kaisha* (company)
- 書類・しょるい: documents; papers
- いじくる: to handle; fiddle with; play around with
- 印鑑・いんかん: official seal
- 押す・おす: press (a seal on paper to make an impression)
- ばかり: only
- 本田・ほんだ: Honda
- 技研・ぎけん: abbreviation of 技術(ぎじゅつ)研究(けんきゅう), that is, "technical research"; Honda Motor Company. Ltd. is, in Japanese, 本田技研工業株式会社・ほんだぎけんこうぎょうかぶしきがいしゃ
- すぐ: soon; right away
- つぶれる・潰れる: "to be crushed"; go bankrupt; fold; collapse
- 専務・せんむ: managing director
- 工場・こうじょう: factory; plant
- 小言(こごと)をいう: to nit-pick; lecture
- おれば: polite form of いれば (if I …)
- たちまち: instantly; in the blink of an eye; immediately
- 破滅・はめつ: ruin; destruction
- お互いに・おたがいに: mutually
- 今日・こんにち: today; the present
- 成功・せいこう: success
- 得(え)る: to attain; acquire
- 大会社・だいがいしゃ: huge corporation
- ただ単(たん)に: simply

- 勤務・きんむ: employment; service; work
- 年数・ねんすう: number of years
- 多い・おおい: many; a large number of
- 課長・かちょう: section head
- 部長・ぶちょう: department head
- 自動的に・じどうてきに: automatically (be promoted)
- 地位・ちい: status; position; rank
- 仕事・しごと: work; a job
- ハン・判: stamp or seal (of approval); works like a signature does in the US [ハンを押(お)したような: cut and dried; invariably (the same); mindless (work); this set phrase is cutomarily written 判で押したような using kanji and で rather than を]
- 進歩・しんぽ: progress
- 退歩(たいほ)する: to retreat; deteriorate; retrogress
- 研究所・けんきゅうじょ: "research facility" [here, referring to Honda]
- 黒(くろ)くなる: "to become black"; get dirty (working)
- 動く・うごく: to move (around) [meaning "work" here]
- 世の中・よのなか: the world; people in general
- 人・ひと: people
- 陣頭指揮・じんとうしき: "to lead at the head of the unit"; for a person in an administrative position to take an active lead in the workplace rather than simply supervising
- 陣頭: at the head of a workforce
- 指揮: lead; conduct
- 間違う・まちがう: to be mistaken/wrong
- 悲壮感・ひそうかん: a feeling of tragic resolve (that if he does not take the lead, the company will fail)
- 自分・じぶん: oneself; I
- 若い・わかい: young
- 間に入る・あいだにはいる: to get in among
- 働く・はたらく: to work
- 不思議・ふしぎ: strange
- 二代目・にだいめ: second generation
- 社長・しゃちょう: company president
- やはり: likewise; too
- 技術者・ぎじゅつしゃ: technician
- 経理・けいり: accounting
- 〜面・めん: field; area of work
- で(出)る: to emerge from; be from
- 選ぶ・えらぶ: to choose; select
- 普通・ふつう: ordimary

得手なものをやれ(抄)

本田宗一郎

　好きこそものの上手といわれるように、好きなことをやらなければいけない。私は会社では好きなことをやる。好きなことというのは得手なんだから、得手以外のことには絶対に口を出さない。わが社はそういう組織でやっている。したがって能率が非常に上がる。

　私が社に来て、書類をいじくったり、印鑑を押してばかりいたら、本田技研はすぐつぶれてしまう。また専務が工場に行って小言をいっておれば、忽ち破滅である。お互いに得手なことをやっているから、今日の成功を得たと思う。

　大会社になると、ただ単に勤務年数が多いから課長、部長と自動的に地位が上がり、仕事もハンを押したようなことばかりやっている。これでは進歩がない。退歩してつぶれてしまう。

　私が研究所で黒くなって動いていると、世の中の人は陣頭指揮だという。これは間違っている。私は陣頭指揮なんて悲壮感ではやっていない。自分が好きだからやっているだけである。私が若い人の間に入って働いているのを不思議に思う人がいる。

　二代目、三代目の社長が、やはり私のように技術者であるなら、私のようにやったらいい。経理面からでた社長が選ばれたとしたら、普通の社長のように印鑑をおしているのもそれでよ

Honda Sōichirō

Honda Sōichirō (1906–91) was born in Shizuoka Prefecture to a blacksmith and bicycle repairman. At sixteen, after graduating from Futama Senior Elementary School, he took a job at an automobile repair shop in Tokyo. At the age of 22, he opened a branch of the shop with his own money near his home, and at 28 he founded a company which produced piston rings. After the war, in 1946, he founded Honda Gijutsu Kenkyujo to equip bicycles with surplus army engines. The Honda Motor Company was founded in 1948. It began with the production of motorcycles and established its prestige through competition in international racing events through the 1950s and 60s. By 1968 it was producing 10 million motorcycles annually. In 1963 the company introduced its first sports car and in 1967 a lightweight passenger car.

By producing race-winning motorcycles and efficient automobiles, Honda helped create the perception that Japanese products were of high quality. Honda believed that the extreme conditions of racing were the best for designing quality motor vehicles, and that the race track is one of the best places for young engineers to learn. After stepping down as president of the company in 1973, Honda fostered cultural exchange, for which he received a number of awards from different countries. He was a sought-after speaker on the international lecture circuit, advocating new administration techniques. In addition to being a devotee of racing cars, Honda enjoyed writing and painting.

E-TE na mono o yare (SHOU)

HON-DA SOU-ICHI-ROU

SUki koso mono no JOU-ZU to iwareru you ni, SUki na koto o yarana-
kereba ikenai. WATASHI wa KAI-SHA de wa SUki na koto o yaru. SUki na koto
to iu no wa E-TE nan da kara, E-TE I-GAI no koto ni wa ZET-TAI ni KUCHI o DA-
sanai. WagaSHA wa sou iu SO-SHIKI de yatte iru. Shitagatte NOU-RITSU
ga HI-JOU ni Agaru.

WATASHI ga SHA ni KIte, SHO-RUI o ijikuttari, IN-KAN o Oshite bakari i-
tara, HON-DA GI-KEN wa sugu tsuburete shimau. Mata SEN-MU ga KOU-JOU ni Itte KO-GOTO o itte oreba, TACHIMAchi HA-METSU de aru. OTAGAi ni E-TE na koto
o yatte iru kara, KON-NICHI no SEI-KOU o Eta to OMOu.

DAI-GAI-SHA ni naru to, tada TAN ni KIN-MU NEN-SUU ga OOi kara KA-CHOU, BU-CHOU to
JI-DOU-TEKI ni CHI-I ga Agari, SHI-GOTO mo *han* o Oshita you na koto bakari
yatte iru. Kore de wa SHIN-PO ga nai. TAI-HO shite tsuburete shimau.

WATASHI ga KEN-KYUU-JO de KUROku natte UGOite iru to, YO no NAKA no HITO wa JIN-TOU SHI-
KI da to iu. Kore wa MA-CHIGAtte iru. WATASHI wa JIN-TOU SHI-KI nante HI-SOU-KAN
de wa yatte inai. JI-BUN ga SUki da kara yatte iru dake de aru.
WATASHI ga WAKAi HITO no AIDA ni HAItte HATARAite iru no o FU-SHI-GI ni OMOu HITO ga iru.

NI-DAI-ME, SAN-DAI-ME no SHA-CHOU ga, yahari WATASHI no you ni GI-JUTSU-SHA de aru nara, WATASHI no you ni yattara ii. KEI-RI-MEN kara deta SHA-CHOU ga ERAbareta
to shitara, FU-TSUU no SHA-CHOU no you ni IN-KAN o oshite iru no mo sore de yo-

Honda Sōichirō's shop in Hamamatsu, which he established at the age of 22.

Honda Dream Model D in 1950. Air-cooled, two-stroke, single cylinder, capacity 98cc, maximum output 3.5ps/4,500rpm, top speed 50km/h.

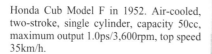

Honda Cub Model F in 1952. Air-cooled, two-stroke, single cylinder, capacity 50cc, maximum output 1.0ps/3,600rpm, top speed 35km/h.

Do What You Are Good At (An Excerpt)

Honda Sōichirō

Just as it is said that [people are] skilled at things because they like [them], people should do what they like. At the company I do the things I like. Because I am good at what I like, I absolutely do not advise on something I'm not good at. We do things at my company with this system. Consequently, efficiency greatly increases.

If I came to the company and only handled and stamped documents, Honda Research would soon go broke. Again, if the managing director were to go to the factory and lecture [people on their jobs], it would be instant destruction. I think that because we respectively do what we are best at, we have this success of today.

When companies get big, simply because one has many years of work experience, one automatically rises in position to section or department head, and one does work which is merely repetitive. With this there is no progress. One loses ground and goes under.

When I am in the research department getting dirty moving around, people [out there] say I'm leading from the front. This is mistaken. I'm not leading from the front with [some] feeling of heroic resolve. I am just doing it because I like it. There are [some] people who think it strange that I work amongst younger people.

If the second or third generation president is an engineer, then, of course, [he] should do as I do. If a president from accounting were to be chosen, then it's enough that he stamps [approval on documents] like a normal president,

- 汗(あせ)まみれ: all sweaty; dripping with sweat; (〜に)まみれる: be covered (with 〜)
- 通用(つうよう)する: to hold valid (for); work (for)
- 外の・ほかの: other; another
- その人(ひと)その人(ひと)によって: according to the person
- やり方(かた): way of
- 当然・とうぜん: natural; usual
- 金・かね: money
- 不得手・ふえて: not good at [negative form of 得手]
- 人(ひと)にやってもらう: to have someone else do (it)
- やらず: not do [= やらないで]
- ことにする: to decide to do something (in a certain way)
- かつて: once; at one point
- 非常に・ひじょうに: extremely; incredibly
- 苦労(くろう)する: to have hard times
- 昭和・しょうわ: Imperial reign name for period from 1926–1989, when Hirohito was Emperor; Japan still uses this type of dating system
- 時・とき: time
- こう考(かんが)える: to think in this way (like this)
- 良品・りょうひん: good products/goods
- 国境なし・こっきょうなし: no national border; borderless
- どんなに: no matter how
- 関税・かんぜい: tariff; customs duty
- 高(たか)くする: to raise
- 障壁・しょうへき: an impediment; barrier
- 品物・しなもの: goods; products
- 入ってくる(来る): to come into
- だから: so; that's why
- 防ぐ・ふせぐ: to prevent
- 国家・こっか: nation; a state (country)
- 施策・しさく: a policy; a measure
- 援護(えんご)する: to protect
- 輸入・ゆにゅう: imports [〜する = to import]
- 制限・せいげん: restriction; limit
- にたよる・に頼る: to depend on; be dependent on
- 永久(えいきゅう)に: eternally; forever
- 続く・つづく: to continue
- 真(しん)の: real/true (protection against imports)
- 輸入防止・ゆにゅうぼうし: a check or hold on imports
- 輸出増進・ゆしゅつぞうしん: increasing exports
- こっち: "this side"; here, indicates Japan [short, informal form of こちら]
- 技術・ぎじゅつ: technology
- あげる・上げる: to raise; improve
- むこう: "over there"; overseas
- よくする: to make better
- 自然(しぜん)と: naturally; as a matter of course
- とまる・止まる: to stop; cease
- 出ていく(行く): to go out (be exported)
- 考え方・かんがえかた: way of thinking
- 根本的・こんぽんてき: fundamental; basic
- 解決・かいけつ: solution; resolution
- 政府・せいふ: government
- なんの役(やく)にたたない: to be of no use; serve no purpose
- おれ・俺: rough, informal for "I," "me" [used by men, mainly among peers]
- おれはおれでやる: to do by oneself (in one's own way)
- 現在・げんざい: the present day; this day and age
- まず: first of all; foremost; can also mean "perhaps"
- 設備・せつび: equipment; facilities
- ものをいう: is what counts [cf. 金(かね)がものをいう: "Money talks"]
- どうしても: no matter what
- 更新(こうしん)する: to renew; upgrade
- 世界的・せかいてき: world-wide; global
- そうかといって: and yet; on the other hand
- 機械・きかい: machinery; equipment
- 入れる・いれる: to bring in; get; install; procure
- 払う・はらう: to pay
- だけど: but
- 入(い)れずにいれば: if (one) doesn't bring in
- 現実・げんじつ: the reality; a hard fact
- また: on the other hand
- フル: from "full"; here (to operate at) full capacity
- 稼動(かどう)する: (of machinery) to operate/function
- 可能性・かのうせい: possibility; potentiality
- 道・みち: path; way; here means せんたく, a choice
- かまう・構う: to mind; care about; matter
- 決心(けっしん)する: to decide; resolve
- 前進(ぜんしん)する: to advance; move forward

いと思う。

　私が汗まみれになって働いているから、本田技研は成功しているというのは、私にだけ通用することであって、外の人には通用しない。その人その人によって社長のやり方が違うのは当然である。

　私は金をいじるのは不得手だから人にやってもらう。私は不得手なことはやらず、得手のことしかやらないことにしている。

　かつて金で非常に苦労したことがある。昭和二十七年の時、私はこう考えた。良品に国境なしということがある。どんなに関税という障壁を高くしても、いい品物は日本へ入ってくる。だからこれを防ぐのに国家の施策で援護してもらって、輸入制限にたよってやるということは永久には続かない。

　真の輸入防止、輸出増進であるなら、これはこっちの技術をあげることだ、むこうのものより品物をよくすることである。そうすれば自然とむこうの品物がこっちに入ってくるのがとまって、こっちから出ていくという考え方、これが根本的な解決で、これをやらないかぎり、政府の施策にたよって障壁をつけてもらったところでなんの役にもたたない。

　だからおれはおれでやるんだという考え方でやるのだが、そうなると現在では、どんなアイデアがあってもまず設備がものをいう。どうしても設備を更新しなければならない。世界的のレベルの設備に更新しないかぎり輸入防止ができない。そうかといって、その機械を入れて払えないでつぶれるかもしれない。だけど入れずにいればつぶれるということは現実だ。またつぶれるかもしらんけれども、それがうまくフル稼動してくれて、もっと大きくなる可能性があるなら道は一つしかない。かまわない、機械を入れることだということに決心をした。そしてそれで大きく前進する事ができた。

ON THE HORIZON
AT THE HONDA MOTOR COMPANY

In partnership with the Itochu trading company and EIN-Engineering, which specializes in recycling equipment, the Honda Motor Company has set up a new venture to recycle plastic scraps left over from car production. The newly formed company will recycle scraps of plastic and saw mill dust into plastics that simulate wood. These new materials will be used for the manufacture of lumber-like products, such as furniture, doors, and wall paneling.

The new plastic materials will have properties that are similar to organic wood. This is an important step towards curbing the massive imports of lumber from forests in Southeast Asia, Canada, and other parts of the world. Japan's own forests seem unable to satisfy its huge appetite for wood products.

The new venture by the Honda Motor Company may prove a significant step toward the preservation of rain forests, while at the same time finding an outlet for the company's scrap materials. April 1997 was the starting date of the new operations.

The company has also produced a highly efficient "hybrid" car which is run by an electric motor and a small combustion engine that uses conventional gasoline. One reason for the car's great efficiency is that it is finely controlled by an embedded computer.

i to OMOu.

WATASHI ga ASEmamire ni natte HATARAite iru kara, HON-DA GI-KEN wa SEI-KOU shite iru to iu no wa, WATASHI ni dake TSUU-YOU suru koto de atte, HOKA no HITO ni wa TSUU-YOU shinai. Sono HITO sono HITO ni yotte SHA-CHOU no yariKATA ga CHIGAu no wa TOU-ZEN de aru.

WATASHI wa KANE o ijiru no wa FU-E-TE da kara HITO ni yatte morau. WATASHI wa FU-E-TE na koto wa yarazu, E-TE no koto shika yaranai koto ni shite iru.

Katsute KANE de HI-JOU ni KU-ROU shita koto ga aru. SHOU-WA NI-JUU-SHICHI-NEN no TOKI, WATASHI wa kou KANGAeta. RYOU-HIN ni KOK-KYOU nashi to iu koto ga aru. Donna ni KAN-ZEI to iu SHOU-HEKI o TAKAku shite mo, ii SHINA-MONO wa NIHON e HAItte kuru. Dakara kore o FUSEgu no ni KOK-KA no SHI-SAKU de EN-GO shite moratte, YU-NYUU SEI-GEN ni tayotte yaru to iu koto wa EI-KYUU ni wa TSUZUkanai.

SHIN no YU-NYUU BOU-SHI, YU-SHUTSU ZOU-SHIN de aru nara, kore wa kotchi no GI-JUTSU o ageru koto da, mukou no mono yori SHINA-MONO o yoku suru koto de aru. Sou sureba SHI-ZEN to mukou no SHINA-MONO ga kotchi ni HAItte kuru no ga tomat-te, kotchi kara DEte iku to iu KANGAeKATA, kore ga KON-PON-TEKI na KAI-KETSU de, kore o yaranai kagiri SEI-FU no SHI-SAKU ni tayotte SHOU-HEKI o tsuke-te moratta tokoro de nan no YAKU ni mo tatanai.

Dakara ore wa ore de yaru n da to iu KANGAeKATA de yaru no da ga, so-u naru to GEN-ZAI de wa, donna *aidea* ga atte mo mazu SETSU-BI ga mono o iu. Doushite mo SETSU-BI o KOU-SHIN shinakereba naranai. SE-KAI-TEKI no *reberu* no SETSU-BI ni KOU-SHIN shinai kagiri YU-NYUU BOU-SHI ga dekinai. Sou ka to itte, sono KI-KAI o Irete HARAenai de tsubureru ka mo shirenai. Dakedo Irezu ni ireba tsubureru to iu koto wa GEN-JITSU da. Mata tsubu-reru ka mo shiran keredomo, sore ga umaku *furu* KA-DOU shite kurete, motto OOkiku naru KA-NOU-SEI ga aru nara MICHI wa HITOtu shika nai. Kamawa-nai, KI-KAI o Ireru koto da to iu koto ni KES-SHIN o shita. Soshite so-re de OOkiku ZEN-SHIN suru KOTO ga dekita.

慣用句: Idiomatic Expressions I

Translate the following into idiomatic English

1. 好きこそ物の上手なれ

「好きこそものの上手なれ」といわれるように本田技研には機械をいじるのが得手な世界的レベルの技術屋が多い。

2. (〜に) 口を出す

本田技研の社長は技術屋で、経理面にはあまり口を出さない。

3. 小言をいう

「もっと輸入防止をするべきだ」と小言をいって政府の施策にたよってばかりいる社長では会社がつぶれてしまう。

4. ハンで押したようなこと

何もアイデアがなく、ハンで押したようなことばかりしている専務は本田技研にはいない。

5. 汗まみれになる

社長は機械いじりが好きで、いつも工場や研究所で若い人と汗まみれになって働いている。

6. 通用する

政府の施策や援護にばかりたよっている専務は本田技研では通用しない。

I think.

That Honda Giken is succeeding because I am getting covered in sweat working is something which works only for me, and doesn't work for other people. It is natural that a president's way of doing things depends on the [kind of] person [he is].

I am no good at manipulating money, so I have someone do it for me. I make a practice of not doing anything I am bad at, and doing only what is my specialty.

Once I had great trouble with money. When it was the year Showa 27, I thought this way: There is the fact that there are no borders for good products. No matter how high one raises tariff barriers, good products will come into Japan. Thus, doing [business] while receiving protection under government policies and depending on import restrictions to prevent this [foreign imports] will not last forever.

If true import prevention is to increase exports, then we must raise our [level of] technology and make [our] products better than those abroad. If we do this, the way of thinking that says foreign products' coming here will naturally cease, and [our products] will leave from here, is the fundamental solution, and as long as we do not do this, the addition of barriers by government policy will serve no purpose at all.

So, I run my business my own way, but with that, at present, no matter what kind of ideas we have, [our] facilities are first of all the deciding factor. No matter what, we must upgrade our facilities. If we do not improve our facilities to a world [class] level, we cannot keep out imports. Even so, we might procure that equipment and go under, being unable to pay for it. But, if I don't procure it, then that we will go under is a reality. Again, we might go bankrupt, but if [our facilities] work well at full [capacity], and if there is the possibility that we may grow even bigger, then there is only one way to go. I don't mind, [so] I decided I would purchase the equipment. And with that I was able to make a great advance forward.

- 当時・とうじ: at that time
- 資本金・しほんきん: capital; funds
- 百万・ひゃくまん: one million
- 億・おく: one hundred million
- 支払い・しはらい: payment
- 困る・こまる: to be in trouble; be in a fix
- ずいぶん・随分: considerably; awfully
- 骨(ほね)を折(お)る: "to break a bone"; have a very hard time
- もちろん: of course
- 技術屋・ぎじゅつや: technician [= 技術者, but more informal with the addition of 屋, which indicates a trade rather than a profession]
- ほう・方: "side"; area (of work)
- ほんとう・本当: real
- 頭(あたま)をかかえる: "to hold one's head (in one's hands)"; be at one's wits' end; be tearing one's hair out
- 身(み)にしみる: "to sink into the body"; feel something deeply; know full well
- 二度(にど)と…ない: (I must) never do again (lit. "a second time")
- (verb)てはいけない: must/should not do
- いけないこと: something that is bad, that shouldn't be done
- なお・尚: even more
- 理論的・りろんてき: logically; rationally
- 踏み切る・ふみきる: to take a decisive step; take the plunge; make a difficult decision
- 英断・えいだん: "excellent decision"; a bold, courageous decision
- 一生を通じて・いっしょうをつうじて: for one's whole life; of a lifetime

　当時会社の資本金が百万円くらいのときに、三億円、四億円
の機械を輸入した。それだから支払いには困ったでしょう。専
務もずいぶん骨を折ったようである。もちろん私は技術屋のほ
うで金は扱ってないから、そのほんとうの苦労はしないけれど
も、専務は頭をかかえてたいへんだったということは私も身に
しみている。二度とこういうことをやってはいけない。いけな
いことではあるけれども、それをやらずにつぶれるということ
はなおいけない。そのとき理論的に私が踏みきらなかったら、
今日の本田技研はない。その踏み切り方はいちばんの英断だっ
たと思う。一生を通じての大英断であった。

慣用句: Idiomatic Expressions II

Translate the following into idiomatic English

7. 良品に国境なし

工場の設備を更新し、世界的レベルの品物を作れば、自然にこっちの品物がむこうに出ていく。「良品に国境なし」といわれるように。

8. (〜が)ものをいう

会社が前進し成功するためには技術と設備がものをいう。

9. 骨を折る

社長は技術屋で経理が不得意らしいから金の扱いで骨を折るのはいつも専務の方だ。

10. 身にしみる

金で苦労したことがあるその社長は、関税という国家の施策にたよって障壁をつけてもらっても社長の成功にはなんの役にもたたないということが身にしみている。

11. (〜に) 踏み切る

社長が設備の更新に踏み切ってから、その会社は大きく前進することになった。

TOU-JI KAI-SHA no SHI-HON-KIN ga HYAKU-MAN-EN kurai no toki ni, SAN-OKU-EN, YON-OKU-EN no KI-KAI o YU-NYUU shita. Sore da kara SHI-HARAi ni wa KOMAtta deshou. SEN-MU mo zuibun HONE o Otta you de aru. Mochiron WATASHI wa GI-JUTSU-YA no hou de KANE wa ATSUKAtte nai kara, sono HON-TOU no KU-ROU wa shinai keredomo, SEN-MU wa ATAMA o kakaete taihen datta to iu koto wa WATASHI mo MI ni shimite iru. NI-DO to kou iu koto o yatte wa ikenai. Ikenai koto de wa aru keredomo, sore o yarazu ni tsubureru to iu koto wa nao ikenai. Sono toki RI-RON-TEKI ni WATASHI ga FUmikiranakattara, KON-NICHI no HON-DA GI-KEN wa nai. Sono FUmiKIriKATA wa ichiban no EI-DAN datta to OMOu. IS-SHOU o TSUUjite no DAI-EI-DAN de atta.

内容理解: Comprehension Exercises

Answer in Japanese

1. 「わが社」の能率が非常にいいのはどうしてでしょうか。
2. 「『陣頭指揮』などという悲壮感でやっているのではない」という本田の真意は?
3. 本田は経理面での経験のある社長でも若い技術者といっしょに黒くなって働くべきだと言っていますか。
4. 「良品に国境なし」、「関税」、「輸入制限」、「輸入増進」、「技術」ということばを使って本田の考えを述べましょう。
5. 「良品」を作るのにもっとも「ものをいう」のは何でしょうか。
6. どうして本田自身より「専務」の方が頭をかかえてたいへんだったのでしょうか。
7. 本田の一生を通じての「大英断」とは?

練習問題: Exercises

True or False ?

1. 大会社ではどんな社長でも本田自身と同じく技術屋の先にたって陣頭指揮でやるべきだ。
2. 勤務年数が多いだけで課長から部長へと自動的に地位が上がり、ハンで押したようなことばかりやっている会社では進歩がない。
3. 技術をあげ、世界的レベルの設備に更新しないかぎり、どんな輸入制限、関税策でもむこうのいい品物がこっちに入ってくるのを防止することはできない。
4. 経理面からでた専務に会社の陣頭指揮をやってもらうことに踏み切ったのが本田社長の一大英断だった。

When the company had only a million yen in capital at the time, I imported three or four trillion yen's worth of equipment. After that, there was trouble with payments. Apparently, the managing director had a hard time of it. Of course, because I was an engineer and not dealing with the money, I did not suffer that real hardship, but that the managing director had his head in his hands, I know deeply in my heart. This kind of thing should never be done again. It was something one should not do, but going under without doing it would have been even worse. At that time, if I had not rationally taken the plunge, there would be no Honda Giken today. I think the way I took that plunge was my boldest decision. It was the boldest decision of my life.

—∾—

語句と語法: Phrases and Usage

- 叩き込む・たたきこむ: "to beat into"; hammer into (a strict, exacting education)
- 教育・きょういく: education
- 必要・ひつよう: necessary
- ぼく・僕: I [informal way for men to refer to themselves]
- 家庭教師・かていきょうし: a tutor [a common job for college students]
- やってて: to be doing [shortened form of やっていて]
- 大学・だいがく: college; university
- 行(い)く: to go [行ってた＝行っていた]
- ころ・頃: a period; "the time when …"
- ぜんぜん…ない: there was absolutely no …
- しおくり: allowance; money from home
- で: so [＝それで]
- おそい: late
- 帰る・かえる: to return to where one is living
- もう: already
- 暗い・くらい: dark
- こん畜生(ちょくしょう): damn, shoot, darn
- いま・今: now
- 勉強(べんきょう)する: to study
- してやらなきゃ: ＝してやらなければいけない; I *am* going to (study)
- やる: to do [here, following the て form of a verb, indicates strong intention]
- これだけ: this much (time)
- 時間(を)ロスする・じかん(を)ろすする: to lose time
- 思う・おもう: to think
- さ: used at the end of sentences mostly by men; informal; can indicate confidence in an assertion
- ああ: a mildly positive response
- たとえば: for example; for instance [the example follows in the second half of the sentence]
- あなた: you
- 似ている・にている: to resemble; be like
- 家・いえ: one's home
- わけ: often used at the end of a sentence of explanations/descriptions
- そうすると: and so; that being so
- 弾く・ひく: to play (a stringed instrument or piano)
- 音楽・おんがく: music
- 成城学園・せいじょうがくえん: name of a school located in Seijo
- 音楽室・おんがくしつ: music room
- 山・やま: mountain
- みたい: like; resembling [colloquial; ＝のような]
- ところ: place
- 田舎・いなか: the countryside; a rural area
- 夜・よる: night
- うん: an 相槌・あいづち, used repeatedly by the listener to show attention and affirmation
- すると: and (then)
- 恐ろしい・おそろしい: scary; frightening
- 笑い・わらい: laughter
- 真暗・ま(っ)くら: completely dark; pitch black
- ひとけのない・人気のない: deserted; without a soul in sight
- 教室・きょうしつ: a classroom
- ってこと: ＝ということ
- いや・嫌: unpleasant; distasteful; awful
- でしょ: informal abbreviation of でしょう
- 自分・じぶん: oneself
- 居間・いま: living room; sitting room
- やつ: person; people [here, informal and familiar usage]
- 羨ましい・うらやましい: enviable
- だから: that's why
- いま(今)でも: even now
- とても: very
- 嬉しい・うれしい: happy
- わかる・分かる: to understand; appreciate
- それだけでも: in that alone [referring to a passage that precedes this excerpt in which he describes how he built his powers of concentration through, for one, playing rugby in junior high school]
- 訓練・くんれん: training
- うける: to receive
- 恵まれる・めぐまれる: to be blessed [passive of めぐむ]
- それから: moreover
- 師匠・ししょう: master; teacher
- 斎藤英雄・さいとうひでお: person's name
- っていう: to be called [informal; ＝という]
- もう(verb past): already
- 亡(な)くなる：to pass away (die); of people [cf. 無(な)くなる: to disappear or be lost (of objects)]
- 先生・せんせい: teacher; a more general term than 師匠 [can be used for doctors, lawyers, learned superiors who are not teachers per se]
- 昔・むかし: old times
- ～流に・りゅうに: in the style of ～

叩き込む教育が必要だ(抄)

小澤征爾と広中平祐の対話

広中　ぼくも家庭教師やっててね、大学へ行ってたころ。ぜんぜん仕送りなかったからね。で、家庭教師やっておそく帰る時にね、もう、暗くなって、こん畜生！　いま勉強してやらなきゃ、と思ってね。これだけ時間ロスしたからさ。

小澤　ああ。たとえばぼくもね、あなたに似てるんだけど、家にピアノがないわけよ。そうすると、ピアノ弾かなきゃ音楽の勉強できないから、成城学園の音楽室が、山みたいなところにあったんだけど、成城は田舎みたいなところだからね。そこへ夜行くわけ。

広中　うん。

小澤　すると恐ろしいわけよね、(笑) 真暗だからさ。ひとけのない教室へいくってことはいやなことでしょ。それ毎日やってた時にね、自分の家の居間にピアノがあって弾けるやつ、羨ましいなと思った。だからいまでもピアノがあるってことは、とても嬉しいわけね。

広中　わかるよ。

小澤　それだけでもぼくは、訓練うけたことでほかの人よりも恵まれたと思う。それからぼくの師匠の斎藤秀雄っていう、もう亡くなっちゃったけど、その先生が、これは昔流に叩き込む

Ozawa Seiji

The conductor Ozawa Seiji was born in 1935 in Manchuria and raised in China until 1941. Once in Japan, he began piano lessons at the age of seven. At sixteen, he entered the prestigious Toho Gakuen Music School in Tokyo, but soon had to give up the piano due to a finger injury incurred in a rugby game. This prompted him to study composing and conducting under well-known cello player Saitō Hideo. He graduated in 1959 and began with conducting student orchestras in Tokyo. He soon left for Europe where he studied with Karl Munchinger and Herbert von Karajan. He won the Besançon International Conductors Competition (1959) and the Koussevitzky Prize (1960) at the Berkshire Music Center. Ozawa's career progressed rapidly. In 1961 he was invited by Leonard Bernstein to accompany the New York Philharmonic during its Japan tour and became its assistant conductor the following year. In 1973 Ozawa was appointed permanent director of the Boston Symphony Orchestra. Since 1992 Mr. Ozawa has also been director of the newly founded Music Festival in the ancient town of Matsumoto.

As to his interactions with the East, he was the first conductor to enter the Republic of China, directing the Beijing Central Orchestra in 1979 for a week. Subsequently, he was invited to bring the Boston Symphony Orchestra for an official cultural visit to China. In 1967, on the occasion of the New York Philharmonic's 125th anniversary, Ozawa conducted the world première of "November Steps" by Takemitsu Tōru, which combined traditional Japanese instruments, such as the *shakuhachi*, with Western classical ones. He expressed the opinion that in contrast to Japanese music, where, for example, the sounds of the flow of water are a natural part of the music score, Western music is more structural and rational. Combining elements of both West and East can sometimes result in great mystical power. Seiji's conducting is delicate and expressive, contrasting softness and tension.

Ozawa believes that having been raised outside of the West gave him extra freedom, which is his real strength. He once likened the concert hall to a kind of public garden with greenery and little birds that chirp and enchant children, and where townspeople gather to enjoy beauty. Conductors create such a temporary garden during a performance. When he speaks of music or conducts, he does it with great passion.

Ozawa Seiji made his debut as operatic conductor in Salzburg, the birthplace of Mozart, with *Così fan tutte* in 1969. He has appeared in Covent Garden, at La Scala in Milan, and the Paris Opera. His clear technique, overflowing vitality, and charm enthrall audiences. Orchestras enjoy working with him and tend to play beautifully under his baton.

Ozawa is an example of how the Japanese respect those who have made their name in the international arena, an accomplishment which is often perceived as greater than domestic success.

TATAkiKOmu KYOU-IKU ga HITSU-YOU da (SHOU)

O-ZAWA SEI-JI to HIRO-NAKA HEI-SUKE no TAI-WA

H: Boku mo KA-TEI KYOU-SHI yatte te ne, DAI-GAKU e itte ta koro. Zenzen
SHI-OKUri nakatta kara ne. De, KA-TEI KYOU-SHI yatte osoku KAEru TOKI ni
ne, mou, KURAku natte, konCHIKU-SHOU! Ima BEN-KYOU shite yarana-
kya, to OMOtte ne. Kore dake JI-KAN *rosu* shita kara sa.

O: Aa. Tatoeba boku mo ne, anata ni NIte ru n da kedo, IE ni *piano* ga nai wake yo. Sou suru to, *piano* HIkanakya ON-GAKU no BEN-
KYOU dekinai kara, SEI-JOU GAKU-EN no ON-GAKU-SHITSU ga, YAMA mitai na tokoro ni
atta n da kedo, SEI-JOU wa INAKA mitai na tokoro da kara ne. Soko
e YORU Iku wake.

H: Un.

O: Suru to OSOroshii wake yo ne, (WARAI) MAK-KURA da kara sa. Hitoke no nai
KYOU-SHITSU e iku tte koto wa iya na koto desho. Sore MAI-NICHI yatte ta
TOKI ni ne, JI-BUN no IE no I-MA ni *piano* ga atte HIkeru yatsu, URAYAma-
shii na to OMOtta. Dakara ima de mo *piano* ga aru tte koto wa,
totemo UREshii wake ne.

H: Wakaru yo.

O: Sore dake de mo boku wa, KUN-REN uketa koto de hoka no HITO yori mo MEGUma-
reta to OMOu. Sore kara boku no SHI-SHOU no SAI-TOU HIDE-O tte iu, mou
NAku natchatta kedo, sono SEN-SEI ga, kore wa MUKASHI-RYUU ni TATAkiKOmu

Ozawa Seiji rehearsing in Shanghai with a Chinese orchestra.

One Needs an Exacting Education (An Excerpt)

A Conversation between Ozawa Seiji & Hironaka Heisuke

Hironaka: I worked as a tutor, you know, when I was attending college. Because I had no
money sent from home at all, you know. So, when I got home late
after tutoring, it was already dark, you know, shoot! Now I'll have to get down
and do my studying, I'd think. I mean, it was because I had lost so much time.

Ozawa: Yeah. For example, I'm like you a bit [in that regard], since we had no
piano in our house. And so, because I had to play the piano or I couldn't study
music, there was the Seijo Gakuen, it was in a place something like a mountain
because Seijo was out there in the countryside. I would go there
at night.

H: Yeah.

O: And it was pretty scary, you know (laughter) since it was completely dark. Going into a deserted
classroom is pretty unnerving business, you know. When I was doing
that everyday, I was so envious of the guys who had a piano in their house's living room
and could play. And that's why even now I'm still very glad I have [my own]
piano.

H: I know what you mean.

O: In that alone [the power of concentration developed early in life], I think that I was luckier than others
because of the training I received. Also, [for] my master, a teacher called Saitō Hideo,
who has already passed away, this old-style strict

- やりかた(方): way of doing
- (verb)～なきゃいけない: must; should ＝～なければいけない [～なきゃ is an informal ending to be used among peers, not a polite one]
- 感じ・かんじ: feeling
- 丁稚・でっち: apprentice [archaic]
- 小僧・こぞう: young boy; errand boy; novice
- 奉公・ほうこう: apprenticeship
- あれ的(てき)に: in that way; like that [colloquial; 的に can be added to many nouns to create adjectives; here, an informal, spoken use]
- もう: "already"; here used as an exclamation
- ～ている以上(いじょう): as long as one is …ing
- やんなきゃ: ＝ やらなきゃ; ＝ やらなければ; if one doesn't do …
- 浮(う)かばれる: "to float (to the top)"; to be saved; "make it" in the world (achieve success)
- っての: ＝ というの
- 音楽なんてもの: this thing called music
- こっち: refers to oneself or the one being educated [informal of こちら]
- 得・とく: advantage; benefit; gain
- なのよ: emphatic for informal conversation; used something like "you know?"
- ま: colloquial for まあ, "anyway"
- 教育方法・きょういくほうほう: education methods
- のんびりする: to take it easy
- のびのび: free and easy
- やっと方がいい: it is better to [Ozawa is finishing Hironaka's sentence here]
- ってこともある: there is also the case/fact that … [ってこと ＝ ということ]
- 場合・ばあい: case; instance
- 若い・わかい: young
- よっぽどの: very; a great [colloquial version of よほど]
- 天才・てんさい: genius
- 別・べつ: different
- きっと: surely
- ぼくら・僕等: us [ら makes a plural (cf. 彼ら・かれら: them)]
- 厳しく・きびしく: strictly
- ～と。: the quotative particle is often used to end sentences; omitted is a phrase like ～(と)いうようにする
- 昔風・むかしふう: old fashioned
- いいかた・言い方: way of saying something; way of putting it
- 非常に・ひじょうに: extremely
- 賛成・さんせい: agreement; approval
- ぼくなんか: a self-deprecatory way to refer to oneself; "someone like me"
- 数学者・すうがくしゃ: mathematician

- 見てて: ＝ 見ていて
- とにかく: in any case; at any rate
- 物凄い・ものすごい: terrific; tremendous [below, same word appears in hiragana]
- 頭(あたま)いい: smart [＝ 頭がいい; particles are often omitted in speech]
- 世の中に・よのなかに: in the world
- 何(なに)か: somehow; for some reason
- 神様・かみさま: god
- 狂う・くるう: to go crazy; go mad
- ときどき・時々: sometimes; now and then
- 間違う・まちがう: to make a mistake; be mistaken
- 何人か・なんにんか: a few people
- ～くらい: to the extent (that one would think …)
- すごい: tremendous
- はーあ: a slightly formal positive response [indicating slight surprise or appreciation (of the speaker's story)]
- 三倍・さんばい: 3 times (the amount of study) [倍 ＝ 2 times]
- 今世紀・こんせいき: this century
- びっくりする: to be surprised
- なかなか: with neg. verb, expresses something difficult to do or which occurs only rarely
- 出てく(来)る・でてくる: to emerge
- 図書館・としょかん: library
- 鉢巻・はちまき: a headband; 鉢巻をする: to wear a headband
- じいっと: unmoving [also, じっと]
- 朝・あさ: morning
- 講義・こうぎ: lecture
- まだ…している: still be (doing …)
- やっぱり: as expected; of course [informal of やはり]
- ぜったいに: absolutely
- もう: perhaps close to "absolutely" [a phase indicating emotional feeling about the level of Mozart's genius]
- 宿る・やどる: to dwell in
- としか思(おも)えない: I could only think that [しか is used with neg. verb to mean "only"; おもう here is in its potential form "can think"]
- いわゆる: so-called
- 演奏・えんそう: (musical) performance
- ～家(か): at the end of a word often indicates a person with professional ability; 演奏家: performing musician
- ～たち: pluralizes nouns and pronouns; 僕たち:we
- 商売・しょうばい: business; trade
- 努力・どりょく: effort; exertion
- 早い・はやい: early [cf. 速(はや)い: fast]
- 起きる・おきる: to get up (in the morning)

やりかただからさ、だから、音楽っていうものは叩き込まれなきゃいけないっていう感じがあるから。——丁稚小僧ってのあるでしょう。

広中　奉公。

小澤　うん、あれ的に。もう、やってる以上はいやでもやんなきゃだめだ、そうしないともう浮かばれないってのがあったから。で、音楽なんてものはね、それでも叩き込まれた方がこっちは得なのよ。ま、いろいろあるでしょ、教育方法に。ノンビリさせた方がいいとか。

広中　そう、ノビノビと。

小澤　やった方がいいってこともあるけど、音楽の場合は若いときに叩き込む——よっぽどの天才は別だけどね、きっと。でもぼくらみたいのは、訓練を厳しく自分でしてやる、と。昔風のいいかただけど、やんなきゃだめだと思う。

広中　ぼくもそういうことに非常に賛成だけどね。ぼくなんか数学者見ててね、とにかく物凄く頭いいやつがいるわけだ、世の中には。何か神様が狂ってさ、ときどき間違って何人かそういうやつを作るんだろうと思うくらい、ものすごく頭のいいやつがいるんだけどさ。そういう人でも、すごい勉強するね。

小澤　はーあ。

広中　とにかく、ふつうの人の三倍は勉強するね。数学者で、今世紀でもびっくりするくらい、なかなか出てこないくらいの数学者だけど、図書館に入って鉢巻をしてね。（笑）フランス人だけどさ、鉢巻をしてじいっと本を見ているわけよ。朝行ってみて、それから講義してまた図書館へ行ってみても、まだじいっとして鉢巻してやってるの。（笑）やっぱり天才でもそういうやり方するんだろうね。

小澤　だけど天才ってのは、音楽でもいたんですよね。たとえばモーツァルトなんかはぜったい天才だった。あれはもう、神さまがモーツァルトの中に宿って音楽作ったとしか思えないんだけどさ。だけども、いわゆる、演奏家、ぼくたちの商売みたいなのはね、やっぱり、努力だな……でも、ぼくなんか恵まれてるわけですよね。たとえば朝早く起きて勉強するの、

Hironaka Heisuke

The mathematician Hironaka Heisuke is in his own right a well-known personality. He was born in 1931 in Yamaguchi Prefecture. A graduate of Kyoto University, he continued his studies at Harvard University. He contributed to mathematics by solving major problems in algebraic geometry. He taught at Harvard and held a joint appointment at Kyoto University. In 1970 he won the most prestigious distinction in mathematics, the international Fields Prize. He also received, in Japan, the Order of Culture in 1975.

Hironaka is much revered by his collegues and, at the same time, remains a highly popular figure in Japan. His wife, Hironaka Wakako is, at the time of this writing, a member of the Japanese Diet, where she has served several terms.

yarikata da kara sa, dakara, ON-GAKU tte iu mono wa TATAkiKOmare-

nakya ikenai tte iu KANji ga aru kara. DET-CHI KO-ZOU tte

no aru deshou.

H: HOU-KOU.

O: Un, areTEKI ni. Mou, yatte ru I-JOU wa iya de mo yannakya

dame da, sou shinai to mou Ukabarenai tte no ga atta kara.

De, ON-GAKU nante mono wa ne, sore de mo TATAkiKOmareta HOU ga kotchi

wa TOKU na no yo. Ma, iroiro aru desho, KYOU-IKU HOU-HOU ni. *Nonbi-*

ri saseta HOU ga ii toka.

H: Sou, *nobinobi* to.

O: Yatta HOU ga ii tte koto mo aru kedo, ON-GAKU no BA-AI wa WAKAi toki

ni TATAkiKOmu—yoppodo no TEN-SAI wa BETSU da kedo ne, kitto. Demo

bokura mitai no wa, KUN-REN o KIBIshiku JI-BUN de shite yaru, to. MUKASHI-FUU

no iikata da kedo, yannakya dame da to OMOu.

H: Boku mo sou iu koto ni HI-JOU ni SAN-SEI da kedo ne. Boku nanka SUU-GAKU-

SHA MIte te ne, tonikaku MONO-SUGOku ATAMA ii yatsu ga iru wake da, YO no

NAKA ni wa. NANI ka KAMI-SAMA ga KURUtte sa, tokidoki MA-CHIGAtte NAN-NIN ka sou

iu yatsu o TSUKUru n darou to OMOu kurai, monosugoku ATAMA no ii

yatsu ga iru n da kedo sa. Sou iu HITO de mo, sugoi BEN-KYOU suru ne.

O: Haaa.

H: Tonikaku, futsuu no HITO no SAN-BAI wa BEN-KYOU suru ne. SUU-GAKU-SHA de, KON-SEI-

KI de mo bikkuri suru kurai, nakanaka DEte konai kurai no SUU-

GAKU-SHA da kedo, TO-SHO-KAN ni HAItte HACHI-MAKI o shite ne. (WARAI) *Furansu-*

JIN da kedo sa, HACHI-MAKI o shite jiitto HON o MIte iru wake yo. ASA I-

tte mite, sore kara KOU-GI shite mata TO-SHO-KAN e Itte mite mo, ma-

da jiitto shite HACHI-MAKI shite yatte ru no. (WARAI) Yappari TEN-SAI de

mo sou iu yariKATA suru n darou ne.

O: Dakedo TEN-SAI tte no wa, ON-GAKU de mo ita n desu yo ne. Tatoeba *Moo-*

tsaruto nanka wa zettai TEN-SAI datta. Are wa mou, KAMI-sa-

ma ga *Mootsaruto* no NAKA ni YADOtte ON-GAKU TSUkutta to shika OMOenai n

da kedo sa. Dakedomo, iwayuru, EN-SOU-KA, bokutachi no SHOU-BAI mi-

tai na no wa ne, yappari, DO-RYOKU da na … demo, boku nanka MEGU-

marete ru wake desu yo ne. Tatoeba ASA HAYAku Okite BEN-KYOU suru no,

WESTERN MUSIC IN JAPAN

Soon after the Meiji Restoration (1868), the Japanese realized that Western Classical Music would help open the gates to Western culture.

It did not take long for Western music to become appreciated for what it truly is. In today's Japan, children are encouraged to learn piano, violin, and other instruments. Over half the children take after-school music lessons, in spite of the high costs to the parents. The Suzuki method encourages a young child to learn violin intuitively by listening repeatedly to the music, rather than from reading scores. The parent is asked to be present during lessons. The method has become a favorite not only in Japan, but also in the West.

That Western classical music is widely appreciated in Japan is shown by the fact that Tokyo has nine symphony orchestras, more than any other city. Neighborhoods and sometimes corporations form their own orchestras. For example, Toshiba Corporation's orchestra performed at Carnegie Hall in 1992.

The rigorous discipline required for serious musical study appeals naturally to the Japanese, who seem to possess the temperament for such endeavors. A ten-year old child will find nothing unusual in having to practice two hours every day. It is no suprise that Gotō Midori started as a violin child virtuoso and soon became one of the most famous soloists.

Besides Western classical music, pop music and jazz are also very popular. *Karaoke*, a Japanese invention*,* has become a favorite form of entertainment in many countries. *Kayō-kyoku* includes several forms of popular music. Since popular musical genres tend to evolve rapidly, what is fashionable today may give way to other genres tomorrow. Do you know what has recently come out of the Tokyo musical scene?

A huge music industry has sprung forth from the Japanese fondness for Western music, as exemplified by the Sony Corporation, the audio and record company, and Yamaha, the manufacturer of pianos, classical guitars, clarinets, electronic keyboards, as well as audio systems for computers.

education, so I have this feeling that this thing called music must be taught
in an exacting way. You know, there's [that thing called] a novice
apprentice.

H: Old-fashioned apprenticeship.

O: Right, like that. As long as you're doing it, you have to do it, even if it's
disagreeable. If you didn't do it that way, you'd never make it in the real world.
Even so, having a strict education was a benefit for those of us who had
it. Anyway, there's a variety, isn't there, in educational methods. [Like] letting the
student take it easy.

H: Right, free and relaxed…

O: … is one good way to do it, but in the case of music, you have to be
exacting—though incredible genius is surely different. But
with people like us, you have to push yourself to train strictly, I think. It's an old-style
way of saying it, but I think you have to do it that way.

H: I also am extremely in favor of that sort of thing. When I look at mathe-
maticians, there are guys out there in the world who are, aside from other things,
incredibly smart. There are people who are so incredibly smart that it's enough to
make me think that god goes crazy and once in a while makes a few of this kind
of person, you know? [But] even those people study tremendously hard.

O: Hmmm.

H: In any case, those people do three times the study of ordinary people. One mathematician, the kind rarely produced, almost [the type] you'd be surprised to see
in this century, goes to the library and puts on his *hachimaki* (laughter). He's
French, but he puts on his *hachimaki* and stares hard at his books. I look in the
morning, then I do a lecture and if I go again to the library and look, [he's] still
there, quietly working with his *hachimaki* on. (laughter) You know, after all, even geniuses
do things that way.

O: But music had its geniuses, too. For example, Mozart
was an absolute genius. Really, I can only think that god
[must have] lived in Mozart and made music.
But [for] so-called performers, the thing which is like a business for us
is none other than effort…. But I'm a lucky
one. For example, I get up early and study,

- いかにも: so clearly; so evidently
- 悲愴に・ひそうに: bravely; with heroic resolve [usually written 悲壮]
- みりゃ: = みれば [informal form]
- 翌週・よくしゅう: the following week [cf. 来週・らいしゅう: next week]
- 音楽会・おんがくかい: music concert
- 金・かね: money [with the conventional honorific お]
- 家族・かぞく: family
- 食わせる・くわせる: "make eat"; to feed [informal]
- 酒・さけ: sake; alcoholic drink
- 飲める・のめる: can drink [potential of のむ]
- うん: yeah; right
- 密接に・みっせつに: closely; intimately
- くっつく: to stick to; be stuck to; be intimately related
- いくら…しても: no matter how much (one does …)
- 食う・くう: "to eat"; make a living [informal]
- ほんといって: to tell the truth [ほんとう has been shortened to ほんと]
- ありがたい: thankful
- チャンス(を)もらう: to be given a chance/opportunity

いかにも悲愴になってやるんだけど、よく考えてみりゃね、そうやって勉強したのを、その翌週音楽会して、それでお金もらって、家族食わせて自分でも酒が飲めるわけだから。

広中　うん。

小澤　勉強することと密接にくっついてるわけだ、商売とがね。それが、いくら勉強してもさ、そういうことできない人もいるわけだよ。で、食うのは別のことで食っているとか。だから、ぼくなんか、ほんといってありがたいと思ってる。チャンスもらっているからね。

〜

慣用句: Idiomatic Expressions

Translate the following into idiomatic English

1. 恵まれる

丁稚小僧式の教育をしてくれたいい師匠がいて、僕はほんとに恵まれたと思っている。

2. 叩き込む

音楽でも数学でも若い時に厳しく叩き込むという教育法に賛成だ。

3. 浮かばれない

音楽では若い時に叩き込まれなければぜったいに浮かばれない。

4. (〜は)別だ

大学のころはあまりノンビリ音楽の勉強ができなかった。自分の家にピアノでもあれば別だっただろうが……。

5. いかにも

あの音楽教室ではいかにもノビノビとした教育をしているらしい。

ikanimo HI-SOU ni natte yaru n da kedo, yoku KANGAete mirya ne,

sou yatte BEN-KYOU shita no o, sono YOKU-SHUU ON-GAKU-KAI shite, sore de oKANE

moratte, KA-ZOKU KUwasete JI-BUN de mo SAKE ga NOmeru wake da kara.

H: Un.

O: BEN-KYOU suru koto to MIS-SETSU ni kuttsuite ru wake da, SHOU-BAI to ga ne. So-

re ga, ikura BEN-KYOU shite mo sa, sou iu koto dekinai HITO mo iru

wake da yo. De, KUu no wa BETSU no koto de KUtte iru toka. Dakara,

boku nanka, honto itte arigatai to OMOtte ru. *Chansu*

moratte iru kara ne.

内容理解: Comprehension Exercises

Answer in Japanese

1. 広中はとても「恵まれた大学生活」を送りましたか。
2. 成城学園へ行っていたころ、小澤はどのようにして厳しく自分を叩き込み、訓練していましたか。
3. 小澤は若い時、どんな人からどのような音楽教育を受けましたか。
4. 小澤と広中は「天才」について、どのような考え方の違い、例を示していますか。
5. 小澤は自分がどのような点で恵まれていると思い、ありがたいと思っていますか。

練習問題: Exercises

True or False ?

1. 小澤の師匠は丁稚小僧を叩き込むような昔流の教育法で学生を訓練していた。
2. 天才的なあるフランスの数学者でもふつうの人の三倍は勉強すると広中は言っている。
3. 小澤が「とても恵まれている」と思うのはモーツァルトのような天才音楽家の作ったものを演奏できるからだ。
4. 演奏家という自分の商売は、自分を厳しく訓練し、勉強することと密接にくっついている商売だから恵まれていると小澤は言っている。

and go resolutely at it, but when I really think about it,

you know, [I take] the study I've done in that way and do a concert the next week, and with that I get money,

and I feed my family and can even have *sake* to drink myself, so…

H: Yes.

O: It's stuck closely together with study, business is, you know. There

are other people who can't do anything like that no matter how hard

they study. So, to eat, they [make a living] by doing something else. So,

someone like me, I feel lucky, to tell the truth, because I've been

given a chance.

語句と語法: Phrases and Usage

- 夜光時計・やこうどけい: "Shining-at-night watch (or clock); luninous watch
- 道世・みちよ: woman's personal name
- 町中・まちなか: in town
- 小さな・ちいさな: small [cf. ちいさい; as with おおきい・おおきな, can be an い or な adj.]
- 個人経営・こじんけいえい: privately run
- アパート: apartment
- 娘・むすめ: daughter
- 住む・すむ: to reside (in a place); inhabit [cf. other "to live" verbs: 暮らす(くらす): "to live, earn a living"; 生きる(いきる): "to live" (be alive)]
- ～畳・じょう: a counter for 畳 (たたみ), reed floor mats [one mat is about 180 cm x 90 cm]
- ～尺・しゃく: an older unit of measurement [one 尺 = 30.3 cm]
- 流し・ながし: a sink; also 流し台 (だい) [cf. 流す: to run (water)]
- AのついたB: B with A stuck on it/included in it
- ありきたり: ordinary; common
- 部屋・へや: a room (apartment/flat)
- 廊下・ろうか: hallway; corridor
- 挟む・はさむ: to sandwich; be placed between two other things
- 並ぶ・ならぶ: to arrange in a line
- 西側・にしがわ: western side
- 窓・まど: window
- ～になっている: to be in a certain state or condition
- 家賃・やちん: rent
- 安い・やすい: cheap; low
- 選ぶ・えらぶ: to choose; select
- 冬・ふゆ: winter
- ～のうち(は)よくても: even if it's good while/during ～
- 夏・なつ: summer
- 西陽・にしび: the afternoon sun or its rays
- 射す・さす: to shine (in, into)
- 午後・ごご: afternoon
- 密閉(みっぺい)する: to make airtight
- 全体・ぜんたい: the whole (room)
- 蒸風呂・むしぶろ: a steam bath
- 一方に・いっぽうに: on one side
- ～しか～ない: is only ～
- 左右・さゆう: left and right
- 隣室・りんしつ: neighboring room [隣 = となり]
- 境・さかい: a border; boundary
- 壁・かべ: wall
- 開けっ放し・あけっぱなし: to leave open [cf. ミルクを出しっ放しにする: to leave the milk out (of the refrigerator)]
- 出入口・でいりぐち: doorway
- すだれ・簾: a screen/blind made of bamboo
- かける: to hang up
- 漸く・ようやく: finally; at long last
- わずかな風・わずかなかぜ: a slight breeze
- 道(みち)をつける: to make a path/way
- 凌ぐ・しのぐ: to bear; endure (the heat)
- ～をするほか verb stem + ようがない: "there is nothing to do other than ～"
- 内職・ないしく: a job done (for income) at home
- はじめる・始める: to start
- 西向き・にしむき: western facing
- かえって: conversely; instead of
- 好都合・こうつごう: beneficial; convenient
- 盛り場・さかりば: entertainment district; drinking district
- 小料理屋・こりょうりや: a small Japanese-style restaurant which serves food and drinks
- 通う・かよう: to commute [cf. 通勤・つうきん: commuting to work; 通学・つうがく: commuting to school]
- 和服・わふく: traditional Japanese clothing [kimono, tabi (see below), etc.]
- 勤め(つとめ)に出(で)る: to go to work/a job
- 一夜・いちや: (in) one night
- 白足袋・しろたび: white tabi [tabi are essentially sturdy socks with a separate division for the big toe, worn with wooden clogs (geta), women's sandals (zōri), etc.]
- 汚れる・よごれる: to get dirty
- 帰宅・きたく: returning home
- 遅い・おそい: late
- 午前中・ごぜんちゅう: during the morning; all morning
- 寝る・ねる: to sleep
- 洗濯・せんたく: laundry
- 間(ま)に合(あ)う: to have enough time
- クリーニング屋(や): a (dry) cleaners
- 一足・いっそく: one pair (of tabi)
- とられる: to be charged
- こぼす: to complain [it is next-door who is complaining]
- 夫・おっと: husband
- 女(おんな)を作(つく)る: to get a girfriend/mistress
- 家・いえ: house
- 帰る・かえる: to return home
- 生活に窮する・せいかつにきゅうする: to have difficulty making a living
- 自分名義・じぶんめいぎ: in her own name
- 処分(しょぶん)する: to sell off; get rid of
- 引越す・ひっこす: to move (to a new house)
- かれこれ: with one thing and another
- 二年・にねん: 2 years
- 居食い(いぐい)する: to live off one's savings
- 忽ち・たちまち: instantly; immediately
- 底(そこ)をつく: "hit bottom"; (one's funds) get all used up
- 財産・ざいさん: property; possessions
- 先にのばす: to stretch into the future; to make ～ last
- ～ため(為)に: in order to ～
- 手段・しゅだん: means; way; method
- 考える・かんがえる: to think (of)
- 幼い・おさない: very young; infantile
- 外・そと: outside (in town)
- かなわず ＝ かなわない: not being able to; not equal to (the task)
- 話・はなし: a story; here, Tamae's complaints

「夜光時計」（抄）

津村節子

　道世は、町中（まちなか）の小さな個人経営のアパートに娘とふたりで住んでいる。六畳一間に三尺の流しのついたありきたりの部屋だ。廊下をはさんで両側に部屋が並んでいるが、道世の部屋は西側が窓になっていた。家賃が安いので西側の部屋を選んだのだが、冬のうちはよくても、夏になると西陽の射す午後は密閉された部屋全体が蒸風呂のようになる。窓は一方にしかなくて左右が隣室との境の壁になっているから、ドアを開けっ放し、出入口にすだれをかけて漸くわずかな風の道をつける（しの）ほか凌ぎようがなかった。しかし、道世が内職をはじめるようになって、この西向きの部屋がかえってその仕事に好都合になった。

　道世の隣室の女は珠江といって、盛り場の小料理屋へ通っていた。和服で勤めに出るので、一夜で白足袋（たび）が汚れる。帰宅が遅く、午前中は寝ているので、毎日の足袋の洗濯が間に合わない。クリーニング屋に出すと、一足五十円から六十円もとられるとこぼしていた。

　夫が女を作って家へ帰らなくなり、生活に窮した道世が自分名義の小さな家を処分してこのアパートに引越して来てからもうかれこれ二年になる。居食いしていては忽ち底をついてしまうわずかな財産を、少しでも先にのばすために生活の手段を考えていたときであった。幼い娘がいては、外へ勤めに出ることもかなわず、その話を

Tsumura Setsuko

Tsumura Setsuko (b. 1928), the second daughter of a silk merchant, lost her mother when she was nine. In 1945 she also lost her father. She spent her adolescence in a factory rather than in a classroom. Two years after the end of the war, she decided to learn a skill to ensure her future financial independence in case she did not marry, since many eligible men had been killed during the war. She enrolled in a dressmaking school, opened her own shop, and hired three seamstresses. Although business was doing well, she closed her shop after two years and went to college to study literature.

She started writing and joined groups that published literary magazines. In 1953 she married the editor of one of these magazines, but the couple had to struggle to make a living. When her husband's part-time business failed, she traveled around with him to sell the leftover stock. She also wrote stories for a girls' magazine. As mother of two young children, however, she found it difficult to continue writing, and she felt guilty about not taking proper care of her children and husband.

In 1965, Tsumura won the Akutagawa Prize, which gave her financial independence and enabled her to devote herself fully to writing. She has been a keen observer of less fortunate women and has written about them with great compassion.

This section has been adapted from *This Kind of Woman: Ten Stories from Japanese Writers, 1960–1976* (Stanford University Press, 1982).

"YA-KOU DO-KEI" (SHOU)

TSU-MURA SETSU-KO

MICHI-YO wa, MACHI-NAKA no CHIIsana KO-JIN KEI-EI no *apaato* ni MUSUME to futari de SUnde iru. ROKU-JOU HITO-MA ni SAN-JAKU no NAGAshi no tsuita arikitari no HE-YA da. ROU-KA o hasande RYOU-GAWA ni HE-YA ga NARAnde iru ga, MICHI-YO no HE-YA wa NISHI-GAWA ga MADO ni natte ita. YA-CHIN ga YASUi no de NISHI-GAWA no HE-YA o ERAnda no da ga, FUYU no uchi wa yokute mo, NATSU ni naru to NISHI-BI no SAsu GO-GO wa MIP-PEI sareta HE-YA ZEN-TAI ga MUSHI-BU-RO no you ni naru. MADO wa IP-POU ni shika nakute SA-YUU ga RIN-SHITSU to no SAKAI no KABE ni natte iru kara, *doa* o AkepPANAshi, DE-IRI-GUCHI ni sudare o kakete YOUYAku wazuka na KAZE no MICHI o tsukeru hoka SHINOgiyou ga nakatta. Shikashi, MICHI-YO ga NAI-SHOKU o hajimeru you ni natte, kono NISHI-MUki no HE-YA ga kaette sono SHI-GOTO ni KOU-TSU-GOU ni natta.

MICHI-YO no RIN-SHITSU no ONNA wa TAMA-E to itte, SAKAriBA no KO-RYOU-RI-YA e KAYOtte ita. WA-FUKU de TSUTOme ni DEru no de, ICHI-YA de SHIRO-TA-BI ga YOGOreru. KI-TAKU ga OSOku, GO-ZEN-CHUU wa NEte iru no de, MAI-NICHI no TA-BI no SEN-TAKU ga MA ni Awanai. *Kuriiningu*YA ni DAsu to, IS-SOKU GO-JUU-EN kara ROKU-JUU-EN mo torareru to koboshite ita.

OTTO ga ONNA o TSUKUtte IE e KAEranaku nari, SEI-KATSU ni KYUU shita MICHI-YO ga JI-BUN MEI-GI no CHIIsana IE o SHO-BUN shite kono *apaato* ni HIK-KOshite KIte kara mou karekore NI-NEN ni naru. I-GUi shite ite wa TACHIMAchi SOKO o tsuite shimau wazuka na ZAI-SAN o, SUKOshi de mo SAKI ni nobasu tame ni SEI-KATSU no SHU-DAN o KANGAete ita toki de atta. OSANAi MUSUME ga ite wa, SOTO e TSUTOme ni DEru koto mo kanawazu, sono HANASHI o

An older apartment building built with an unusual combination of wood and concrete.

Privately operated apartment buildings.

"Luminous Watch" (An Excerpt)

Tsumura Setsuko

Michiyo lives in a small privately managed apartment in town together with her daughter. It is an ordinary six-mat room with a 90-cm sink. There are rooms sandwiching the hall on both sides, and on the west of Michiyo's room's was a window. Because the rent is cheap she chose the room on the west side, and even though the winter was nice, when it became summer, in the afternoon with the shining western sun, the entire closed-in room would become like a steam bath. There was a window only on one side, and left and right were the boundary walls for the neighboring rooms, so the only way to make it bearable was to leave the door open, hang a bamboo blind in the entry, and make a small path for a faint breeze. But when Michiyo started working at home, this west facing room was, on the contrary, beneficial to her work.

The woman next-door to Michiyo was called Tamae, and she went to work at a small bar in the entertainment district. She went to work in Japanese clothing, so her white tabi became dirty in a single night. She returned late and slept during the morning, so she didn't have time for an everyday washing of her tabi. If sent [them] to the cleaners, she complained that for a pair it took from 50 to 60 yen.

With one thing and another, it was already two years since Michiyo's husband had gotten another woman and not come back, and she, hard up for her livelihood, had sold the small house registered in her name and moved into this apartment. It was a time when she was thinking, in order to stretch into the future even a little the small funds she had, which would quickly hit bottom if she were to live off her savings, of a means to [make a] living. With a young daughter she was unable to go out to

- 聞く・きく: to hear; listen
- 思いつく・おもいつく: to strike on (an idea); to think of
- 資本・しほん: capital; funds; money
- 技術・ぎじゅつ: skill
- いる・要る: to need
- と言(い)えば: if ~ is the case; speaking in terms of ~
- 案外・あんがい: unexpectedly; surprisingly
- 客・きゃく: customer
- 客がつく: to get customers
- ~のではないか: I wonder if … [often used as a non-forceful way of suggesting ideas]
- たかが: at most; no more (than); merely
- 重労働・じゅうろうどう: heavy labor
- ~ではあるまい: shouldn't be; is not likely to be [= ではないだろう]
- 朝・あさ: morning
- 晩・ばん: night
- 朝(あさ)から晩(ばん)まで: all day; from morning to night [= 一日中(いちにちじゅう)]
- 休(やす)みなく: without rest/a break
- 働(はたら)きつづける: to continue to work
- 造花・ぞうか: artificial (handmade) flowers
- 手袋・てぶくろ: gloves [手: hand; 袋: bag]
- 刺繍・ししゅう: embroidery
- ~より: (more) than ~
- 中間搾取・ちゅうかんさくしゅ: "intermediate exploitation"; middleman
- ~がないだけ: if only because there isn't a ~ (middleman)
- 格段に・かくだんに: especially; exceptionally
- 割(わり)がいい: the rate/return is good
- 無論・むろん: of course; without question [= もちろん]
- きれい・奇麗: clean; nice; pretty
- 贅沢(ぜいたく)を言(い)う: "to talk of luxury"; to ask/expect too much
- ~ていられない: cannot (afford to) be doing ~
- 案・あん: an idea; a plan
- ひどく: terribly; awfully [colloquial usage]
- 乗気(のりき)になる: to show interest in; be enthusiastic about
- だって: even [= でも]
- 出す・だす: to give out; provide/supply
- うちの店(みせ): うち can mean "my" or "I/me"; 店 = shop, restaurant
- 近所・きんじょ: neighborhood
- してあげる: to do (for someone)
- 喜(よろこ)んで~をする: to be glad to do ~ [喜ぶ: to be happy; be glad]

- 皮切りに・かわきりに: as a start
- 今(いま)では: right now (as compared with the past)
- 固定客・こていきゃく: steady/firm/regular customers
- 持つ・もつ: to have
- 最低・さいてい: a minimum; the least
- 月収・げっしゅう: monthly income/earnings
- くだる: to be less than; fall below
- 集(あつ)めに回(まわ)る: to go around to collect
- 仕上がる・しあがる: to be completed; be finished up
- 配達(はいたつ)する: to deliver
- 初(はじ)めのうち: at the beginning
- 食物・たべもの: food
- 食器・しょっき: dishes (for eating)
- 水商売・みずしょうばい: the "water trade"; the world of bars and bar hostesses
- 抵抗・ていこう: resistance; reluctance
- 口(くち)さがない: gossipy; slanderous
- 住人・じゅうにん: residents; inhabitants
- 見栄・みえ: the desire to put up a good front; vanity; pride
- そうでなくてさえ: even if it weren't so
- ふたり暮(ぐ)らし: two people living together
- ~による: depending on ~; based on ~
- 生活(せいかつ)する: to make a living
- 噂(うわさ)する: to gossip; spread rumors
- verb ~合(あ)う: to ~ together/mutually/to one another
- しかし: however; on the other hand
- 経済的・けいざいてき: economical
- 援助・えんじょ: support; assistance; help
- 勘ぐる・かんぐる: to guess at someone's true intent or situation
- 公・おおやけ: public
- Aより~Bしたほうがいい: better to do B than A
- また: furthermore; in addition
- ふえる・増える: to increase; rise; gain
- 到底・とうてい: (cannot) possibly; absolutely (can't)
- 処理(しょり)する: to manage; handle
- verb~しきれる: to do completely [cf. たべきれない: (I) can't eat it all]
- 裏庭・うらにわ: a backyard; a back garden
- 共同・きょうどう: common; joint
- 洗濯場・せんたくば: a place to do laundry
- 夥しい・おびただしい: innumerable; countless
- 持ち出す・もちだす: to carry out

聞いた道世は足袋の洗濯という仕事を思いついたのである。これは、資本も技術もいらない。

　一足三十円で洗うと言えば、案外客もつくのではないか。たかが足袋である。一日二十足洗ってもそんな重労働ではあるまい。二十足で六百円。朝から晩まで休みなく働きつづけて一日三百五十円にしかならない造花や手袋の刺繍より中間搾取がないだけ格段に割りがいい。無論きれいな仕事ではないが、そんな贅沢は言っていられなかった。

　その案を珠江に話してみると、彼女はひどく乗気になった。

　「私だけだって一月二十足や三十足は出すわ。うちの店に働いている人が二人いるし、近所の店の人たちにも話してあげる。一足三十円なら、みんな喜んで出すわよ」

　珠江の店を皮切りに道世はいまでは五十数人の固定客を持っている。一人一月最低二十足出すから千足の足袋を洗い、月収は三万を下らない。一週間に二日足袋を集めに回り、その時仕上がった足袋を配達する。

　はじめのうち、道世は部屋の小さな流しで集めてきた足袋を洗っていた。食物や食器を洗う流しで、水商売の女たちの足袋を洗うことにはかなりの抵抗があったが、そんな内職を口さがないアパートの住人たちに知られたくない見栄があった。そうでなくてさえ、娘とふたり暮らしの道世が、何によって生活しているのか人々は噂し合っているらしい。

　しかし、経済的な援助をしている男がいるのではないかなどと勘ぐられるよりは、むしろ足袋洗いの内職をしていることを公にしたほうがよいとも思い、また、仕事がふえてくると到底小さな流しなどでは処理しきれなくなって、彼女はアパートの裏庭にある共同洗濯場へ夥しい足袋を持ち出すようになった。

THE SINGLE MOTHER

The story is told with much empathy for Michiyo, a single mother. In Japan, single mothers are still the exception, although slowly becoming more numerous. They face economic and social discrimination. In Japanese society, it is the wife who has to piece the household together, irrespective of any problems her husband might occasion. The blame for a broken marriage tends to fall on the wife. For the sake of the child, everything must appear normal on the surface. There is also a common fear that a proliferation of single mothers will seriously disrupt the good functioning of society. In the story, Michyio, as a single mother, has to face great hardships. The author has captured in vivid detail the plight of the single mother in Japan.

KIita MICHI-YO wa TA-BI no SEN-TAKU to iu SHI-GOTO o OMOitsuita no de aru. Kore wa, SHI-HON mo GI-JUTSU mo iranai.

IS-SOKU SAN-JUU-EN de ARAu to Ieba, AN-GAI KYAKU mo tsuku no de wa nai ka. Takaga TA-BI de aru. ICHI-NICHI NI-JUS-SOKU ARAtte mo sonna JUU-ROU-DOU de wa aru mai. NI-JUS-SOKU de ROP-PYAKU-EN. ASA kara BAN made YASUmi naku HATARAkitsuzukete ICHI-NICHI SAN-BYAKU GO-JUU-EN ni shika naranai ZOU-KA ya TE-BUKURO no SHI-SHUU yori CHUU-KAN SAKU-SHU ga nai dake KAKU-DAN ni WAri ga ii. MU-RON kirei na SHI-GOTO de wa nai ga, sonna ZEI-TAKU wa Itte irare-nakatta.

Sono AN o TAMA-E ni HANAshite miru to, KANO-JO wa hidoku NORI-KI ni natta.

"WATASHI dake datte HITO-TSUKI NI-JUS-SOKU ya SAN-JUS-SOKU wa DAsu wa. Uchi no MISE ni HATARAite iru HITO ga FUTA-RI iru shi, KIN-JO no MISE no HITOtachi ni mo HANAshite ageru. IS-SOKU SAN-JUU-EN nara, minna YOROKOnde DAsu wa yo"

TAMA-E no MISE o KAWA-KIri ni MICHI-YO wa ima de wa GO-JUU-SUU-NIN no KO-TEI-KYAKU o MOtte i-ru. HITO-RI HITO-TSUKI SAI-TEI NI-JUS-SOKU DAsu kara SEN-ZOKU no TA-BI o ARAi, GES-SHUU wa SAN-MAN o KUDAranai. IS-SHUU-KAN ni FUTSU-KA TA-BI o ATSUme ni MAWAri, sono TOKI SHI-Agatta TA-BI o HAI-TATSU suru.

Hajime no uchi, MICHI-YO wa HE-YA no CHIIsana NAGAshi de ATSUmete kita TA-BI o ARAt-te ita. TABE-MONO ya SHOK-KI o ARAu NAGAshi de, MIZU-SHOU-BAI no ONNAtachi no TA-BI o ARAu ko-to ni wa kanari no TEI-KOU ga atta ga, sonna NAI-SHOKU o KUCHIsaganai *apaato* no JUU-NINtachi ni SHIraretaku nai MI-E ga atta. Sou de nakute sae, MUSUME to futariGUrashi no MICHI-YO ga, NANI ni yotte SEI-KATSU shite iru no ka HITO-BITO wa UWASA shi-Atte iru rashii.

Shikashi, KEI-ZAI-TEKI na EN-JO o shite iru OTOKO ga iru no de wa nai ka nado to KAN-gurareru yori wa, mushiro TA-BI-ARAi no NAI-SHOKU o shite iru koto o OOYAKE ni shita hou ga yoi to mo OMOi, mata, SHI-GOTO ga fuete kuru to TOU-TEI CHIIsana NAGAshi na-do de wa SHO-RI shikirenaku natte, KANO-JO wa *apaato* no URA-NIWA ni aru KYOU-DOU SEN-TAKU-BA e OBITADAshii TA-BI o MOchiDAsu you ni natta.

LUMINOUS WATCH

Michiyo, the main character of the story, is a single mother with a five-year old child, Chikako, and whose husband has abandoned her for another woman. Michiyo's financial resources are rapidly diminishing, so she needs another source of income. Since she has to take care of Chikako, she cannot work outside of the home. Moreover, she has no real qualifications. But then she has a brilliant idea: washing the *tabi* of women who work in bars! Her little home business is a success, but she still feels lonely. She becomes attached to a man, Kadota, whom she sees everyday at noon in the park and ends up inviting to her small apartment. To her surprise, he accepts. Kadota has been concealing from his wife the fact that he was fired from his job a few months earlier. He begins to feel very comfortable in the home of hard-working Michiyo.

Meanwhile, Michiyo's husband wants to divorce her, an additional source of stress, especially in that Michiyo has to answer the many questions Chikako has about her father. Chikako is confused as to the identity of the man who spends so much time around her mother. Is he her father? Hadn't Michiyo said that her father was ill and away from home for the last two years? Just as Michiyo begins to sort out all that is happening in her life and is happy to have a man around the house, the police inform her that her husband has committed suicide. But it turns out that it is Kadota, in a fit of depression, who has committed suicide. He has left Michiyo his only belonging, a luminous watch. At this point, Kadota's wife storms into Michiyo's apartment, accusing her falsely of having driven her husband to despair, and tears the luminous watch from Michiyo's hands.

This excerpt is taken from a 25-page *tanpen shōsetsu* (short-length story).

work, so Michiyo, hearing that story, struck on the idea of washing tabi as a job. This needed no capital or skill.

Were she to offer to wash a pair for 30 yen, she wondered if customers wouldn't come to her. They were only tabi [after all]. Even washing twenty pairs a day shouldn't be that heavy a job. At twenty pairs, 600 yen. It was a considerably better rate than working from morning to night without a break on artificial flowers or embroidering gloves which would only yield 350 yen a day, if only because there was no middleman. Of course, it wasn't nice work, but she couldn't afford the luxury of saying such things as that.

When she ventured to tell Tamae of her idea, she was terribly enthusiastic.

"I alone will give you twenty or thirty pair a month. There are two others working at my place, and I'll talk to the people in the neighborhood shops for you. At 30 yen a pair everyone will gladly give them to you."

With Tamae's place as a start, Michiyo had about fifty solid customers by now. Each person put out at least twenty pairs a month so she had one thousand pairs to wash, and her monthly earnings didn't go below 30,000 yen. Two days out of the week she went around to collect the tabi, and delivered the cleaned ones at that time.

At the beginning, Michiyo was washing the tabi she had collected in the small sink in her room. She had [felt] considerable resistance to washing bar hostess' tabi in the sink where she washed food and dishes, but she had a pride which didn't want that sort of work known by the loose-mouthed residents in the apartment. Even without that [being known] it seemed people were spreading rumors about what Michiyo, living as a pair with her daughter, was doing to support herself.

But, rather than have it be suspected that there might be a man giving her economic aid, she thought it better to make it public that she was doing in-house work washing tabi, and also, when her work increased and she began to be completely unable to handle it all in the small sink, she began to carry the huge amounts of tabi out to the public laundry area in the back garden to the apartment.

- 盥・たらい: a (wash)tub; basin
- 並べる・ならべる: to line up; to arrange
- いっぱい・一杯: full, entire
- コンクリート: concrete
- たたき: a concrete slab/floor
- 水道栓・すいどうせん: a tap; faucet
- 屋根・やね: roof
- 雨・あめ: rain
- 意外に・いがいに: unexpectedly
- 時間がかかる: "it takes time"
- 予め・あらかじめ: ahead of time; in advance
- 洗剤・せんざい: soap; (laundry) detergent
- 溶かす・とかす: to dissolve
- 湯・ゆ: hot water
- ～に漬(つ)ける: to soak in ～
- 予(あらかじ)め～しておく: to do ～ ahead of time
- 浮く・うく: to float to the surface
- ところで: as soon as; at that point
- ブラシ: brush
- 爪先・つまさき: tips of the toes [here referring to the toes of the tabi]
- 細い・ほそい: thin
- 針金・はりがね: wire
- 束ねる・たばねる: to bundle up
- 特別・とくべつ: special
- おちる・落ちる: to come out [of a stain or grime]
- 黄ばむ・きばむ: to yellow (with age)
- 漂白・ひょうはく: bleach
- 薄糊・うすのり: light (うすい) starch (のり)
- 干す・ほす: to (hang out) to dry
- 洗濯機・せんたくき: a washing machine
- 放り込む・ほうりこむ: to throw into
- 決して … ない: certainly does not …; definitely does not …
- 数・かず: number
- 多い・おおい: large (number); many
- 午前中いっぱい: all morning
- 陽・ひ: the sun; rays of the sun
- 洗い上がる・あらいあがる: to wash completely; finish washing

　共同洗濯場といっても、盥を二つも並べればいっぱいのコンクリートのたたきに、水道栓が一つあるだけである。屋根がないから雨の日は洗濯をすることができない。

　足袋の洗濯は、意外に時間のかかるものである。予め三十分ほど洗剤を溶かした湯に漬けておき、汚れが浮いてきたところで一つ一つブラシで洗う。爪先は、細い針金を束ねた特別のブラシで洗わねばおちない。黄ばんでいるものは漂白し、薄糊をつけてから干す。洗濯機などに放り込んだのでは決してきれいにならない。数の多いときは午前中いっぱいかかるので、午後から陽の射す西側の窓は洗い上がった足袋を干すのに好都合であった。

慣用句: Idiomatic Expressions

Translate the following into idiomatic English.

1. 〜ほか〜ようがない

共同洗濯場は屋根がないから雨の日は台所の流し台で洗う<u>ほかやりようがない</u>。

2. 底をつく

内職だけでは道世の月収は三週間ほどで<u>底をつく</u>ような生活だった。

3. （〜も）かなわない

娘とふたり暮らしでは、自由に職を選ぶことも<u>かなわない</u>、そこで、道世は水商売
の女たちの足袋洗いの内職を始めることにした。

4. 贅沢を言っていられない

生活に窮した道世は足袋洗いの内職のことをアパートの住人に知られたくないなど
と<u>贅沢を言っていられない</u>と思い、共同洗濯場へ足袋を持ち出すことにした。

5. 乗気である（〜になる）

水商売の女たちの足袋を洗うという仕事に道世ははじめあまり<u>乗気でなかった</u>。

6. 口さがない

経済的な援助をしてくれる男がいるのではないかなどと<u>口さがない</u>アパートの住人
たちに噂されることに道世はかなり抵抗を感じていた。

KYOU-DOU SEN-TAKU-BA to itte mo, TARAI o FUTA-TSU mo NARAbereba ippai no *konkuri-ito* no tataki ni, SUI-DOU-SEN ga HITOtsu aru dake de aru. YA-NE ga nai kara AME no HI wa SEN-TAKU o suru koto ga dekinai.

TA-BI no SEN-TAKU wa, I-GAI ni JI-KAN no kakaru mono de aru. ARAKAJIme SAN-JUP-PUN hodo SEN-ZAI o TOkashita YU ni TSUkete oki, YOGOre ga Uite kita tokoro de HITOtsu HITO-tsu *burashi* de ARAu. TSUMA-SAKI wa, HOSOi HARI-GANE o TABAneta TOKU-BETSU no *burashi* de ARAwane-ba ochinai. KIbande iru mono wa HYOU-HAKU shi, USU-NORI o tsukete kara HOsu. SEN-TAKU-KI nado ni HOUriKOnda no de wa KESshite kirei ni naranai. KAZU no OOi toki wa GO-ZEN-CHUU ippai kakaru no de, GO-GO kara HI no SAsu NISHI-GAWA no MADO wa ARA-iAgatta TA-BI o HOsu no ni KOU-TSU-GOU de atta.

内容理解: Comprehension Questions

Answer in Japanese

1. 道世は誰とどんなアパートに住んでいますか。
2. 隣室にはどんな人が住んでいますか。
3. 道世はどんな仕事を思いつきましたか。
4. 足袋洗いの仕事はどうして造花や手袋の刺繍より割りがいいのでしょうか。
5. 足袋洗いの「案」について珠江はどう思いましたか。
6. はじめのうち道世は自分の仕事に対してどんな抵抗を感じていましたか。
7. どうして道世は内職していることを公にした方がいいと思うようになりましたか。
8. 足袋洗いの内職は資本も技術もいらないかんたんな仕事でしょうか。
9. どうして家賃の安い道世のアパートは内職に好都合でしたか。

練習問題: Exercises

True or False ?

1. 西陽の射す家賃の安いアパートは道世の内職にはかえって好都合だった。
2. 足袋の洗濯という内職は資本も技術もいらないし、それほど重労働でもないが造花や刺繍の仕事よりは格段割りが悪い。
3. 道世が水商売の女たちの足袋洗いの内職を始める前から、口さがないアパートの住人たちは娘とふたり暮らしの道世が何によって生活しているのか噂し合っているらしかった。
4. 道世が共同洗濯場へ足袋を持ち出すようになったのは食物や食器を洗う小さな流しで水商売の女たちの足袋を洗うことにかなり抵抗を感じていたからだ。

Even called a "public laundry," it was only a concrete floor, [its space] filled up after two washtubs were arranged on it, with a single faucet. There was no roof, so on rainy days she could not do laundry.

Laundering tabi is a thing that takes more time than one thinks. Before anything else they are soaked for at least 30 minutes in hot water with detergent dissolved in it, and are washed one by one with a brush as the stains float to the surface. The toes must be washed with a special brush of bundled thin wire. Yellowed ones are bleached and hung to dry after a light starching. Throwing them in a washing machine will definitely not get them clean. When the numbers of them were great, because it took all morning, the window on the west side where the sun shone after noon was convenient for drying the tabi she had finished washing.

語句と語法: Phrases and Usage

- 怪傑・かいけつ: a person with strange powers; a "wonder man/woman"
- 主婦・しゅふ: housewife
- 仮面・かめん: a mask [～仮面 is a common ending for masked television or comic superheroes]
- ～歳・さい: ～ years old [commonly, 才]
- ふつう・普通: ordinary
- でも: but
- 空飛ぶ・そらとぶ: to fly the skies [without を after 空, a modifier]
- 怪傑主婦仮面: loosely, the "Mysterious Masked Housewife"
- ～として: as (a) ～
- 悪人・あくにん: evil people; bad guys
- 退治(たいじ)する: to exterminate; vanquish; stamp out
- まわる・回る: to go around
- 家・いえ: "home" rather than "house," since she lives in an アパート (apartment)
- 恰好・かっこう: appearance; how one is dressed
- たいてい・大抵: largely; usually
- ジーパン: jeans
- トレーナー: "trainer"; a sweatshirt
- ほんとうのことをいうと: to tell the truth
- 家事・かじ: household chores
- ～をするには: in order to do ～
- スリップ: slip (clothing)
- 一枚・いちまい: one [枚 is a counter for thin flat objects]
- ～がいちばん(一番)いい: "to be number one"; be best
- おもってる: = おもっている [in informal language, い is often dropped]
- それなら: if that (i.e., if she wears a slip)
- 料理・りょうり: food; meals
- 作る・つくる: to make; prepare (food)
- 暑い・あつい: hot; warm
- 眠い・ねむい: sleepy
- 猫・ねこ: cat
- 「みじめ」: cat's name ["miserable" (or, sad, wretched, pitiable)]
- ～を連(つ)れて … いく: to take ～ (somewhere)
- ベッド: bed
- 入る・はいる: to get into
- 昼寝(ひるね)をする: to take a nap
- 夫・おっと: husband [cf. 主人(しゅじん), which has the additional meaning of "master"]
- お願い(おねがい)だから: I'm asking you, please …
- ＮＨＫ・えぬえっちけい: a public broadcaster supported by national laws which allow collecting fees

- 集金・しゅうきん: collecting money
- おじいさん: old man
- ～の前に: before/in front of (the NHK man)
- 下着・したぎ: underwear
- 出(で)る: to appear
- verb-てくれよ: "please ～" [informal, slightly emotional plea]
- 泣く・なく: to cry; weep [here used in the sense of "beg"]
- 頼む・たのむ: to request (a favor); ask; beg
- 妥協(だきょう)する: to compromise; come to terms
- 会社・かいしゃ: company; corporation
- 送り出す・おくりだす: to send ～ off (to work)
- 掃除・そうじ: cleaning
- 洗濯・せんたく: laundry; the wash
- 励む・はげむ: to work hard at
- 鑑・かがみ: a model; paragon
- それから: after that; then
- 一休み(ひとやすみ)する: to take a break; take a breather
- テレビ: television
- 新金色夜叉・しんこんじきやしゃ: a new TV version of the famous 1897 novel "Golden Demon" by Ozaki Kouyou
- 百年の恋・ひゃくねんのこい: "the hundred-year love"
- 再放送・さいほうそう: a rebroadcast
- とか … とか: indicates a non-inclusive list
- 緊張(きんちょう)する: to feel tense
- 仕事・しごと: work
- 電話・でんわ: telephone
- 鳴る・なる: to ring
- 時間帯・じかんたい: time frame; period of time; time of day
- 正義の味方・せいぎのみかた: ally/friend (味方) of justice (正義)
- ～をやる: to do (as a job)
- ～と決(き)めてある: to have decided that ～
- 帰宅(きたく)する: to come home; return
- ～時間までに: by the time ～
- ちゃんと: properly; duly; correctly
- 晩御飯・ばんごはん: evening meal; dinner
- ～ておかなくちゃならない: must; have to; lit. "if one doesn't do, it won't do" [= ～ておかなければなりません]
- 約束・やくそく: a promise
- パート: a "part" time job (from English)
- 出(で)る: to go to work; go out to work
- 守る・まもる: to keep (a promise)

「怪傑主婦仮面」より

高橋源一郎

（1）

　ハルミさんは二十七歳のふつうの主婦だ。でも、ふつうの主婦でない時には、空飛ぶ「怪傑主婦仮面」として悪人を退治してまわる。

　家にいる時、ハルミさんの恰好（かっこう）はたいていジーパンにトレーナーである。ほんとうのことをいうと家事をするには、スリップ一枚がいちばんいいとハルミさんは思ってる。それなら料理を作る時に暑くないし、眠くなったらすぐ猫（ねこ）の「みじめ」を連れてベッドに入り昼寝をすることができるからだ。

　でも、ハルミさんの夫のヒロシさんが「お願いだから、NHKの集金のおじいさんの前に下着で出ないでくれよ」と泣いて頼むので、ハルミさんは妥協したのだ。

　ハルミさんはヒロシさんを会社に送りだすと、掃除と洗濯（せんたく）に励む。主婦の鑑（かがみ）だ。それから、一休みするとテレビを見る。『新金色夜叉・百年の恋（こんじきやしゃ）』とか再放送の『ありがとう』とか。

　テレビの時間が終わると、ハルミさんは少し緊張する。「怪傑主婦仮面」の仕事の電話が鳴る時間帯だからだ。

　ハルミさんは「正義の味方」をやるのは三時から五時までと決めてある。ヒロシさんが帰宅する時間までにはちゃんと晩御飯を作っておかなくちゃならない。そういう約束で、「正義の味方」のパートに出ているのだ。約束は守らなくちゃならない。

Takahashi Gen'ichirō

Born in 1951 in Hiroshima, Takahashi Gen'ichirō made his literary debut in 1981 with a short story entitled さよならギャングたち *Good-bye Gangs* (Kodansha), which won him the prestigious Gunzō New Writers prize. *Gunzō* is a serious literary magazine, in which, among other well-known works, appeared a serialized novel by Mishima Yukio. Takahashi also wrote 虹の彼方に (*Over the Rainbow*). He has also translated Jay McInerney's *Bright Lights, Big City* into Japanese, and has won the Mishima Yukio Award. Baseball is one of his favorite topics, about which he has written an entire volume. The short story *The Imitation of Leibnitz* (*New Japanese Voices*, Atlantic Monthly Press, 1992) is about baseball.

"KAI-KETSU SHU-FU KA-MEN" yori

TAKA-HASHI GEN-ICHI-ROU

(1)

Harumi-san wa NI-JUU-NANA-SAI no futsuu no SHU-FU da. Demo, futsuu no SHU-FU de nai TOKI ni wa, SORA-TObu "KAI-KETSU SHU-FU KA-MEN" toshite AKU-NIN o TAI-JI shite mawaru.

IE ni iru TOKI, *Harumi*-san no KAK-KOU wa taitei *jiipan* ni *toreenaa* de a-ru. Hontou no koto o iu to KA-JI o suru ni wa, *surippu* ICHI-MAI ga ichiban ii to *Harumi*-san wa OMOtte ru. Sore nara RYOU-RI o TSUKUru TOKI ni ATSUku nai shi, NEMU-ku nattara sugu NEKO no "Mijime" o TSUrete *beddo* ni HAIri HIRU-NE o suru koto ga dekiru kara da.

Demo, *Harumi*-san no OTTO no *Hiroshi*-san ga "oNEGAi da kara, ENU-EICHI-KEI no SHUU-KIN no ojii-san no MAE ni SHITA-GI de DEnai de kure yo" to NAite TANOmu no de, *Harumi*-sa-n wa DA-KYOU shita no da.

Harumi-san wa *Hiroshi*-san o KAI-SHA ni OKUridasu to, SOU-JI to SEN-TAKU ni HAGEmu. SHU-FU no KAGAMI da. Sore kara, HITO-YASUmi suru to *terebi* o MIru. "SHIN-KON-JIKI-YA-SHA・HYAKU-NEN no KOI" toka SAI-HOU-SOU no "arigatou" toka.

Terebi no JI-KAN ga Owaru to, *Harumi*-san wa SUKOshi KIN-CHOU suru. "KAI-KETSU SHU-FU KA-MEN" no SHI-GOTO no DEN-WA ga NAru JI-KAN-TAI da kara da.

Harumi-san wa "SEI-GI no MI-KATA" o yaru no wa SAN-JI kara GO-JI made to KImete a-ru. *Hiroshi*-san ga KI-TAKU suru JI-KAN made ni wa chanto BAN-GO-HAN o TSUKUtte okana-kucha naranai. Sou iu YAKU-SOKU de, "SEI-GI no MI-KATA" no *paato* ni DEte iru no da. YAKU-SOKU wa MAMOranakucha naranai.

NHK stickers on doors showing that the occupants are registered users of the public TV network.

"The Mysterious Masked Housewife" (An Excerpt)

Takahashi Gen'ichirō

(1)

Harumi is an ordinary 27-year-old housewife. But when she isn't an ordinary housewife, she goes around vanquishing villains as the flying "Mysterious Masked Housewife."

When at home, Harumi's garb is usually a sweatshirt with jeans. To tell the truth, Harumi thinks a slip is best for doing housework. It's because, if [she's only wearing] that, it isn't too hot when making meals, and if she gets sleepy, she can quickly take the cat, "Mijime," get into bed, and take a nap.

But Harumi's husband, Hiroshi, cried out and pleaded with her, "I'm begging you, don't appear before the old man collecting money for NHK in your underwear," so Harumi compromised.

When Harumi has sent her husband off to work, she applies herself to cleaning and laundry. She's a model housewife. After that, she takes a little rest and she watches television. [Things like] "Hundred Year Romance" or rebroadcasts of "Arigatou."

When television time ends Harumi gets a little tense. It is because it is the time of day for the phone to ring about work as the "Mysterious Masked Housewife."

Harumi's working as the "Ally of Justice" is set at from three to five o'clock. By the time Hiroshi returns home she must have dinner made. With that promise, she is going out to do her part-time job as an "Ally of Justice." Promises must be kept.

- ジリジリジリ: ringalingaling
- おや: What?; Oh?
- 〜をとる: to pick up
- すいません: "Sorry to bother you" [colloquial for すみません]
- 出勤(しゅっきん)する: to go to work; leave for one's job
- いってくる: informal of「いってきます」; the cat, if it could speak, would say「いってらっしゃい」
- 悪・あく: evil
- 戦う・たたかう: to fight; do battle
- 立上がる・たちあがる: to stand up; rise up (to take action)
- 最初・さいしょ: first
- もちろん・勿論: of course
- 着替え・きがえ: changing clothes
- ところで: by the way; incidentally
- みなさん・皆さん: everyone; ladies and gentlemen [directed at the reader]
- 格好(かっこう)をする: to have (such and such) an appearance; to look like (superwoman); dress like
- お思いになる・おおもいになる: to think [formal]
- スーパーマン: superman
- スーパーウーマン: superwoman
- 同じ・おなじ: same
- AみたいなB: a B which looks like an A
- にきまっている: (something) is certainly/necessarily a certain way
- 少し・すこし: a little; a tiny bit
- 違う・ちがう: to be different
- たしかに・確かに: certainly; to be sure
- 昔・むかし: old days; long ago
- タイツ: tights
- 〜をはく: to wear [of pants, clothing one steps into]
- わたしは: the narrator shifts directly to Harumi's thoughts here
- エアロビクス: aerobics
- 習う・ならう: to learn; take lessons
- カルチャーセンター: "culture center"; community center for arts, crafts, exercise, etc.
- 通う・かよう: to go to; commute to
- 「〜じゃないわ」: the narrator has shifted to Harumi, first person
- 姿・すがた: form; appearance
- いや: negates previous statement
- 厳密に・げんみつに: strictly
- スーパー: supermarket
- 買う・かう: to buy
- やつ: one thing/object [colloquial for mono]
- 着る・きる: to wear (shirts etc.)
- KENZO: expensive brand name of Takada Kenzo, stationed in Paris

- マント: a cape [from French "manteau"]
- だって?: what about a...? [author pretends reader has asked about a cape]
- あんなもの: anything like that
- 高速・こうそく: high speed
- 首・くび: neck
- (首)がしまる: to tighten around the neck
- 痛い・いたい: painful; hurts
- そのかわり: in place of that; instead
- サングラス: sunglasses
- は/をする: here, "wear" (sunglasses) [also: 〜をかける、〜をつける]
- もしかして: perhaps; just maybe
- フォーカスする: coll.; slang; to have one's picture taken unawares [from the sensationalist magazine Focus]
- 上司・じょうし: superiors; bosses
- ばれる: (a secret) gets out; be found out; be discovered
- 普段・ふだん: common; usual; everyday
- 風圧・ふうあつ: wind pressure
- 飛(と)んでしまう: to be blown away
- 水泳・すいえい: swimming
- 使う・つかう: to use
- ゴーグル: goggles
- そうそう: "oh yes"
- 忘れる・わすれる: to forget
- 必需品・ひつじゅひん: an absolute necessity; a necessary item
- 背中・せなか: one's back
- 背負う・せおう: to carry/shoulder
- ナップザック: a knapsack
- 東急ハンズ: Tokyu Hands [a department store with many specialty and unusual items]
- 後・あと: after [preceding verbs must be in past tense]
- 買(か)い物(もの)する: to shop; to go shopping (for groceries)
- たいへん・大変: hard-pressed; not easy (work)
- なのである: ＝なのです; slightly formal; used stylistically here
- 変身(へんしん)する: to transform into (one's superhero costume)
- 〜階建て・〜かい/がいだて: a 〜 floor (building)
- 公団住宅・こうだんじゅうたく: public housing
- ベランダ: a small verandah or balcony outside an apartment
- 出(で)る: go out onto (the verandah)
- ちょうど・丁度: just as; exactly when
- 布団・ふとん: Japanese bedding; futon [people often air futons outside]
- とりこむ・取り込む: to take in (laundry etc.)
- 隣・となり: next door; neighboring
- 声(こえ)をかける: to call to
- ええ: "yes"

ジリジリジリ。おや、電話だ。ハルミさんは電話をとる。「ハルミさん？すいません、『怪傑主婦仮面』出勤してください」
「『みじめ』、わたし、仕事にいってくるね」
ハルミさんは悪と戦うために立ち上がった。

（2）

「怪傑主婦仮面」として出勤するためにハルミさんが最初にやらなくちゃならないのは、もちろん着替えである。

ところで、みなさんは「怪傑主婦仮面」がどんな恰好（かっこう）をしているとお思いになるだろうか。これはもう、空を飛ぶのだから、スーパーマン（スーパーウーマンも同じだが）みたいな恰好に決まっているといいたいのだが、少し違う。

たしかに、昔の「正義の味方」は、タイツをはいて飛んでいたかもしれない。でもわたしはエアロビクスを習いにカルチャーセンターに通う主婦じゃないわ。ハルミさんはそう思っている。だから、ハルミさんはジーパンにトレーナーという姿で空を飛ぶ。そうだ、主婦をやってる時と同じ恰好だ。いや、厳密にいうと違うか。主婦をやってる時のトレーナーはスーパーで買った千九百円のやつだが、「正義の味方」のパートに出かける時に着ていくのは「KENZO」の九千八百円のやつだからだ。

マントだって？あんなものは着ないよ。高速で空を飛んでいると首がしまってきて痛いんだ。その代わり、サングラスはする。つけないと目が痛いし、もしかしてフォーカスされた時、夫のヒロシさんの会社の上司にばれたりしないようにだ。もちろん、普通のサングラスでは風圧で飛んでしまうから、水泳で使うゴーグルみたいなやつだ。

そうそう、忘れていた。「怪傑主婦仮面」の必需品は背中に背負ったナップザック（東急ハンズで買ったやつ）だ。悪を退治した後は、スーパーで買物して帰らなくちゃならない。「怪傑主婦仮面」はたいへんなのである。

（3）

「怪傑主婦仮面」に変身したハルミさんは八階建ての公団住宅の六階のベランダに出た。ちょうど布団（ふとん）をとりこんでいた隣の家のマサコさんがハルミさんに声をかけた。
「ハルミさん、パートですか？」
「ええ」

WOMEN IN TODAY'S JAPAN 1

Women fulfill diverse roles in Japanese society. In the family, they hold a position of responsibility and often control the purse strings, allotting a monthly allowance (お小遣い・おこづかい) to their husbands. In the workplace, women are usually paid less for the same work, which is not unique to Japan, and their chances for advancement are much less than those of men. Also, if a woman needs to take a leave due to pregnancy or child care, she may feel that she is obligated to quit her job. This automatically cuts her chances of advancement within a single workplace. After a hiatus of several years, she will reenter the workforce, but she will have lost seniority. At this stage, she will typically serve as temporary labor, for which there is a strong demand.

The belief is still common that a woman who works is merely trying to find a husband, which lowers her status in the workplace. In offices, women are expected to do the "feminine" jobs, such as serving tea or photocopying. However, the situation is slowly changing. Being a career woman is increasingly becoming a viable option. With the presently low birth rate and increase of the aging population, the number of men who will enter the professional work force may not be sufficient. Will women be called upon to fill the gaps? There are signs indicating that young women are preparing to become professionals in increasing numbers.

Jirijirijiri. Oya, DEN-WA da. *Harumi*-san wa DEN-WA o toru. "*Harumi*-san? Suimasen, 'KAI-KETSU SHU-FU KA-MEN' SHUK-KIN shite kudasai"

"'Mijime', watashi, SHI-GOTO ni itte kuru ne"

Harumi-san wa AKU to TATAKAu tame ni TAchiAgatta.

(2)

"KAI-KETSU SHU-FU KA-MEN" toshite SHUK-KIN suru tame ni *Harumi*-san ga SAI-SHO ni yaranakucha naranai no wa, mochiron KI-GAe de aru.

Tokoro de, mina-san wa "KAI-KETSU SHU-FU KA-MEN" ga donna KAK-KOU o shite iru to o-OMOi ni naru darou ka. Kore wa mou, SORA o TObu no da kara, *suupaaman* (*suupaauuman* mo ONAji da ga) mitai na KAK-KOU ni KImatte iru to iitai no da ga, SUKOshi CHIGAu.

Tashika ni, MUKASHI no "SEI-GI no MI-KATA" wa, *taitsu* o haite TOnde ita kamo shirenai. Demo watashi wa *earobikusu* o NARAi ni *karuchaasentaa* ni KAYOu SHU-FU ja nai wa. *Harumi*-san wa sou OMOtte iru. Dakara, *Harumi*-san wa *jiipan* ni *toreenaa* to iu SUGATA de SORA o TObu. Sou da, SHU-FU o yatte ru TOKI to ONAji KAK-KOU da. Iya, GEN-MITSU ni iu to CHIGAu ka. SHU-FU o yatte ru TOKI no *toreenaa* wa *suupaa* de KAtta SEN-KYUU-HYAKU-EN no yatsu da ga, "SEI-GI no MI-KATA" no *paato* ni DEkakeru TOKI ni KIte iku no wa "KENZO" no KYUU-SEN-HAP-PYAKU-EN no yatsu da kara da.

Manto datte? Anna mono wa KInai yo. KOU-SOKU de SORA o TOnde iru to KUBI ga shimatte kite ITAi n da. Sono KAwari, *sangurasu* wa suru. Tsukenai to ME ga ITAi shi, moshi ka shite *fookasu* sareta TOKI, OTTO no *Hiroshi*-san no KAI-SHA no JOU-SHI ni baretari shinai you ni da. Mochiron, FU-TSUU no *sangurasu* de wa FUU-ATSU de TOnde shimau kara, SUI-EI de TSUKAu *googuru* mitai na yatsu da.

Sou sou, WASUrete ita. "KAI-KETSU SHU-FU KA-MEN" no HITSU-JU-HIN wa SE-NAKA ni SE-Otta *nappuzakku* (TOU-KYUU *hanzu* de KAtta yatsu) da. AKU o TAI-JI shita ATO wa, *suupaa* de KAI-MONO shite KAEranakucha naranai. "KAI-KETSU SHU-FU KA-MEN" wa taihen na no de aru.

(3)

"KAI-KETSU SHU-FU KA-MEN" ni HEN-SHIN shita *Harumi*-san wa HACHI-KAI-DAte no KOU-DAN-JUU-TAKU no ROK-KAI no *beranda* ni DEta. Choudo FU-TON o torikonde ita TONARI no IE no *Masako*-san ga *Harumi*-san ni KOE o kaketa.

"*Harumi*-san, *paato* desu ka?"

"Ee"

WOMEN IN TODAY'S JAPAN II

In some of the areas which were traditionally closed to married and child-bearing women, there has been much progress. For example, it is now accepted that women combine a writing career with family and home responsibilities. Also, there are several women members of the Japanese Diet who are married and have even raised a family, which was unthinkable not long ago. Hironaka Wakako is a member of the Diet. She is also the wife of famous mathematician Hironaka Heisuke (see *One Needs an Exacting Education*, p. 82).

Dingalingaling. Oh, it's the phone. Harumi picks up the phone. "Harumi? Excuse me, please come in to work [as the] 'Mysterious Masked Housewife.'"

"'Mijime,' I'll go to work and be back, O.K.?"

Harumi rose up to do battle with evil.

(2)

In order to go to work as the "Mysterious Masked Housewife," the first thing Harumi has to do is, of course, to change.

By the way, how do all of you think the "Mysterious Masked Housewife" might be dressed? As to that, why, since she flies in the sky, I'd like to say that she's dressed like superman (and it's the same for superwoman), but it's not quite like that.

To be sure, the old time "Allies of Justice" might have been flying [while] wearing tights. But I'm not some housewife going to the Culture Center to learn aerobics, you know. This is what Harumi thinks. So, Harumi flies in a sweatshirt with jeans. Yes, it is in fact the same garb as when she is a housewife. No, to be rigorous about it, that's wrong. That's because the sweatshirt for when she is a housewife is one she bought for 1,900 yen at the supermarket, but the one she wears when she goes to work part-time as an "Ally of Justice" is a 9000-yen one from KENZO.

A cloak, you say? She doesn't wear anything like that. When flying through the air at high speed, it tightens around your neck and hurts. In place of that, she wears sunglasses. If she doesn't put them on, her eyes hurt, and it is also so that if [by chance] she is caught on camera, it won't become known to her husband Hiroshi's superiors at the office. Of course, her usual sunglasses would be blown away by the wind pressure, so these are one's like the goggles used for swimming.

Oh yes, I had forgotten. A necessary item for the "Mysterious Masked Housewife" is the knap-sack (one bought at Tokyu Hands) borne on her back. After vanquishing evil, she has to shop at the supermarket and return home. It's very tough being a "Mysterious Masked Housewife."

(3)

Harumi, having transformed into the "Mysterious Masked Housewife," went out on the sixth floor verandah of their eight-story public housing. The next-door neighbor, Masako, who was just then bringing in her futons, spoke to Harumi.

"Harumi, is it [time for your] part-time job?"

"Yes"

- じゃあ: Well…; In that case
- 雨(あめ)が降(ふ)ったら: if it rains
- 洗濯物・せんたくもの: laundry
- verb 〜ておく: (do 〜) ahead of time, for a future purpose; "I'll go ahead and (take in your laundry)"
- あの: used when hesitating ("umm…") or at the beginning of sentences to get attention, when suggesting things, etc.
- 鍵・かぎ: a key
- 新聞入れ・しんぶんいれ: a box/container into which the newspaper is delivered
- 中・なか: inside
- お互いさま: it's mutual ("we all [have to] help each other out")
- 「じゃあ、ちょっと悪(あく)を退治(たいじ)してきます」: a play on the usual 「いってきます」 when leaving for work etc.
- に向(む)かって: to; toward; in the direction of
- ビュン！: Whoosh!
- 高度・こうど: altitude
- ぐんぐん: quickly; rapidly
- あげていく: to go on increasing (altitude)
- 手(て)を振(ふ)る: to wave a hand; wave at
- いっぱい: "full"; many [here, similar to たくさん]
- マイホーム: "My Home" [one's own home]
- 棟・むね: ridge (of a roof); apartment block
- なんだか: somehow; in some way
- ブルーな: blue; melancholy; sad
- 気(き)持(も)ち: feeling
- ありがちな: apt/prone to (exist in housewife superheroes)
- 心的・しんてき: mental; psychological
- 傾向・けいこう: trend; tendency
- 「〜なんだって」: "I hear that 〜"; "it is said that 〜"
- そりゃ: = それは [an affective/emotive expression (here, used in the explanation of why Harumi feels "blue")]
- 成層圏・せいそうけん: the stratosphere
- 別・べつ: different
- 許可(きょか)する: to permit; allow (legally)
- 百・ひゃく: a hundred
- メートル: a meter [sometimes symbolized by 米]
- 前後・ぜんご: about; around (500 m.)
- 光化学(こうかがく)スモッグ: photochemical smog
- 毎日・まいにち: everyday; daily
- 天然素材・てんねんそざい: natural ingredients
- シャンプー: shampoo
- リンス: rinse; conditioner
- 洗髪(せんぱつ)する: to wash one's hair [cf. 髪(かみ)を洗う(あらう)]
- 枝毛・えだげ: split ends
- ばっかり: = ばかり "only" with emphasis
- キューティクル: cuticle (hair's protective layer)
- にちがいない: without a doubt
- 最近・さいきん: recently; lately
- ニキビ: acne; pimples
- まで: even
- できる: to develop

- 直射日光・ちょくしゃにっこう: direct rays of the sun
- あたる: to be struck by; exposed to
- シミ・染み: blemish
- 直る・なおる: to get better; cure
- 時々・ときどき: sometimes
- 挫ける・くじける: to give in; be discouraged
- だって: because of course …
- 〜なんだもの: used to give reasons [typically used by women]
- 担当地域・たんとうちいき: an area of responsibility
- 山手線・やまのてせん: a loop line in Tokyo
- 内側・うちがわ: inside [here, referring to a location inside the loop formed by the Yamanote Line]
- 北半分・きたはんぶん: the north half
- 区・く: a district; ward
- あたり: vicinity; general area
- 女子大生・じょしだいせい: women college students
- 南側・みなみがわ: the south side
- 受け持つ・うけもつ: to be in charge of
- 聞いた話では・きいたはなしでは: according to what she had heard
- ほとんど・殆ど: almost completely; almost all
- 常勤・じょうきん: a full-time job
- 多(おお)いそうだ: she heard (they were) many
- そんなもの: that kind of thing; the way it is
- 近くに・ちかくに: close by; nearby
- 盛り場・さかりば: entertainment district (usually with many bars)
- 〜ことがある: to have (had the experience of) 〜
- とても: very; extremely
- 派手(はで)な: gaudy; garish; ostentatious; "loud" (clothing)
- 髪・かみ: hair
- (〜は)揃(そろ)って: (they were) all 〜
- どの〜も: every one of the (college women)
- 肩(かた)パット: shoulder pads
- 服・ふく: clothing
- 「ねえ、奥(おく)さん」: ねえ: a way of addressing someone (especially when seeking understanding/consent) [奥さん is used to address another's wife]
- いくら〜だからって: no matter if (they're college students)
- いちおう・一応: at least; after a fashion
- そのへん(を): (they should at least draw the line) at that
- わきまえる・弁える: to discriminate; know
- verb 〜てもらわないとねえ: if we can't have them (dress better)…right? [after と、こまる (it's no good; will not do) or a similar phrase is omitted]
- 後で・あとで: after; following
- verb 〜たびに・度に: every time (one 〜s)
- グチ(愚痴)をこぼす: to "spill" complaints; grumble
- 相槌(あいづち)をうつ(打つ): the habit of saying はい、ええ. etc. as a polite indication one is listening
- 内心・ないしん: in one's heart; one's real feelings
- 複雑・ふくざつ: complex; mixed
- なんといっても: no matter what is said

「じゃあ、雨が降ったら、洗濯物とりこんでおきますね」

「あの、鍵は新聞入れの中です。いつも、すいませんね」

「お互いさまよ」

「じゃあ、ちょっと悪を退治してきます」

「行ってらっしゃい」

　ハルミさんはベランダから空に向かって飛びだした。ビュン！

　ハルミさんは高度をぐんぐん上げていく。マサコさんが手を振っているのが見える。公団住宅がいっぱい見える。ハルミさんにはどれが自分とヒロシさんのマイホームのある棟なのかわからない。なんだかブルーな気持ちだ。でも、これは空飛ぶ正義の味方にありがちな心的傾向なんだって。そりゃ、成層圏を飛ぶなら別だけど、「正義の味方」に許可されている高度五百メートル前後は光化学スモッグで一杯なのだ。毎日、天然素材のシャンプーとリンスで洗髪しているのに枝毛ばかりだ。キューティクルなんかみんなとれちゃったにちがいない。最近はニキビまでできてきたし、直射日光にあたるから、シミは直らない。そのことを考えると、ハルミさんは時々、泣きたくなる。でも、そんなことで挫けちゃいけない。ハルミさんは心の中でそう思う。

　だって、わたしは「怪傑主婦仮面」なんだもの。

（4）

　「怪傑主婦仮面」ハルミさんの担当地域は、山手線の内側の北半分、豊島区・北区・文京区あたりだ。中央線から南側、千代田区・渋谷区・港区あたりは「怪傑女子大生仮面」たちが受け持っている。

　ハルミさんの聞いた話では、北半分の「怪傑主婦仮面」はほとんど主婦のパートなのに、南半分の「怪傑女子大生仮面」は常勤が多いそうだ。そんなものなんだろうか。新宿の近くに悪を退治にいくと、渋谷の盛り場で悪を退治している「正義の味方」たちの姿が見えることがある。みんなとても派手な恰好をしているのだ。髪は揃って長いし、どの「怪傑女子大生仮面」も肩パットの入った服を着ている。

「ねえ、奥さん。いくら、女子大生だからって、いちおう『正義の味方』という仕事をしてるんだから、そのへんわきまえてもらわないとねえ」

　ハルミさんの後で五時から「怪傑主婦仮面」のパートをやっているテルコさんは、会うたびにグチをこぼす。ハルミさんは「そうねえ」と相槌をうつけれど、内心は複雑だ。なんといっても「正義の味方」なん

The entrance to the Tokyu Hands speciality department store in Ikebukuro, Tokyo.

Aerial view of typical public housing complex in Tokyo.

"Jaa, AME ga FUttara, SEN-TAKU-MONO torikonde okimasu ne"

"Ano, KAGI wa SHIN-BUN-Ire no NAKA desu. Itsumo, suimasen ne"

"OTAGAisama yo"

"Jaa, chotto AKU o TAI-JI shite kimasu"

"Itterasshai"

Harumi-san wa *beranda* kara SORA ni MUkatte TObidashita. *Byun!*"

Harumi-san wa KOU-DO o gungun Agete iku. *Masako*-san ga TE o FUtte i-
ru no ga MIeru. KOU-DAN-JUU-TAKU ga ippai MIeru. *Harumi*-san ni wa dore ga JI-BUN
to *Hiroshi*-san no *maihoomu* no aru MUNE na no ka wakaranai. Nan da ka *buruu*
na KI-MOchi da. Demo, kore wa SORA-TObu SEI-GI no MI-KATA ni arigachi na SHIN-TEKI KEI-KOU nan
datte. Sorya, SEI-SOU-KEN o TObu nara BETSU da kedo, "SEI-GI no MI-KATA" ni KYO-KA sarete iru KOU-DO GO-HYAKU *meetoru* ZEN-GO wa KOU-KA-GAKU *sumoggu* de IP-PAI na no da. MAI-NICHI, TEN-
NEN SO-ZAI no *shanpuu* to *rinsu* de SEN-PATSU shite iru no ni EDA-GE bakari da. *Kyuu-
tikuru* nanka minna torechatta ni chigai nai. SAI-KIN wa *nikibi* made de-
kite kita shi, CHOKU-SHA NIK-KOU ni ataru kara, *shimi* wa NAOranai. Sono koto o KANGAe-
ru to, *Harumi*-san wa TOKI-DOKI, NAkitaku naru. Demo, sonna koto de KUJIkecha
ikenai. *Harumi*-san wa KOKORO no NAKA de sou OMOu.

Datte, watashi wa "KAI-KETSU SHU-FU KA-MEN" nan da mono.

(4)

"KAI-KETSU SHU-FU KA-MEN" *Harumi*-san no TAN-TOU CHI-IKI wa, YAMA(no)-TE-SEN no KITA-HAN-BUN,
TO-SHIMA-KU–KITA-KU–BUN-KYOU-KU atari da. CHUU-OU-SEN kara MINAMI-GAWA, CHI-YO-DA-KU–SHIBU-YA-KU–
MINATO-KU atari wa "KAI-KETSU JO-SHI-DAI-SEI KA-MEN" tachi ga UkeMOtte iru.

Harumi-san no KIita HANASHI de wa, KITA-HAN-BUN no "KAI-KETSU SHU-FU KA-MEN" wa hotondo SHU-
FU no *paato* na no ni, MINAMI-HAN-BUN no "KAI-KETSU JO-SHI-DAI-SEI KA-MEN" wa JOU-KIN ga OOi sou da.
Sonna mono nan darou ka. SHIN-JUKU no CHIKAku ni AKU o TAI-JI ni iku to, SHIBU-YA no SAKAri-
BA de AKU o TAI-JI shite iru "SEI-GI no MI-KATA" tachi no SUGATA ga MIeru koto ga aru. Mi-
nna totemo HA-DE na KAK-KOU o shite iru no da. KAMI wa SOROtte NAGAi shi, dono "KAI-KETSU
JO-SHI-DAI-SEI KA-MEN" mo KATA*patto* no HAItta FUKU o KIte iru.

"Nee, OKU-san. Ikura, JO-SHI-DAI-SEI da kara tte, ichiou 'SEI-GI no MI-KATA'
to iu SHI-GOTO o shite iru n da kara, sono hen wakimaete morawanai to nee"

Harumi-san no ATO de GO-JI kara "KAI-KETSU SHU-FU KA-MEN" no *paato* o yatte iru *Teruko*-san wa, Au tabi ni *guchi* o kobosu. *Harumi*-san wa "sou nee" to
AI-ZUCHI o utsu keredo, NAI-SHIN wa FUKU-ZATSU da. Nan to itte mo "SEI-GI no MI-KATA" nan

Central Shinjuku; one of the liveliest areas in Tokyo.

Central Shibuya; a popular gathering place for Tokyo youth.

"Well, if it rains, I'll take in your laundry."

"Oh, the key is in the newspaper box. I'm sorry [about this] all the time."

"We have to help each other out."

"Well, I'll be back after I go vanquish evil."

"[See you when you return]."

Harumi flew off into the air from the verandah. Whoosh!

Harumi rapidly increased her altitude. She could see Masako waving her hand. She could see lots of public apartment buildings. Harumi could not tell which was the building with her own and Hiroshi's "home sweet home." It's a somewhat depressing feeling. It is said this is a mental tendency which sky-flying "Allies of Justice" are likely to have. Sure, it would be different if [she were] flying in the stratosphere, but the 500 meter or so altitude permitted for "Allies of Justice" is full of photochemical smog. Even though she washes her hair with a natural ingredient shampoo and rinse everyday, she has nothing but split ends. Doubtless all the cuticles have been stripped away. Recently she has even started to get acne, and because she is exposed to direct sunlight, the blemishes won't get better. When she thinks of this, sometimes Harumi wants to cry. But she can't let things like that get her down. In her heart Harumi thinks so.

Because, [of course], I am a "Mysterious Masked Housewife!"

(4)

Harumi the "Mysterious Masked Housewife's" area of responsibility is the northern half of the inside of the Yamanote line—around the Toshima, Kita, and Bunkyo wards. The area south of the Chuo Line—in the vicinity of the Chiyoda, Shibuya, and Minato wards—is taken on by the "Mysterious Masked College Girls."

From what Harumi has heard, although the northern part's "Mysterious Masked Housewives" are nearly all part-time housewives, the southern part's "Mysterious Masked College Girls" have a lot of full-timers. She wonders if that is how it is. When she vanquishes evil near Shinjuku, she has occasions where she can see the form of an "Ally of Justice" vanquishing evil in Shibuya's amusement district. They are all in the most garish costumes. They all have long hair, and all the "Mysterious Masked College Girls" wear clothing with shoulder pads.

"Don't you agree, Mrs. No matter if they say they're women college students, at least since they're doing work as "Allies of Justice," they should behave a little more discreetly …, you know?"

Teruko, who follows Harumi from five o'clock in doing her "Mysterious Masked Housewife" part-time work, complains every time they meet. Harumi responds lightly with a "That's true," but her inside feelings are more complex. Whatever is said, because they are "Allies of Justice"

- こざっぱりとした: neat and trim (in appearance)
- verb〜てほしい(欲しい): to wish someone would 〜; want someone to 〜
- きちんと (〜すれば): properly; punctually; scrupulously
- さえすれば: if only (this is done)
- どんな〜をしようと: whatever a persons does
- 自由(じゆう)なような気(き)がする: to feel that one is free (to …)
- いけない！: "Oh no!"
- 空中・くうちゅう: mid-air
- 叫ぶ・さけぶ: to shout; yell
- 考え事(かんがえごと)をする: to be thinking about something
- verb〜ながらAをする: to do A while 〜ing
- あやうい・危うい: "dangerous"; almost; nearly
- 目的地・もくてきち: destination
- 通りすぎる・とおりすぎる: to pass by; go past
- ところ: (to be on) the point (of … ing)
- ホバリングする: to hover
- ポケット: pocket
- メモ: a memo; a note
- とりだす・取り出す: to take out
- 地面・じめん: ground; surface of the earth
- 見下ろす・みおろす: to look down (on)
- 谷中・やなか: place name
- 墓地・ぼち: cemetery; graveyard
- 根津神社・ねずじんじゃ: Nezu Shrine
- 離れる・はなれる: to separate from [はなれた: distant]
- 不忍池・しのばずいけ: Shinobazu Pond
- 光る・ひかる: to glimmer; shine
- 着く・つく: to arrive; reach (a destination)
- 身震(みぶる)いをする: to shudder; tremble
- 待ち受ける・まちうける: to wait for; lie in wait
- 急降下(きゅうこうか)する: to swoop down
- いきなり: all of a sudden; as if out of nowhere
- 降る・ふる: to drop; fall [降ってくる: come falling down]
- 度胆(どぎも)を抜(ぬ)かれる: to be utterly dumbfounded
- なんだ: what!
- てめえ: = 手前(てまえ); you [slang; many people who "talk tough" turn the last syllables into え sounds:「いてえ！」= いたい ("Ouch! It hurts!")]
- 名前・なまえ: name
- 地上げ・じあげ: "land-raising" [i.e., to raise the level of low-lying land by fill; now, the forcing of people out of land or house by land sharks, making them sign over property under duress]
- 現場・げんば: a site; location
- 到着(とうちゃく)する: to arrive
- 出没(しゅつぼつ)する: to haunt/infest; appear here and there
- あんた: you [colloquial and less polite version of *anata*]
- おとなしくかえりなさい: "go home quietly" [the type of speech that might be directed at children]
- 堂々と・どうどうと: in an imposing manner; stately
- 濃紺・のうこん: dark blue
- 背広・せびろ: suit
- ワイシャツ: dress shirts [needn't be "white"; from Eng. "white shirt"]
- サラリーマン: "salaryman"; a corporate office worker
- 〜らしい: = のような; apparently; seemingly

- ところ: here, appearance, characteristic
- 妙(みょう)に: strangely; oddly
- 不自然・ふしぜん: unnatural; odd
- 肩(かた)をいからせる: to square one's shoulders
- 突っ立つ・つったつ: stand erect [here, perhaps "imposingly"]
- 頭・あたま: head; hairstyle
- ヤクザ屋: gangsters [屋 often indicates a person in business]
- 〜といわれる: to be called 〜
- パンチパーマ: "punch perm" [a Japanese-made English term (和製英語); short cut with tiny curls/fine wave permed in]
- 後ろ・うしろ: behind; in back of
- ダンプカー: dump truck
- 台・だい: a counter for autos or large equipment
- エンジン: engine; motor
- ぶるぶるいわせる: to rev up (the engine)
- いくら〜しても: no matter how much one 〜s
- おどす: to threaten; menace
- 立ち退く・たちのく: to leave; move out; evacuate
- 最後に・さいごに: lastly; in the end
- ダンプ ＝ダンプカー
- 突入(とつにゅう)する: to rush into; charge in
- 軍団・ぐんだん: an army corps [here, a band of gangsters]
- やり方・やりかた: a way of doing something
- このアマ: derogatory term for women [used as a threat]
- 粋がる・いきがる: to put on airs; be stuck up; grandstand
- verb〜てんじゃねえ: a tough guy way to say "don't 〜" [a mother might say to a child「〜ているのじゃありませんよ！」]
- 家ごと・いえごと: along with the house [ごと following nouns means that the noun plus something else is effecting by an action]
- 轢く・ひく: to run over; crash into [ひいちまう＝ひいてしまう]
- 奥底・おくそこ: the depths; deep down
- 怒り・いかり: anger; rage
- エネルギー: energy
- ものすごい: incredible; fantastic
- 勢い・いきおい: power; impetus; force
- こみあげる・込み上げる: to well up
- 黙ったまま・だまった まま: "without saying a word"
- 間・あいだ: a gap; space between
- 通り抜ける・とおりぬける: to pass between
- つかつかと: unhesitatingly; straight towards
- 近寄る・ちかよる: to approach; draw close to
- 両手・りょうて: both hands
- ナンバープレート: license plate
- 掴む・つかむ: to grasp; grip
- べりりっ: sound of metal ripping
- 縦に・たてに: vertically; straight up and down
- 真っ二つ・まっぷたつ: exactly in two
- 裂ける・さける: to split; be torn
- 振返る・ふりかえる: to look back
- 後(うし)ろも見(み)ずに: without looking back
- 逃げる・にげる: to flee; run away; escape
- お茶でものんで: used to ask people to sit for a while and talk
- 厚意・こうい: good favor; courtesy
- うれしい・嬉しい: happy; glad; gratifying
- 〜件・けん: a counter for "cases," jobs to be taken care of

　だから、こざっぱりとした恰好でいてほしいとも思うし、きちんと悪を退治さえすればどんな恰好をしようと自由なような気もするのだ。
「いけない！」ハルミさんは空中で叫んだ。
　考え事をしながら飛んでいたので、あやうく目的地を通りすぎてしまうところだったのだ。ハルミさんはホバリングしながら、ジーパンのポケットからメモをとりだすと、地面を見下ろした。北に谷中墓地、南に根津神社、少し離れたところに不忍池が光ってみえた。
「着いたわ！」
　ハルミさんは身震いすると、待ち受ける悪に向かって急降下していった。
（５）
　男たちは、空からいきなり主婦が降ってきたので、度胆を抜かれていた。
「なん、なんだ、てめえは！」
「わたしの名前は『怪傑主婦仮面』」
　ハルミさんは自分が「地上げ」の現場に到着したことを知った。そうだと思ったのよね。文京区に出没する悪は最近、ほとんどこれなのである。
「あんたたち、おとなしく帰りなさい」ハルミさんは堂々と言った。
　濃紺の背広にワイシャツにネクタイといういかにもサラリーマンらしいところが妙に不自然な男が二人、肩をいからせてハルミさんの前に突っ立っていた。でも、頭はヤクザ屋さんのトレードマークといわれるパンチパーマだ。男たちの後ろではダンプカーが一台エンジンをぶるぶるいわせている。いくら脅しても立ち退かないと、最後にはダンプやブルドーザーを突入させるのが「地上げ」軍団のやり方なのだ。
「てめえ、このアマ、粋がってんじゃねえよ。家ごとダンプで轢いちまうぞ」
　ハルミさんは、体の奥底から怒りのエネルギーがものすごい勢いでこみあげてくるのがわかった。
　ハルミさんは、黙ったまま男たちの間を通り抜け、つかつかとダンプに近寄ると、両手でナンバープレートのあたりを掴んだ。ベリリッ。ダンプカーは縦に真っ二つに裂けた。ハルミさんは振り返った。男たちは後ろも見ずに逃げていくところだった。
「ありがとう！ありがとう！『怪傑主婦仮面』、どうかお茶でも飲んでいってください」
「ご厚意はうれしいんですけど、五時までにあと二件、悪を退治しなく

Shinobazu Pond festooned with lotus plants.

da kara, kozappari to shita KAK-KOU de ite hoshii to mo OMOu shi, kichin to AKU o

TAI-JI sae sureba donna KAK-KOU o shiyou to JI-YUU na you na KI mo suru no da.

"Ikenai!" *Harumi*-san wa KUU-CHUU de SAKEnda.

KANGAeGOTO o shinagara TOnde ita no de, ayauku MOKU-TEKI-CHI o TOOrisugite shima-

u tokoro datta no da. *Harumi*-san wa *hobaringu* shinagara, *jiipan* no *po-*

ketto kara *memo* o toridasu to, JI-MEN o MI-Oroshita. KITA ni YANAKA BO-CHI, MINAMI ni

NE-ZU JIN-JA, SUKOshi HANAreta tokoro ni SHINOBAZU no IKE ga HIKAtte mieta.

"TSUita wa!"

Harumi-san wa MI-BURUI suru to, MAchiUkeru AKU ni MUkatte KYUU-KOU-KA shite itta.

(5)

OTOKOtachi wa, SORA kara ikinari SHU-FU ga FUtte kita no de, DO-GIMO o NUkarete ita.

"Nan, nan da, temee wa!"

"Watashi no NA-MAE wa 'KAI-KETSU SHU-FU KA-MEN'"

Harumi-san wa JI-BUN ga "JI-Age" no GEN-BA ni TOU-CHAKU shita koto o SHItta. Sou

da to OMOtta no yo ne. BUN-KYOU-KU ni SHUTSU-BOTSU suru AKU wa SAI-KIN, hotondo kore na no de aru.

"Antatachi, otonashiku KAErinasai" *Harumi*-san wa DOU-DOU to Itta.

NOU-KON no SE-BIRO ni *waishatsu* ni *nekutai* to iu ikanimo *sarariiman* rashi-

i tokoro ga MYOU ni FU-SHI-ZEN na OTOKO ga FUTA-RI, KATA o ikarasete *Harumi*-san no MAE ni TSU-

tTAtte ita. Demo, ATAMA wa *yakuza*YA-san no *toreedomaaku* to iwareru *pa-*

nchipaama da. OTOKOtachi no USHIro de wa *danpukaa* ga ICHI-DAI *enjin* o buruburu

iwasete iru. Ikura ODOKAshite mo TAchiNOkanai to, SAI-GO ni wa *danpu* ya *buru-*

doozaa o TOTSU-NYUU saseru no ga "JI-Age" GUN-DAN no yariKATA na no da.

"Temee, kono *ama*, IKIgatte n ja nee yo. IEgoto *danpu* de HIichima-

u zo"

Harumi-san wa, KARADA no OKU-SOKO kara IKAri no *enerugii* ga monosugoi IKIOi de ko-

miagete kuru no ga wakatta.

Harumi-san wa, DAMAtta mama OTOKOtachi no AIDA o TOOriNUke, tsukatsuka to *danpu*

ni CHIKA-YOru to, RYOU-TE de *nanbaapureeto* no atari o TSUKAnda. *Beriritt. Da-*

npukaa wa TATE ni MApPUTAtsu ni SAketa. *Harumi*-san wa FUriKAEtta. OTOKOtachi wa

USHIro mo MIzu ni NIgete iku tokoro datta.

"Arigatou! Arigatou! 'KAI-KETSU SHU-FU KA-MEN', douka oCHA de mo NOnde i-

tte kudasai"

"GoKOU-I wa ureshii n desu kedo, GO-JI made ni ato NI-KEN, AKU o TAI-JI shinaku-

Women in Today's Japan

慣用句: Idiomatic Expressions I

Translate the following into idiomatic English

1. 恰好をする

「正義の味方」のパートをしている時、ハルミさんはタイツ姿ではなく、たいていジーパンに「ＫＥＮＺＯ」のトレーナーという恰好をして空を飛ぶ。

2. （〜に）決まっている

ダンプやブルドーザーがあり、肩をいからせたパンチパーマの男たちがいるから、ここは「地上げ」の現場に決まっている。

3. （〜に）変身する

エプロン姿のハルミさんが「正義の味方」のパートに出るためにまずやらなければならないことは、「怪傑主婦仮面」に変身することだ。

4. 〜なら別だ

主婦が派手な恰好でパートに出かけるのはどうだろうか…。女子大生なら別だけど。

5. そんなものなんだろうか

ダンプやブルドーザーなどを使って脅すというのが「地上げ」のやり方らしいが、そんなものなんだろうか。

she wants them to look tidy, but if they just vanquish evil

properly, she also feels that they are free to wear whatever they want.

"Oh no!" Harumi shouted in mid-air.

She had been thinking about things while she had been flying and had come dangerously close to

passing her destination. Harumi, while hovering, took her memo pad from the pocket of her jeans,

and looked down at the ground. In the north was the Yanaka Cemetery, south

was Nezu Shrine, and a little separated [from the others] Shinobazu Pond glittered.

"I've arrived!"

Harumi, with a shudder, zoomed down towards the awaiting evil.

(5)

The men, since a housewife had come falling from the sky without warning, were completely dumbfounded.

"Wha…, what [the hell] are you!"

"My name is the 'Mysterious Masked Housewife.'"

Harumi knew she had arrived at the "land-raising" site. I thought it would be so, you know.

The evil which infested Bunkyo ward recently is almost all of this [type].

"You all go home quietly now," Harumi said in a dignified manner.

Two men, in dark blue suits, white shirts, and neckties, whose salary-man like character

was strangely unnatural, squared their shoulders and were standing [unmoving] in front of

Harumi. But their heads had what is called Mr. Gangster's trademark: the "punch

perm." Behind the men a dump truck is revving

its engine. When you don't leave, no matter how often threatened, it is the "land-raising" gang's

way of operating to finally charge in with a dump truck or bulldozer.

"You, you bitch, don't be putting on airs! We'll run you and your house down with the dump

truck!"

Harumi could tell that, from the depths of her body, the energy of her rage was welling

up with incredible energy.

Harumi, without a word, passed between the men, closed in on the dump truck

without hesitation, and grabbed it near the license plate with both hands. Rrripp! The

dump truck split perfectly in two along a vertical line. Harumi looked back over her shoulder. The men,

without looking back, were running away.

"Thank you! Thank you! 'Mysterious Masked Housewife,' please come [they said] and have some tea

with us"

"I'm happy for the thought, but by five o'clock I have two other cases where I must vanquish

- 〜なくちゃいけない: = なければいけません
- いや: here, "no, I mean …"
- 再び・ふたたび: again; a second time
- 大空・おおぞら: the great sky (blue yonder)
- 羽ばたく・はばたく: "to flap (one's) wings"; take off
- 「〜というか」: (or) should I say …
- 個所・かしょ: counter for places, locations
- 撃退(げきたい)する: to repel; drive off
- 老人・ろうじん: old people
- 狙う・ねらう: to aim at; target
- マルチ商法(しょうほう): "multilevel marketing plan": a heavily regulated venture which lures unknowing investors with the promise of increased profits
- 一味・いちみ: a gang; ring; band
- 本部・ほんぶ: main office
- 襲撃(しゅうげき)する: to raid/assault
- 集める・あつめる: to collect
- 金・かね: money
- 返す・かえす: to return; give back
- 腕・うで: arm
- はめる・嵌める: wear (on one's wrist)
- ディズニー: Disney [probably a Mickey Mouse watch or some other character]
- 時計・とけい: a clock or watch [腕時計(うでどけい) is specific for "watch"]
- 〜時(じ)を回(まわ)ろうとしていた: it was about to turn 〜 o'clock
- 大声・おおごえ: a loud voice
- 全速力・ぜんそくりょく: full/maximum speed
- スーパーマーケット: supermarket
- 一直線に・いっちょくせんに: directly ["in a direct line"]
- ドア: door
- 呼鈴・よびりん: doorbell
- 鳴らす・ならす: to ring (a bell)
- ばたばた: a quick and repetitive flapping or bustling sound
- 誰か・だれか: someone
- 走る・はしる: to run

- 音・おと: sound
- 聞こえる・きこえる: to (be able to) hear; be audible
- ノブ: knob; door handle
- がちゃがちゃ: the metallic sound of things touching/rubbing together
- 響く・ひびく: to reverberate; sound
- エプロン姿(すがた): (in her) aproned form
- 現れる・あらわれる: to appear
- お帰りなさい: "Welcome home" [standard phrase]
- ただいま: "I'm back" [standard phrase]
- そっと: on the sly; secretly
- 目(め)をやる: to glance at; look at
- テーブル: table
- ぬくぬく: warm
- 美味しい・おいしい: delicious; tasty
- 並ぶ・ならぶ: be lined up [cf. 並べる: to line up]
- 気づく・きづく: to notice
- きっと: certainly; without a doubt
- 忙しい・いそがしい: busy
- にちがいない: there's no mistake
- ひま・暇: free time; leisure
- 〜までやる: to do even 〜
- ご苦労様・ごくろうさま: "Thanks for your hard efforts" [usually used towards subordinates or people one is intimate with; お疲れ様・おつかれさま is better for people of higher status]
- なんの、なんの: "Oh, it's nothing"
- にこにこする: to smile
- 鞄・かばん: a bag (for documents); briefcase
- ご飯・ごはん: meal
- お風呂・おふろ: a bath
- 世・よ: the world
- 存在(そんざい)する: to exist
- (〜)かぎり: as long as 〜
- やめる: to stop; quit; give up
- (〜する)わけにはいかない: one cannot (stop fighting evil)

ちゃいけないんです」

　ハルミさんは、いや「怪傑主婦仮面」は再び、大空に向かって羽ばたいたのだった。

(6)

　そうやってハルミさんが、というか「怪傑主婦仮面」が「地上げ屋」を二個所で撃退し、老人を狙うマルチ商法一味の本部を襲撃して、集めた金を老人たちに返した時、ハルミさんの腕にはめられたディズニー時計はもう五時を回ろうとしていた。

「あっ！」ハルミさんは大声で叫んだ。「いけない！帰らなくちゃ」

　ハルミさんは全速力で飛んだ。スーパーマーケットに向かって一直線に。

　ヒロシさんはドアの前で呼鈴を鳴らした。バタバタと誰かが走ってくる音が聞こえ、ノブががちゃがちゃ響き、そしてエプロン姿のハルミさんの姿が現れた。

「お帰りなさい」

「ただいま」

　ヒロシさんはそっとキッチンに目をやった。テーブルの上にはぬくぬくして美味しいものがたくさん並んでいた。ヒロシさんはハルミさんが「KENZO」のトレーナーを着ていることに気づいた。今日もきっと、悪を退治するのに忙しかったにちがいない。トレーナーを着替えるひまもなく晩御飯を作っていたんだろう。

「ハルミさん」ヒロシさんは言った。

「なあに」

「『怪傑主婦仮面』として悪を退治するだけでもたいへんなのに、主婦までやって、ご苦労さま」

「なんの、なんの」ハルミさんはニコニコしながらそう答えると、ヒロシさんの鞄を受け取った。

「あなた、ご飯にします？それともお風呂？」

　この世に悪が存在するかぎり、ハルミさんは「怪傑主婦仮面」のパートをやめるわけにいかないのだ。

❧

慣用句: Idiomatic Expressions II

Translate the following into idiomatic English

6. いくら～だからって（だからといって）

いくらヤクザだからって、「地上げ」を堂々とやるような悪人はどうしても退治しなければならない。

7. 愚痴をこぼす

テルコさんは、「怪傑女子大生仮面」の恰好が派手だと愚痴をこぼしている。

8. 度胆を抜く（抜かれる）

ダンプカーを真っ二つに裂いてしまったハルミさんを見て、男たちは度胆を抜かれ、ばたばたと逃げだした。

9. （～する）わけにはいかない

ハルミさんが「怪傑主婦仮面」のパートをやっていることがもしヒロシさんの会社の人に知られたら、ヒロシさんは困ってしまう。だから、パートに出かける時は変身しないわけにはいかないのだ。

cha ikenai n desu"

Harumi-san wa, iya "KAI-KETSU SHU-FU KA-MEN" wa FUTATAbi, OO-ZORA ni MUkatte HAbata-ita no datta.

(6)

Sou yatte Harumi-san ga, to iu ka "KAI-KETSU SHU-FU KA-MEN" ga "JI-AgeYA"
o NI-KA-SHO de GEKI-TAI shi, ROU-JIN o NERAu maruchiSHOU-HOU ICHI-MI no HON-BU o SHUU-GEKI shite, ATSUme-
ta KANE o ROU-JINtachi ni KAEshita TOKI, Harumi-san no UDE ni hamerareta dizuniiDO-
KEI wa mou GO-JI o MAWArou to shite ita.

"Att!" Harumi-san wa OO-GOE de SAKEnda. "Ikenai! KAEranakucha"
Harumi-san wa ZEN-SOKU-RYOKU de TOnda. Suupaamaaketto ni MUkatte IT-CHOKU-SEN ni.

Hiroshi-san wa doa no MAE de YOBI-RIN o NArashita. Batabata to DARE ka ga HASHItte kuru OTO ga KIkoe, nobu ga gachagacha HIBIki, soshite epuronSUGATA no Harumi-sa-
n no SUGATA ga ARAWAreta.

"Okaerinasai"

"Tadaima"

Hiroshi-san wa sotto kitchin ni ME o yatta. Teeburu no UE ni wa nukunu-
ku shite OIshii mono ga takusan NARAnde ita. Hiroshi-san wa Harumi-san ga
"KENZO" no toreenaa o KIte iru koto ni KIzuita. KYOU mo kitto, AKU
o TAI-JI suru no ni ISOGAshikatta ni chigai nai. Toreenaa o KI-GAeru hima mo
naku BAN-GO-HAN o TSUKUtte ita n darou.

"Harumi-san" Hiroshi-san wa Itta.

"Naani"

"'KAI-KETSU SHU-FU KA-MEN' toshite AKU o TAI-JI suru dake de mo taihen na no ni, SHU-FU made yatte, goKU-ROUsama"

"Nanno, nanno" Harumi-san wa nikoniko shinagara sou KOTAeru to, Hiroshi-san no KABAN o UkeTOtta.

"Anata, goHAN ni shimasu? Sore to mo oFU-RO?"

Kono YO ni AKU ga SON-ZAI suru kagiri, Harumi-san wa "KAI-KETSU SHU-FU KA-MEN" no paato o yameru wake ni ikanai no da.

—❧—

内容理解: Comprehension Questions

Answer in Japanese

1. 「ふつうの主婦」でいる時のハルミさんはどんな恰好をしているのでしょうか。
2. どうして家事をするにはスリップ一枚がいいとハルミさんは思っていますか。
3. ハルミさんはどうしてテレビの時間が終わると少し緊張するのでしょうか。
4. 「正義の味方」のパートに出かける時のハルミさんの恰好は？
5. どうしてナップザックは「怪傑主婦仮面」の必需品なのでしょうか。
6. 空飛ぶ正義の味方はどんな気持ちになりがちですか。
7. ハルミさんと「怪傑女子大生仮面」たちの担当地域はそれぞれどこでしょうか。
8. 「怪傑女子大生仮面」たちの恰好は？それについてハルミさんともう一人の「主婦仮面」のテルコさんはそれぞれどう思っていますか。
9. ハルミさんは今日どんな悪を退治しましたか。
10. ハルミさんはどうして「怪傑主婦仮面」のパートをやめるわけにはいかないと思っているのでしょうか。

練習問題: Exercises

True or False ?

1. 正義の味方・怪傑主婦仮面として悪人を退治してまわるからハルミさんは「主婦の鏡」だ。
2. 空を飛ぶ時のハルミさんはサングラスに「ＫＥＮＺＯ」のトレーナーで、昔のスーパーマンやスーパーウーマンのような恰好をしている。
3. ハルミさんは自分の仕事のあと五時からパートをやっているテルコさんと同じように「怪傑女子大生仮面」たちには派手な恰好をしてほしくない、と思っている。
4. 主人のヒロシさんはハルミさんの「ＫＥＮＺＯ」トレーナーに気づいて、今日も悪の退治で忙しい日だったにちがいないと思った。

evil."

Harumi, or rather the "Mysterious Masked Housewife," again faced the sky
and took off.

(6)

In this way Harumi, or the "Mysterious Masked Housewife" drove off "land-raising"
men in two spots and attacked the main office of a multilevel marketing plan targeting the elderly, and
when she had returned the money she collected to the elderly [victims], the Disney watch
on Harumi's arm was already about to turn five o'clock.

"Ah!" Harumi shouted loudly. "This won't do! I've gotta get back!"

Harumi flew at full speed. In a straight line in the direction of the supermarket.

Hiroshi, [standing] before the door, rang the bell. He heard the pattering
sound of someone running, the knob clicked and then Harumi's form, dressed in her apron,
appeared.

"Welcome home."

"I'm back."

Hiroshi sneaked a glance at the kitchen. On top of the table were many warm
delicious things lined up. Hiroshi noticed that Harumi was
wearing her "KENZO" sweatshirt. Today, too, she must have been
busy vanquishing evil. She had probably made dinner without having time
to change her sweatshirt.

"Harumi," said Hiroshi.

"Yes, Dear?"

"Even though vanquishing evil as the 'Mysterious Masked Housewife' alone is pretty tough, thanks
for being a housewife, too."

"Oh, it's nothing," Harumi replied, smiling, and she took Hiroshi's
bag.

"Dear, will you eat first? Or would you like to take a bath?"

As long as evil exists in this world, Harumi can't give up her part-
time job as the "Mysterious Masked Housewife."

━━━◆◆━━━

Tawara Machi

Tawara Machi was born in Osaka in 1962. She graduated from Waseda University's literature department. In 1988 she won a prize for サラダ記念日 (Salad Anniversary). Tawara often draws her themes from her experiences as a high school teacher in Kanagawa Prefecture.

サラダ記念日 became an instant bestseller, due to her bold attempt to blend the traditional tanka form with colloquial language. Its language is also accessible to younger readers, which contributes greatly to the author's popularity. This is a departure from the more classical and traditional language that is usually encountered in tanka (cf. "Japanese Poetic Form" on page 260). The themes of Tawara's tanka are love and human emotions in the setting of modern life, amidst the various seasonal changes. These themes are part of a long tradition in Japan. Tawara Machi has expressed them in everyday language, which is why her work is so popular.

「サラダ記念日」より　　　俵万智

ゆく河の流れを何にたとえてもたとえきれない水底（みなそこ）の石

明日まで一緒にいたい心だけホームに置いて乗る終電車

なんとなく冬は心も寒くなる電話料金増えて木枯らし

「この味がいいね」と君が言ったから七月六日はサラダ記念日

——❧——

"Sarada KI-NEN-BI" yori　　　TAWARA MA-CHI

Yuku KAWA no NAGAre o NANI ni tatoete mo tatoekirenai MINA-SOKO no ISHI

A-SHITA made IS-SHO ni itai KOKORO dake *hoomu* ni Oite NOru SHUU-DEN-SHA

Nantonaku FUYU wa KOKORO mo SAMUku naru DEN-WA RYOU-KIN FUete KO-GArashi

"Kono AJI ga ii ne" to KIMI ga Itta kara SHICHI-GATSU MUI-KA wa *sarada* KI-NEN-BI

——❧——

Salad Anniversary selections　　　Tawara Machi

The current of the flowing river, unlike anything it's compared to, the stone at the bottom.

Leaving my heart that only wants to be together until tomorrow on the platform, getting on the last train.

Somehow winter makes the heart, too, grow cold, the phone bills increase, the biting wind.

"This tastes good," you said, and so July sixth is our salad anniversary.

語句と語法: Phrases and Usage

- 独自・どくじ: original; one's own (unique)
- 研究・けんきゅう: research; investigation; study
- たいのおかしら: "head of a sea bream"; sea beam, with the head and tail intact, is served on particularly felicitous occasions
- ある日(ひ): one day
- 主人・しゅじん: husband [cf. 夫・おっと, which is also used by a wife to refer to her husband; in reference to someone else's husband, the honorific prefix ご is customarily added to 主人]
- ちょっと: for a second
- 指輪・ゆびわ: a ring
- 貸す・かす: to lend [opposite: 借りる・かりる: to borrow]
- verbてくれ: informal request/command usually from a social equal or superior
- 驚く・おどろく: to be surprised; startled
- この人・このひと: this person [indicates her husband]
- 買(か)ってやろう: will buy for her [やる is a verb meaning "to give" to a social inferior or in very informal situations]
- のであろうか: could it be? [= のだろうか]
- いつだったか: when it was (I don't know) [cf. なんだったか; どこだったか]
- 結婚(けっこん)する: to get married
- もらってみたい: もらう = "receive"; て form + みたい: "want to see (what it is like) to receive (a ring)" [common are やってみる, 見てみる, and 待ってみる]
- どんな~でもいい: any kind of ~ is OK [a variation: どんなに (adj. て form)もいい: it's OK no matter how (adj.) it is]
- 安物・やすもの: a "cheap" thing [of low quality and inexpensive]
- 事・こと: matter [here, nominalizes preceding verb; i.e., もらう事 = receiving]
- 意義・いぎ: significance; importance
- あなた: you [= 主人; a common way wives address their husbands directly]
- 選ぶ・えらぶ: to choose; pick out
- 渡す・わたす: to hand to; pass to; give
- 夢・ゆめ: a dream; hope; aspiration
- そういう友人(ゆうじん): friends like that [refers to previous sentence: i.e., friends whose husbands had chosen and bought them rings]
- みる(見る)と: when I see
- うらやましい・羨ましい: envious
- ~してしまう: しまう has two meanings as used with other verbs: 1) do completely, 2) to emphasize an (irreversibly) bad result; -てしまう or -でしまう can be contracted to -ちゃう and -じゃう respectively

- ~では: = じゃ if (it's after we're already married)
- もう意味(いみ)はない: there's no meaning to it anymore [もう can also mean "already" with past tense or future tense verb]
- 話(はなし)をする: to tell (about); speak (about)
- 際・さい: when [often used in formal speech meaning "occasion"; here synonymous with とき]
- 非常(ひじょう)に: very; extremely
- 悔いる・くいる: to regret [one's own acts]
- まさか: surely [followed by a negative; conveys a sense of disbelief]
- 思い出す・おもいだす: to remember; recall
- 今(いま)さらながら: at this late date; after all that's happened
- 急に・きゅうに: suddenly
- 可愛らしい・かわいらしい: darling
- おもえてくる: to come to seem; begin to feel
- 粋な・いきな: chic; refined
- プレゼント: present [cf. 贈り物・おくりもの]
- 妻・つま: wife
- 内緒(ないしょ)で: in secret
- サイズ: size [= おおきさ]
- 調べる・しらべる: to investigate; look into
- さりげない: as if it were nothing; nonchalantly
- 驚かせる・おどろかせる: to surprise/startle someone
- ~くらい: extent; enough (to); sufficient (to)
- 洒落た・しゃれた: thoughtful; tasteful
- 演出・えんしゅつ: production (as if for stage or film)
- verbばよい: would be good if ~
- ~ものを: although [cf. ~ものの; ~のに]
- こうやって: in this way [= こういうふうに]
- 直接・ちょくせつ: directly
- 不器用・ぶきよう: clumsy; awkward
- ところ: point; aspect
- 彼・かれ: he [her husband]
- 朴訥・ぼくとつ: simple; artless; unsophisticated
- 良さ・よさ: a good point [noun form of よい=いい; adding さ to any adj. in place of い will nominalize it]
- 想い・おもい: feelings and imaginings
- 胸(むね)がいっぱい: "one's chest gets full"; to be full of emotion

独自の研究

さくらももこ 「たいのおかしら」より

　ある日主人が「ちょっと指輪を貸してくれ」と言うので私は驚いた。

　この人は私に指輪を買ってやろうと思っているのであろうか。いつだったか私が「結婚する前に、指輪をもらってみたかった。どんな安物でもいいから、指輪をもらう事に意義があった。あなたが選んであなたの手から渡してくれる事に夢があった。そういう友人を見るとうらやましかったが、結婚してしまってからではもう意味はない」というような話をした際、主人は非常に悔いていた。そんな事はたやすい事であったのに、全く気がつかなかったと後悔していた。

　まさかその事を思い出し、今さらながら私に指輪をやろうと……!?

　私は急にこの人が可愛らしく思えてきた。そんな粋なプレゼントなら、妻に内緒でサイズを調べ、さりげなく渡して驚かせるくらいの洒落た演出を考えればよいものを、こうやって直接「指輪を貸してくれ」と言ってしまう不器用なところが彼の朴訥な良さなのだ。

　そのような想いで胸がいっぱいになった私は「もういい

Sakura Momoko

Sakura Momoko was born in 1965 in Shizuoka Prefecture. She began writing *manga*, or comic books, in high school. After graduating from Shizuoka Eiwa Jōgakuin Tanki Daigaku with a degree in Japanese literature, she took a job for a short time at a publishing company while drawing comics on the side. She then left that position to devote herself full-time to *manga*. In 1987 she began a comic strip entitled *Chibi Maruko-chan* which was serialized in the magazine *Ribon*. It should be noted that Chibi ちび is a colloquial term for "small." In 1989 *Chibi Maruko-chan* won the Kodansha Manga award.

A TV cartoon series was made from the comic strip and also became a hit. It tells of the trials, tribulations, dreams, and joys of Chibi, an elementary school girl. Sakura Momoko draws from her own experiences to present us with a delightful dramatization of everyday life.

This selection is from her best-selling collection of essays *Tai no Okashira*.

DOKU-JI no KEN-KYUU

Sakura Momoko "Tai no Okashira" yori

Aru HI SHU-JIN ga "chotto YUBI-WA o KAshite kure" to Iu no de
WATASHI wa ODOROita.

Kono HITO wa WATASHI ni YUBI-WA o KAtte yarou to OMOtte iru no de aro-
u ka. Itsu datta ka WATASHI ga "KEK-KON suru MAE ni, YUBI-WA o moratte
mitakatta. Donna YASU-MONO de mo ii kara, YUBI-WA o morau KOTO ni
IGI ga atta. Anata ga ERAnde anata no TE kara WATAshite kureru KOTO ni YUME ga atta. Sou iu YUU-JIN o MIru to urayamashikat-
ta ga, KEK-KON shite shimatte kara de wa mou I-MI wa nai" to iu
you na HANASHI o shita SAI, SHU-JIN wa HI-JOU ni KUite ita. Sonna KOTO wa
tayasui KOTO de atta no ni, MATTAku KI ga tsukanakatta to KOU-KAI shite ita.

Masaka sono KOTO o OMOiDAshi, IMAsaranagara WATASHI ni YUBI-WA o yaro-
u to …!?

WATASHI wa KYUU ni kono HITO ga KA-WAIrashiku OMOete kita. Sonna IKI na *purezento* nara, TSUMA ni NAI-SHO de *saizu* o SHIRAbe, sarigenaku WATAshite ODOROkaseru kurai no SHA-REta EN-SHUTSU o KANGAereba yoi mono o, ko-
u yatte CHOKU-SETSU "YUBI-WA o KAshite kure" to Itte shimau BU-KI-YOU
na tokoro ga KARE no BOKU-TOTSU na YOsa na no da.

Sono you na OMOi de MUNE ga ippai ni natta WATASHI wa "mou ii

Page from Sakura Momoko's comic book *Chibi Maruko-chan*, vol. 3.

A Personal Study

From "*Tai no Okashira*" Sakura Momoko

One day I was surprised because my husband said, "Lend me your ring for a second."

I wondered if he was thinking of buying a ring for me. Some time ago I told him: "I wanted to receive a ring before we got married. Even a cheap one would be all right, because there was meaning in receiving a ring. It was my dream that it would be one that you chose and passed to me with your own hand. I was jealous when I saw friends like that, but it's meaningless now that we're already married."
My husband really regretted [not giving me one] when I told him that. Although something like that would have been simple [to do], he was sorry he hadn't noticed at all.

Could it be that he had remembered what I said and was thinking of giving me a ring after such a long time …!?

Suddenly my husband seemed so darling to me. Although, with a special present such as this a husband should think to make more of a special production of it, investigating his wife's ring size in secret and surprising her by casually handing it to her, but his clumsy way of directly saying "lend me your ring" like that is an artless good point that he has.

Happily carried away by such thoughts as this, I told him, "I don't need

- なんて: anything like (a ring); (a ring) or anything like that
- その気持ち(きもち)で充分(じゅうぶん): those (your) feelings alone are enough
- いる・要る: to need
- ジェスチャー: a gesture
- 加える・くわえる: to add
- 輝く・かがやく: to shine; sparkle
- 笑顔・えがお: a "smiling face"; smile
- 笑顔を満面に浮かべる・えがおをまんめんにうかべる: "to (make) float a smile on one's whole face"; to be all smiles
- とにかく: anyway; in any case
- 言い張る・いいはる: to keep saying; insist
- ここは: "here"; at this juncture; at this point in time
- ひとつ: "one"; indicates a sense of resolve or appeal in facing a difficult situation; often combined, as here, with ここは
- 意地を張らずに・いじをはらずに: without being stubborn [意地 is the spirit or attitude of doing/getting what one wants]
- 役目・やくめ: a role
- 両親・りょうしん: parents
- いただく: used with から or に, is a polite もらう "to receive" from a social superior
- 結婚指輪・けっこんゆびわ: a wedding ring
- 差し出す・さしだす: to hold out
- 無言・むごん: "no word"; (in) silence
- 受け取る・うけとる: "to receive and take"; to take
- ちょうど: just; perfectly
- 大きさ・おおきさ: size
- 入れ物・いれもの: a container
- ～まで: until ~; (go) so far as to ~
- 調達(ちょうたつ)する: to procure
- ～となると: if (と) it's the case that ~
- もしかしたら: maybe; perhaps
- どこか: somewhere
- 宝石屋・ほうせきや: a jewelry store [屋 means "store"]
- 注文(ちゅうもん)する: to order
- 申訳ない・もうしわけない: to feel sorry about
- ～と共に・とともに: along with ~
- 照れ臭い・てれくさい: embarrassed; self-conscious
- ぎこちない: awkward; clumsy; stiff
- 気分・きぶん: feeling
- 独りで・ひとりで: alone; by oneself [cf. 一人で]
- 赤面・せきめん: "red-faced"; blushing
- verb-始める・はじめる: start to (verb)
- えっ！: expression of surprise; "What?!"
- 平常・へいじょう: normal
- 戻る・もどる: to return
- 口調・くちょう: a tone of voice
- 手品・てじな: a magic trick; magic
- 日常生活・にちじょうせいかつ: daily life
- ですます調(ちょう): the second kanji from 口調・くちょう "tone" indicates formal speech (see translation)

- 例の・れいの: the usual; the customary
- 以外・いがい: other than
- 考(かんが)えられない: cannot think of; be unthinkable
- ニワトリ: a chicken [animal names are often written in katakana]
- キョトンとした: vacantly; stupidly; with amazement
- ぼっ立つ・ぼったつ: combination of ぼうっとする "space out" and 立つ "stand"
- 宇宙・うちゅう: space; the universe
- 果て・はて: the edge of; the further reaches of
- 放り出す・ほうりだす: to throw out
- 様な・ような: like; (I felt) as if (I had been cast into space)
- 気(き)がする: to have a feeling
- 構う・かまう: to mind; pay attention to
- 進める・すすめる: to go on; proceed
- なにがどうなっている(のだ)か: "(I didn't know) what was becoming how"; had no clue what was going on
- 不思議・ふしぎ: mysterious; strange; marvelous
- 技・わざ: technique
- 一部・いちぶ: one part
- 始終・しじゅう: "beginning and end"; all of
- 一部始終: all of something; from start to finish
- 見せる・みせる: to show
- 満足(まんぞく)する: to be satisfied
- (な adj.)げに: seemingly; as if (adj.)
- 満足気に・まんぞくげに: (seemingly) satisfied
- 笑う・わらう: to laugh
- 当然・とうぜん: of course
- 返される・かえされる: (passive) be returned (to one)
- 無用・むよう: "no use"; useless
- 先ほど・さきほど: just before (now); a while ago
- 莫大・ばくだい: huge
- 期待・きたい: expectation
- 抱く・いだく: to hold; entertain (hope)
- 恥じる・はじる: to be embarrassed; be ashamed
- なんと adj.: "what a (adj.)"
- 愚か・おろか: foolish
- どうか: "somehow (or other)"; used in making a request or expressing a desire
- 気(き)がつく: to notice
- ほしい: hope (something happens)
- いつも通り・いつもどおり: just as always
- ～として: as
- 目(め)に映(うつ)る: to be projected in someone's eyes
- ～verbように…: another verb is omitted here (i.e., 祈る・いのる: to pray) "I hope/I pray I appeared only as…"
- 己・おのれ: oneself
- 恥ずかしさ・はずかしさ: embarrassment [さ in place of い nominalizes the adj. for "embarrassed," はずかしい]
- 激情・げきじょう: strong or violent emotion
- 押し流される・おしながされる: to be overwhelmed (by)

から、指輪なんて。その気持ちだけで充分だよ」と、"いらない"というジェスチャーまで加えて輝く笑顔を満面に浮かべた。

それでも主人は「とにかく貸してくれ」と言い張るので、私もここはひとつ意地を張らずに渡すのが役目であろうと思い、彼の両親からいただいた結婚指輪を差し出した。

主人はそれを無言で受け取ると、小さなプラスチックケースに入れた。指輪にちょうど良い大きさの入れ物である。あんな物まで調達してきているとなると、もしかしたらもうどこかの宝石屋に注文してあるのかもしれない。私は何か申し訳なくなると共に、照れ臭いようなぎこちない気分になっていた。

独りで赤面してぎこちなくなっている私に向かって主人は「はい、このプラスチックケースをよく見てください。いいですか」と言い始めた。

私は「えっ！！」と思い、赤面の顔は平常に戻った。あの口調は彼が手品をやる時の口調だ。日常生活において急に"ですます調"になるのは例の手品の時以外に考えられない。

私は驚いたニワトリのように首を少し前にしてキョトンとしたままぼっ立っていた。宇宙の果てに放り出された様な気がした。

主人はそんな事には全く構わず手品を進めていった。何がどうなっているのだか知らないが主人は私の指輪を使って不思議な技の一部始終を見せ「ものすごく驚いただろ」と満足気に笑っていた。当然指輪はすぐ返された。手品がおわれば無用である。

私は先ほど自分が莫大（ばくだい）な期待を抱いていた事を恥じた。なんと愚かな人間である事よ。私があんなに期待してしまった事を、この夫は気がついたであろうか。どうか気がついていないでほしい。いつも通り、手品をするのを見ているだけの妻として、彼の目に映っていましたように……と、私は己（おのれ）の恥ずかしさの激情に押し流されていた。そんな私

Page from Sakura Momoko's comic book *Chibi Maruko-chan*, vol. 3.

kara, YUBI-WA nante. Sono KI-MOchi dake de JUU-BUN da yo" to, "iranai" to iu *jesuchaa* made KUWAete KAGAYAku E-GAO o MAN-MEN ni U-
kabeta.

Sore de mo SHU-JIN wa "tonikaku KAshite kure" to IiHAru no de,
WATASHI mo koko wa hitotsu I-JI o HArazuni WATAsu no ga YAKU-ME de arou to
OMOi, KARE no RYOU-SHIN kara itadaita KEK-KON YUBI-WA o SAshiDAshita.

SHU-JIN wa sore o MU-GON de UkeTOru to, CHIIsana *purasuchikku keesu* ni Ireta. YUBI-WA ni choudo YOi OOkisa no IreMONO de aru.
Anna MONO made CHOU-TATSU shite kite iru to naru to, moshikashitara mo-
u doko ka no HOU-SEKI-YA ni CHUU-MON shite aru no kamo shirenai. WATASHI wa NANI
ka MOUshiWAKE naku naru to TOMO ni, TEreKUSAi you na gikochinai KI-BUN
ni natte ita.

HITOri de SEKI-MEN shite gikochinaku natte iru WATASHI ni MUkatte SHU-JIN
wa "hai, kono *purasuchikku keesu* o yoku MIte kudasai.
Ii desu ka" to IiHAJImeta.

WATASHI wa "ett!!" to OMOi, SEKI-MEN no KAO wa HEI-JOU ni MODOtta. A-
no KU-CHOU wa KARE ga TE-JINA o yaru TOKI no KU-CHOU da. NICHI-JOU SEI-KATSU ni oite KYUU
ni "desumasu CHOU" ni naru no wa REI no TE-JINA no TOKI I-GAI ni KANGAerare-
nai.

WATASHI wa ODOROita *niwatori* no you ni KUBI o SUKOshi MAE ni shite *kyoton*
to shita mama botTAtte ita. U-CHUU no HAte ni HOUriDAsareta YOU
na KI ga shita.

SHU-JIN wa sonna KOTO ni wa MATTAku KAMAwazu TE-JINA o SUSUmete itta. NANI
ga dou natte iru no da ka SHIranai ga SHU-JIN wa WATASHI no YUBI-WA o TSUKAtte FU-SHI-GI na WAZA no ICHI-BU SHI-JUU o MIse "monosugoku ODOROita daro"
to MAN-ZOKU-GE ni WARAtte ita. TOU-ZEN YUBI-WA wa sugu KAEsareta. TE-JINA ga
owareba MU-YOU de aru.

WATASHI wa SAKIhodo JI-BUN ga BAKU-DAI na KI-TAI o IDAite ita KOTO o HAjita.
Nan to OROka na NIN-GEN de aru KOTO yo. WATASHI ga anna ni KI-TAI shite shimatta KOTO o, kono OTTO wa KI ga tsuita de arou ka. Dou ka KI ga tsuite inai de hoshii. ItsumoDOOri, TE-JINA o suru no o MIte i-
ru dake no TSUMA toshite, KARE no ME ni UTSUtte imashita you ni … to,
WATASHI wa ONORE no HAzukashisa no GEKI-JOU ni OshiNAGAsarete ita. Sonna WATASHI

THE SHŌTO SHŌTO STORY

The *shōto shōto* ショートショート (short-short) story is a favorite literary genre in contemporary Japan. Sakura Momoko's *Dokuji no Kenkyū* is a fine example of its type. There are even special editions of *shōto shōto* anthologies that are tailored for a person's ride on the subway. In a society where people have tight schedules, a *shōto shōto* is most welcome, especially if it manages to lift a person away from the daily round into a world of fantasy.

The uncontested master of the *shōto shōto* story is Hoshi Shin'ichi (1926–98), who published over 1,000 such stories, often in the realm of science fiction.

We have included one of Hoshi Shin'ichi's short-short stories (see pages 156 & 158), and encourage the student to read other of his works. Among his works is *Mōso Ginkō*, for which he was awarded the Nihon Suiri Sakka Kyōkai prize in 1968.

a ring or anything anymore! Your feelings alone are enough," and I even added a gesture indicating "I don't need it" and floated a sparkling smile across my face.

Despite that, my husband persisted, saying "Anyway, give me the ring," and so, thinking that, all right, my role here is to simply hand it over without being stubborn, I held out the wedding ring I had received from his parents.

My husband, upon taking the ring without a word, put it into a small plastic case. It was just the right size container for a ring. If he had gone all the way to procure something like that, maybe, just maybe, he has already placed an order at a jeweler's somewhere! Along with feeling somehow apologetic, I was getting an uncomfortable feeling something like embarrassment.

Now turning towards me as I sat there by myself blushing, growing uncomfortable, my husband started to speak: "All right, now take a very good look at this plastic case. Are you ready?"

I thought "What!" and my blushing face returned to normal. That tone of voice is the tone he always uses when he does his magic tricks. I couldn't think of any time he suddenly began using such formal language in our everyday lives other than during these well-known magic tricks.

I stood there with my neck stuck slightly forward like a startled chicken, struck dumbfounded. I felt as if I had been expelled into the outer reaches of space.

My husband, not paying the least bit of attention to that, proceeded with his trick. I had no idea what was going on, but my husband, using my ring, showed me all of some mysterious trick and laughed, seemingly satisfied, saying, "I bet that really surprised you, huh?" Of course, my ring was returned immediately. When the trick ended, he had no use for it.

I was embarrassed that I had earlier entertained such huge expectations. What a fool I was! Had this husband [of mine] noticed that I had held such expectations? I really hoped that somehow he hadn't noticed. Praying that I had appeared to his eyes as his wife simply watching him perform one of his magic tricks in the same way I always did, I was swept away by the depth of my own embarrassment. My husband faced me in my

- 〜に向(む)かって: facing 〜
- ッけ: a rhetorical or substantive interrogative following た or だ which indicates recollection by the speaker
- 一番(いちばん)デリケート: most delicate
- 部分・ぶぶん: a part; area
- グサッと: indicates a strong stabbing action [onomatopoetic]
- 刺す・さす: to stab; stick
- 恥じ隠し・はじかくし: hiding (one's) embarrassment
- 〜のため: can mean "because of" or "in order to"
- 居(い)ても立(た)ってもいられない: a set phrase; "I couldn't stand being there" [so upset one doesn't know what to do]
- ピョンピョン: a springing sound
- 飛び跳ねる・とびはねる: to jump up (suddenly); fly up
- ちがうもん: "You're wrong" [at the end of a sentence もん, a shortened form of もの, is used to emphatically state a reason or make an argument. It often sounds childish, as it does here]
- 絶叫(ぜっきょう)する: to cry out; scream
- しか…ない: しか is used with a negative verb to mean "only"
- 為す術がない・なすすべがない: "there was nothing I could do"; [used with しか (see above comment): "I could only (do…)"]
- 超魔術・ちょうまじゅつ: "super magic"; prob. stage magic before a large audience
- 凝る・こる: to be absorbed in; be crazy about
- 以来・いらい: since
- 披露(ひろう)する: to present; show
- 光景・こうけい: a scene
- ありふれた: commonplace; familiar
- 唐突・とうとつ: sudden; unexpected [＝突然・とつぜん]
- 開始・かいし: a start; beginning
- 合図・あいず: a signal; sign
- verb ばかり: used with a past tense verb: (to have) just (started)
- たびたび: frequently; often
- タネ: here, a secret or trick
- 見破る・みやぶる: to see through (a trick or deception)
- (その)たびに: every time (that occurred)
- たまる・溜まる: to build up
- 様子・ようす: appearance
- 遂に・ついに: finally
- 本気・ほんき: serious; earnest
- 心構え・こころがまえ: state of mind; attitude
- ねじ曲がる・ねじまがる: to be twisted (ねじた) and bent (まがる)
- 証拠・しょうこ: proof
- 素直・すなお: unaffected; unpretentious; unprotesting; submissive [usually seen as a desirable quality]
- 受け容れる・うけいれる: to accept
- 与える・あたえる: to give; convey
- 娯楽・ごらく: amusement
- なんとかする: (to do) somehow or other, one way or another
- 下卑た・げびた: mean; dirty; low
- 精神・せいしん: spirit; (state of) mind
- 観る・みる: to watch; see; observe
- 言い放つ・いいはなつ: to declare; assert
- なるほど: of course; "I see"

- 感心(かんしん)する: to be impressed
- 特に・とくに: especially; in particular
- 追求・ついきゅう: pursuit
- やめる: to quit; stop
- 「へーすごい」:「へー」alone is like "wow!"; すごい can mean "fabulous!," "great!"
- 等・など: etc. [indicates other things of a given genre]
- 手頃・てごろ: handy; convenient; suitable
- 絶賛・ぜっさん: highest praise
- 方法・ほうほう: a method
- 幾つか・いくつか: several; a few
- 身(み)につける: to learn/acquire
- 逆鱗(げきりん)に触れる(ふれる): to cause the anger (of a superior)
- 観賞・かんしょう: admire; enjoy
- 〜法・ほう: method of 〜
- 見出す・みいだす: to find out; uncover
- 〜verb ていく: to go on (verb)-ing
- 近頃・ちかごろ: lately; recently
- 〜するようになる: to grow to do 〜
- 三年・さんねん: it is a common saying that learning even basic skills (e.g., holding a brush for calligraphy) takes three years
- 何事も・なにごとも: anything
- 改めて・あらためて: anew
- そもそも: in the first place; originally
- 興味・きょうみ: interest
- 少年・しょうねん: a young boy [cf. 青年・せいねん: a young man]
- きっかけ: a spur; the original cause/reason
- タバコ: cigarette(s)
- 宙・ちゅう: space; mid-air
- 浮かせる・うかせる: to make float [causative form of the verb うく]
- 移動(いどう)する: to move
- 様々・さまざま: various
- 現象・げんしょう: a phenomenon; a marvelous happening
- 次々・つぎつぎ: one after the other
- やってのける: to pull off; accomplish
- いたく: "painfully"; tremendously
- 感動(かんどう)する: to be moved
- し＝して: verb stem from 〜ます form ＝〜て form of verb
- コツコツ: an onomotapoetic phrase for working at something in a steady, regular way
- 地道に・じみちに: steadily; step by step
- 手に入れる・てにいれる: to buy; obtain
- わからぬ＝わからない
- いつの間(ま)にか: before one knows it; in a flash
- 用品・ようひん: articles; paraphernalia
- 部屋・へや: a room
- ゴロゴロ: refers to a great many objects lying about [onomatopoetic]
- 集まる・あつまる: (things) collect [intrans. verb; cf. 集める]
- 冊・さつ: a counter for bound volumes/books
- 読破(どくは)する: to read (a difficult or lengthy book); peruse

に向かって主人は「指輪、くれると思ったっけ？」と一番
デリケートな部分をグサッと刺してきた。

　私は恥隠しのため、居ても立ってもいられなくなり、ピョンピョン飛びはねながら「ちがうもんちがうもん」と絶叫し続けるしか為す術がなかった。

　主人が手品や超魔術に凝り出したのは三年前からである。以来、彼が日常に手品を持ち込み披露するという光景は我が家ではありふれたものになった。唐突な "ですます調" が手品開始の合図である。

　彼が手品を始めたばかりの頃は、たびたび私にタネを見破られ、そのたびにストレスがたまっていた様子であった。ある日遂に彼は本気で怒り、「タネを見破ろうという心構えで手品を見るのは心がねじ曲がっている証拠だ。もっと素直に驚きを受け容れろ。手品というものは "驚き" を与えてくれる娯楽なのだ。何とかしてタネを見破ってやろうなどという下卑た精神で観るものではない」と言い放った。

　私は「なるほど」と感心し、それ以来特にタネを見破ろうという追求をやめた。そして「へーすごい」等という手頃な絶賛の方法を幾つか身につけ、彼の逆鱗に触れない観賞法を見出していった。

　近頃では、本当に不思議だと感じる事もするようになってきた。三年も研究すると、何事もうまくなるものだと改めて思う。

　そもそも彼が手品に興味を持ち始めたのは一人の少年がきっかけであった。

　まだ中学生だと言うその少年は、タバコを宙に浮かせたり、コインをあっちからこっちに移動させたり、考えられない様々な現象を次々と我々の目の前でやってのけた。

　主人はいたく感動し、以来手品の研究をコツコツと地道にするようになったのである。

　どこで手に入れるのだか分からぬが、いつの間にか手品用品が部屋にゴロゴロ集まってきた。手品本も何冊か読破している様子である。

Short-Short Story

by Hoshi Shin'ichi

魔法の大金 —— 星新一

　まともに働くのがきらいで、酒を飲んで遊んでばかりいたエヌ氏は、ついに身動きがとれなくなってしまった。金がなくなり、なんとかしなければならない状態になったのだ。

　しかし、依然として、まともに働く気にはならなかった。思案したあげく、彼は、魔法にたよろうと思いついた。そして、図書館に出かけて古い本を読みあさり、なんとかその秘法らしきものを知るとができた。熱のこもった祈りであった。それに応じて、やがて煙とともに妙な人物が出現し、エヌ氏に話しかけた。

　「わしは悪魔だ。」

　「これはありがたい。みごとに成功したようだな。こううまくゆくとは……」

　エヌ氏がつぶやいていると、悪魔が言った。

　「呼び出したのは、なにか用があるからか」

　「もちろんでございます。ぜひ、わたしをお助け下さい」

　「願いをかなえてやってもよい。だが、一回だけだぞ」

　「けっこうでございます。じつは、財産がなく困っているところでございます」

　「では、財産を作ってやろう。城がいいか、美術品がいいか、王冠がいいか、それとも名馬はどうだ」

　「いずれも結構でございますが、できましたら紙幣にしていただきとうございます。現代では、なにをするにも便利ですから」

　「よし。では、それにしよう。しかし、紙幣とはどんなものだ」

　「はい、このようなものでございます」

　エヌ氏はとっておきの一枚の高額紙幣を出した。悪魔はそれを眺めながら言った。

　「これをどれくらい欲しいのだ」

　「はい、百枚、いや、千枚、できれば一万枚ほど……」

　「お安いご用だ」

　と悪魔は息を吹きかけた。たちまち、そこに紙幣の山ができあがった。一万枚はありそうだ。手に取ってみると、どれが見本に渡した一枚か、まったくわからない出来だ。エヌ氏は目を丸くした。

　「すばらしいお力です」

　「これでいいか」

　「ありがとうございます。なんとお礼を申しあげたものか……」

　「では、さらばじゃ」

　と悪魔は消えた。エヌ氏は紙幣をカバンにつめ、銀行に運んだ。家においておくのは不用心だからだ。銀行の窓口の人は、それを受取って驚いたような口調で言った。

　「大金でございますね。どこで手にお入れになったのですか」

　「なんでもうけたのかを、説明しなくてはいけないのか」

　「いえ、普通の場合ならかまいませんが、この紙幣はどれもこれも同じ番号ですので……」

MA-HOU no TAI-KIN —— HOSHI SHIN-ICHI

　Matomo ni HATARAku no ga kirai de, SAKE o NOnde ASOnde bakari ita enu-SHI wa, tsui ni MI-UGOki ga torenaku natte shimatta. KANE ga naku nari, nan to ka shinakereba naranai JOU-TAI ni natta no da.

　Shikashi, I-ZEN toshite, matomo ni HATARAku KI ni wa naranakatta. SHI-AN shita ageku, KARE wa, MA-HOU ni tayorou to OMOitsuita. Soshite, TO-SHO-KAN ni DEkakete FURUi HON o YOmiasari, nan to ka sono HI-HOU rashiki mono o SHIru koto ga dekita. NETSU no komotta INOri de atta. Sore ni OUjite, yagate KEMURI to tomo ni MYOU na JIN-BUTSU ga SHUTSU-GEN shi, enu-SHI ni HANAshikaketa.

　"Washi wa AKU-MA da."

　"Kore wa arigatai. Migoto ni SEI-KOU shita you da na. Kou umaku yuku to wa …"

　Enu-SHI ga tsubuyaite iru to, AKU-MA ga Itta.

　"YObiDAshita no wa, nani ka YOU ga aru kara ka"

　"Mochiron de gozaimasu. Zehi, watashi o oTASUke KUDAsai"

　"NEGAi o kanaete yatte mo yoi. Da ga, IK-KAI dake da zo"

　"Kekkou de gozaimasu. Jitsu wa, ZAI-SAN ga naku KOMAtte iru tokoro de gozaimasu"

　"Dewa, ZAI-SAN o TSUKUtte yarou. SHIRO ga ii ka, BI-JUTSU-HIN ga ii ka, OU-KAN ga ii ka, sore to mo MEI-BA wa dou da"

ni MUkatte SHU-JIN wa "YUBI-WA, kureru to OMOtta kke?" to ICHI-BAN
derikeeto na BU-BUN o gusatto SAshite kita.

WATASHI wa HAJI-KAKUshi no tame, Ite mo TAtte mo irarenaku nari, p-
yonpyon TObihanenagara "chigau mon chigau mon" to ZEK-
KYOU shiTSUZUkeru shika NAsu SUBE ga nakatta.

SHU-JIN ga TE-JINA ya CHOU-MA-JUTSU ni KOriDAshita no wa SAN-NEN MAE kara de aru.
I-RAI, KARE ga NICHI-JOU ni TE-JINA o MOchiKOmi HI-ROU suru to iu KOU-KEI wa WA-
gaYA de wa arifureta mono ni natta. TOU-TOTSU na "desumasu CHOU"
ga TE-JINA KAI-SHI no AI-ZU de aru.

KARE ga TE-JINA o HAJImeta bakari no KORO wa, tabitabi WATASHI ni tane o MI-
YABUrare, sono tabi ni sutoresu ga tamatte ita YOU-SU de atta.
Aru HI TSUI ni KARE wa HON-KI de OKOri, "tane o MI-YABUrou to iu KOKORO-GAMAe
de TE-JINA o MIru no wa KOKORO ga nejiMAgatte iru SHOU-KO da. Motto SU-
NAO ni ODOROki o UkeIrero. TE-JINA to iu mono wa 'ODORO-ki' o ATAe-
te kureru GO-RAKU na no da. NAN to ka shite tane o MI-YABUtte yarou nado to iu GE-BIta SEI-SHIN de MIru mono de wa nai" to IiHANAtta.

WATASHI wa "naruhodo" to KAN-SHIN shi, sore I-RAI TOKU ni tane o MI-YABUro-
u to iu TSUI-KYUU o yameta. Soshite "hee sugoi" NADO to iu TE-
GORO na ZES-SAN no HOU-HOU o IKUtsu ka MI ni tsuke, KARE no GEKI-RIN ni FUrenai KAN-
SHOU-HOU o MI-IDAshite itta.

CHIKA-GORO de wa, HON-TOU ni FU-SHI-GI da to KANjiru KOTO mo suru you ni natte kita. SAN-NEN mo KEN-KYUU suru to, NANI-GOTO mo umaku naru mono da to ARATA-
mete OMOu.

Somosomo KARE ga TE-JINA ni KYOU-MI o MOchiHAJImeta no wa HITO-RI no SHOU-NEN ga
kikkake de atta.

Mada CHUU-GAKU-SEI da to iu sono SHOU-NEN wa, tabako o CHUU ni Ukaseta-
ri, koin o atchi kara kotchi ni I-DOU sasetari, KANGAerare-
nai SAMA-ZAMA na GEN-SHOU o TSUGI-TSUGI to WARE-WARE no ME no MAE de yatte noketa.

SHU-JIN wa itaku KAN-DOU shi, I-RAI TE-JINA no KEN-KYUU o kotsukotsu to JI-MICHI
ni suru you ni natta no de aru.

Doko de TE ni Ireru no da ka WAkaranu ga, itsu no MA ni ka TE-JINA
YOU-HIN ga HE-YA ni gorogoro ATSUmatte kita. TE-JINA-BON mo NAN-SATSU ka DOKU-HA
shite iru YOU-SU de aru.

"Izuremo KEK-KOU de gozaimasu ga, dekimashitara SHI-HEI ni shite itadakitou gozaimasu. GEN-DAI de wa, nani o suru ni mo BEN-RI de-su kara"

"Yoshi. Dewa, sore ni shiyou. Shikashi, SHI-HEI to wa donna mono da"

"Hai, Kono you na mono de gozaimasu"

Enu-SHI wa totteoki no ICHI-MAI no KOU-GAKU-SHI-HEI o DAshita. AKU-MA wa sore o NAGAmenagara Itta.

"Kore o dore kurai HOshii no da."

"Hai, HYAKU-MAI, iya, SEN-MAI, dekireba ICHI-MAN-MAI hodo …"

"OYASUi goYOU da"

to AKU-MA wa IKI o FUkikaketa. Tachimachi, soko ni SHI-HEI no YAMA ga dekiagatta. ICHI-MAN-MAI wa arisou da. TE ni TOtte miru to, do-re ga MI-HON ni WATAshita ICHI-MAI ka, mattaku wakaranai DEKI da. Enu-SHI wa ME o MARUku shita.

"Subarashii oCHIKARA desu"

"Kore de ii ka"

"Arigatou gozaimasu. Nanto oREI o MOUshiageta mono ka …"

"Dewa, saraba ja"

to AKU-MA wa KIeta. Enu-SHI wa SHI-HEI o *kaban* ni tsume, GIN-KOU ni HAKOnda. IE ni oite oku no wa BU-YOU-JIN da kara da. GIN-KOU no MADO-GUCHI no HITO wa, sore o UKE-TOtte ODOROita you na KU-CHOU de Itta.

"TAI-KIN de gozaimasu ne. Doko de TE ni oIre ni natta no desu ka"

"Nan de mouketa no ka o, SETSU-MEI shinakute wa ikenai no ka"

"Ie, FU-TSUU no BA-AI nara kamaimasen ga, kono SHI-HEI wa dore mo kore mo ONAji BAN-GOU desu no de …"

The Magic Fortune —— Hoshi Shin'ichi

Mr. N, who hated honest work and only sat around drinking alcohol, at last became completely destitute. His money had run out, and he had gotten into a state where he had to do something about it.

But, as ever, he didn't get the will to do honest work. After long reflection, he hit upon the idea of relying on magic. And so, he departed for the library and scanned old books, and somehow was able to learn of something that appeared to be that secret method. It was fervent prayer. In response to that, before long, a strange figure appeared along with smoke and spoke to Mr. N.

"I am a demon."

"This is great. It seems I've succeeded wonderfully. I didn't think things would go this well …"

"As for your calling me out, is it because you have some business?"

"But of course. By all means, I hope you will help me."

"I can grant you a request. But, [I'll] only do it once."

"That would be splendid. Actually, I am troubled because I have no wealth."

"Then I will create a fortune for you. Is a castle good, or works of art, or a royal crown, or maybe a splendid horse?"

"Those are all fine, but if possible I would like to get paper money. In these times, it is useful whatever one does."

"Good. Then let us make it that. But, what is paper money?"

"Here, it is this type of thing."

Mr. N brought out his one specially kept high-denomination bill. The demon, while looking at it, said,

"And how many of these do you want?"

"Well, one hundred, … no, a thousand, if possible, about ten thousand …"

"No sooner said than done,"

said the demon, who blew a breath on [the bill]. In an instant a mountain of bills had appeared. There seemed to be ten thousand. When he took one in his hand, it was of such a make that he couldn't at all tell which was the sample he handed over. Mr. N was astonished.

"What a splendid power."

"Is this alright?"

"Thank you. I don't know how I should thank you …"

"Then, farewell."

said the demon, who then vanished. Mr. N stuffed the bills into a bag and carried them to the bank. [He did so] because it would be unsafe to leave them in the house. The person at the bank [teller] window took them and said in a surprised tone,

"You have a huge fortune here, don't you. Where did you acquire it, [sir]?"

"Do I have to tell you how I made the money?"

"No, we wouldn't mind at all if it were an ordinary case, but these bills are, every last one of them, of the same serial number …"

embarrassment, thrusting hard at my most tender spot: "So you thought I was going to give you a ring, did you?"

To hide my embarrassment, completely at my wits end as I was, there was nothing I could do but bounce up and down and yell continuously "You're wrong! You're wrong!"

My husband started to go crazy over slight of hand tricks and other magic three years ago. Thereafter, scenes where he would bring home magic tricks and perform them became a common occurrence in our house. His sudden switch into formal language is the signal for the start of the trick.

When he had just started his slight of hand tricks I often saw through the secret, and it seemed that every time this happened it was more stressful for him. One day he finally got seriously angry and declared, "Your always trying to see through the trick is proof of your twisted heart [personality]. Try to accept the surprise of the trick a little more open-mindedly. This thing called magic is entertainment that gives us a 'surprise.' It isn't something you watch with the mean spirit of somehow trying to see through the secret of the trick."

Impressed by this I thought, "Oh, I see," and since then I have stopped particularly trying to see through his tricks. I have mastered a few convenient forms of praise, like saying, "Wow, that's neat," and have found a way of appreciating without incurring his wrath.

Recently, it has even gotten so that I feel they really are mysterious. I realize anew that if you work at something for as long as three years you really do get better at it, no matter what it is.

Originally, it was a single youth who made him take an interest in magic tricks.

This young boy, still in junior high school, made a cigarette float in mid-air, moved coins from here to there, and pulled off a variety of marvels you couldn't imagine, one after the other, right before our eyes.

My husband, tremendously impressed, thereafter slowly but surely began to study magic.

I don't know where he gets them, but before I knew it there was magic paraphernalia lying collected all over the room. It also seemed that he had read through several books on magic.

- 超能力・ちょうのうりょく: supernatural ability
- 名(な)のつく: (anything) with the name ~ [の＝が]
- 番組・ばんぐみ: a (TV, radio) program
- 放送(ほうそう)する: to broadcast
- 必ず・かならず: without fail
- チェックする: to check (out); watch
- 独自に・どくじに: in one's own (unique) way
- 惜しまず・おしまず: unsparing(ly) [here 「に」 is omitted; おしむ can mean "to be reluctant, stingy"]
- マメに: (to work) hard without complaint, seriously, and with minute attention to detail, carefully; painstakingly
- 努力(どりょく)をする: to make an effort
- 姿勢・しせい: an attitude; posture
- 見習う・みならう: to watch and learn from
- 多少・たしょう: somewhat; to a certain extent
- 経る・へる: to pass
- ～に関(かん)して: concerning ~
- 知識・ちしき: knowledge
- 当時・とうじ: at that time [needs an antecedent]
- 習字・しゅうじ: (brush) calligraphy
- このままでは: at this rate
- 進歩・しんぽ: progress
- ～わけがない: there is no good reason ~ (I can receive a ring)
- 進める・すすめる: to advance/further (my research)
- ～(する)ことにする: decide to do ~
- 縁(えん)のない: have no relation to [の＝が]
- 世界・せかい: world [can also mean a smaller world (e.g., of politics)]
- 自分(じぶん)なりに: in my own way
- 文字・もじ: written characters; letters
- 全く・まったく: completely
- まずは: first of all
- 筆・ふで: a brush (for calligraphy)
- 買わなければ・かわなければ: "I must buy…" [かわなければならない where the ならない is omitted]

　TVで“マジック”“超魔術”“超能力”と名のつく番組が放送されれば必ずチェックし独自に楽しんでいる。

　このように、自分が興味を持ったものには惜しまずマメに努力をする姿勢は見習うべきところである。私もあの不思議な中学生を見た時には、多少手品に興味を持ったのだ。しかし三年経った今でも手品に関しての知識は当時と全く変わっていない。

　このままではあまり良くない。何も進歩のない女になってしまう。指輪などもらえるわけがない。

　そう思い、私は習字を習うことにした。手品とは縁のない習字の世界で、自分なりに文字の研究を進めてゆこうと思っている。

　まずは筆を買わなければ。

－⚬⚬⚬－

慣用句: Idiomatic Expressions

Translate the following into idiomatic English

1. 今さらながら

魔術には前から興味がないので今さらながら手品本買っても仕方がない。

2. さりげなく〜 する

主人が新しい手品を披露するたびに私は「へー、すごい」とさりげなく感心したふりをする。

3. 居ても立ってもいられない

高価な指輪を主人がくれるのかと思い、私は居ても立ってもいられなかった。

4. 〜しか為す術がない

お客さんにすぐ手品のタネを見破られ、私は手品の先生に「すみません、すみません」と言うしか為す術がなかった。

5. （〜の）逆鱗に触れる

彼は手品の本ばかり読んでいて全く勉強しないので先生の逆鱗に触れたのだろう。

6. 改めて〜する

三年経っても習字の進歩がないので、改めて習字の難しさを感じる。

7. （〜を）やってのける

主人はポケットの中から次々と宝石の指輪を取り出すという術をやってのけた。

8. コツコツと地道に〜する

習字が上手になるにはコツコツと地道に練習をするしか方法がない。

9. まめに努力する

まめに努力すれば必ず字は上手になりますよ。

10. 〜なりに

主人は超魔術に興味を持ちはじめ、いろいろな本やテレビ番組などで主人なりに研究しているようだ。

TEREBI de "*majikku*" "CHOU-MA-JUTSU" "CHOU-NOU-RYOKU" to NA no tsuku BAN-GUMI ga HOU-SOU sarereba KANARAzu *chekku* shi DOKU-JI ni TANOshinde iru.

Kono you ni, JI-BUN ga KYOU-MI o MOtta mono ni wa Oshimazu *mame* ni DO-RYOKU o suru SHI-SEI wa MI-NARAu beki tokoro de aru. WATASHI mo ano FU-SHI-GI na CHUU-GAKU-SEI o MIta TOKI ni wa, TA-SHOU TE-JINA ni KYOU-MI o MOtta no da. Shikashi SAN-NEN TAtta IMA de mo TE-JINA ni KANshite no CHI-SHIKI wa TOU-JI to MATTAku KAwatte inai.

Kono mama de wa amari YOku nai. NANI mo SHIN-PO no nai ONNA ni nat-te shimau. YUBI-WA nado moraeru wake ga nai.

Sou OMOi, WATASHI wa SHUU-JI o NARAu koto ni shita. TE-JINA to wa EN no na-i SHUU-JI no SE-KAI de, JI-BUN nari ni MO-JI no KEN-KYUU o SUSUmete yukou to OMOtte iru.

Mazu wa FUDE o KAwanakereba.

内容理解: Comprehension Exercises

Answer in Japanese

1. 筆者は「結婚指輪」について、どんな夢があったのでしょうか。
2. 筆者によると「主人」のどんなところが朴訥な良さなのでしょうか。
3. 筆者はどうして照れ臭いようなぎこちない気分になっていたのでしょうか。
4. 「主人」が"ですます調"になるのはどんな時ですか。
5. 筆者はどうして恥隠しのため、居ても立ってもいられなくなったのでしょうか。
6. 「主人」によると手品はどんな精神で観るものなのでしょうか。
7. 「主人」が手品に興味を持ち始めたのは何がきっかけでしたか。
8. 筆者は「主人」のどのような姿勢を見習うべきだと言っていますか。
9. 筆者は「進歩のある女」になるためにどんな「研究」をしようと思っていますか。

練習問題: Exercises

True or False ?

1. 「どんな安物でいいから結婚する前に指輪をもらってみたかった」という「私」の話を聞いて「主人」は内緒でサイズを調べ、さりげなく渡して驚かせようと洒落た演出を考えはじめた。
2. 主人が指輪をくれるのかと期待を抱いていた自分の気持に「主人」は全く気がつかなかった。
3. 「主人」は三年も手品や超魔術に凝っているが、あまり進歩がない。
4. 自分が興味を持ったものには惜しまずまめに努力する「主人」の姿勢に見習うべきだと思い、私は私なりに習字を習い、文字の研究を進めようと思うようになった。

Whenever a program called "magic," "super magic," or "supernatural abilities" came on TV he always watched and enjoyed it in his own unique way.

This sort of attitude he has towards making unsparing, diligent efforts to work at something he's interested in is something I should learn from. When I saw that marvelous junior high student I also became somewhat interested in magic. But my knowledge of magic now, three years later, hasn't changed a bit since then.

Things are not very good as they are. I'll end up being a woman who hasn't made anything of herself. There's no way I could get a ring.

Thinking this, I decided to start learning calligraphy. I'm thinking that in the world of calligraphy, with no relation to magic tricks, I will advance my study of letters in my own way.

But first things first, I have to buy a brush.

語句と語法: Phrases and Usage

- 価格・かかく: price; value [an economic term; cf. 値段・ねだん]
- 破壊・はかい: destroying; demolishing
- 価格破壊: described in the text, the phenomenon where a significant number of consumers shift to bargain goods, which seem to be below cost judged from past standards
- 不況・ふきょう: a recession [cf. 好況(こうきょう)、好景気(こうけいき), prosperous times]
- ～下・か: under (recession)
- 売上げ・うりあげ: sales; takings; proceeds
- 伸ばす・のばす: to extend; increase; expand
- 商売・しょうばい: business; trade
- 郊外・こうがい: suburbs [this does not, for the most part, mean big lawns etc., but newly developed apartment complexes and residential areas]
- ～を中心に・ちゅうしんに: "with ～ at the center"; centered around ～
- 多～・た: many [cf. 多い・おおい]
- 店舗・てんぽ: a store; a shop
- 展開(てんかい)をする: to develop [here, implies a large-scale operation to set up many stores]
- 大型・おおがた: large size or scale
- ディスカウント・ショップ: discount store
- 紳士服・しんしふく: men's clothing
- ～服・ふく: clothing [cf. 洋服(ようふく): Western clothes; 和服(わふく): Japanese clothing]
- スキー: ski
- ～用品・ようひん: goods/accessories for ～
- ～といった: (things) like ～ [common for listing examples; = というような]
- 特定・とくてい: specific; particular
- 分野・ぶんや: field; area
- 特化(とっか)する: to specialize in (a particular type of goods)
- 専門店・せんもんてん: specialty store
- 最寄り品・もよりひん: necessities and other goods which consumers tend to buy at the nearest store, without paying attention to quality [もより: the nearest, nearby]
- 高級・こうきゅう: high quality
- ブランド商品(しょうひん): brand (name) goods
- 安い・やすい: cheap
- 売れる・うれる: to sell (intrans. verb)
- 扱う・あつかう: to deal in; to handle
- 店・みせ: a store; shop
- 共通(きょうつう)する: to have in common
- 流通・りゅうつう: distribution
- 販売・はんばい: sales; marketing
- ～にかかるコスト: the cost to (do) ～
- 極限・きょくげん: absolute limit; utmost degree
- ～まで: up to/until ～ (a certain point)
- 抑える・おさえる: to hold down (a price); to restrain

- 可能な・かのうな: possible
- 最(さい)～: to the full extent [as a prefix means もっとも "most" or "least"]
- 最低限・さいていげん: a minimum
- 提供(ていきょう)する: to provide; supply
- 点・てん: point [here, means something like "(common) characteristic"]
- 従来・じゅうらい: up to now; from before; conventional
- 感覚・かんかく: feeling; sensibility
- ～からすると: from the (perspective, viewpoint, fact)
- 原価・げんか: cost (of production); unit price
- 下回る・したまわる: to fall under (a certain amount) [cf. 上回る・うわまわる]
- ～としか … おもえない: can only think that …
- 低(てい)～: low [cf. 低い・ひくい]
- 個人消費・こじんしょうひ: personal consumption
- 主力・しゅりょく: the main force or body; driving force
- 廉価・れんか: budget/low price
- シフトする: to shift (from A to B)
- 現象・げんしょう: phenomenon
- 呼(よ)ばれる: to be called [cf. 呼ぶ: to call]
- 背景・はいけい: background
- として: as
- アジア: Asia
- 製品・せいひん: products
- 輸入・ゆにゅう: import [cf. 輸出・ゆしゅつ: export]
- 第一・だいいち: first
- 消費者・しょうひしゃ: consumer
- 志向・しこう: orientation (toward high quality products); inclination
- 高級志向・こうきゅうしこう: an inclination to buy high quality (goods)
- 低価格志向・ていかかくしこう: inclination towards low prices
- ～へと変化(へんか)する: to change to ～
- 第二・だいに: second
- ～だからこそ: exactly because of ～
- 伸(の)びる: to expand
- こうした: this kind (of)
- 駅前商店街・えきまえしょうてんがい: shopping district [usually refers to a concentration of stores in an area near, or along a street leading to, a train station]
- 新興・しんこう: new; rising
- 住宅地・じゅうたくち: a residental area
- 控える・ひかえる: to have nearby [can also mean "to wait" and "to refrain"]
- 顕著・けんちょ: obvious; conspicuous
- み(見)られる: can be seen
- 進出(しんしゅつ)する: to advance; make inroads

価格破壊

日下公人

　この不況下に大きく売上を伸ばしている商売がある。郊外を中心に多店舗展開をしている大型の「ディスカウント・ショップ」がそれである。紳士服やスキー用品といった特定分野に特化した専門店もあれば、最寄り品から高級ブランド商品まで、安く売れるものならなんでも扱うという店もある。

　これらのディスカウント・ショップに共通しているのは、流通・販売にかかるコストを極限まで抑えて、可能な最低限の価格で商品を提供する点にある。従来の感覚からすると原価を下回っているとしか思えない低価格で商品が販売され、個人消費の主力がそうした廉価商品へとシフトしている現象は、「価格破壊」と呼ばれる。

　価格破壊現象の背景としては、アジアからの製品輸入が第一で、消費者の志向が高級志向から低価格志向へと変化したことが第二である。ディスカウント商売は不況だからこそ伸びたというわけである。

　また、こうした現象が、デパートもなければ駅前商店街もないような新興の住宅地を控えた郊外で、とくに顕著にみられることからすると、ディスカウント・ショップが進

THE JAPANESE ECONOMY

The Japanese economy was termed a "miracle" during its period of intense growth during the seventies and eighties. The rate at which it grew was such that today's generation is perhaps five or six times richer than its parents.

But in the early nineties the so-called bubble economy burst. The stock market tumbled. Land prices dropped, leaving many young couples with loans far greater than their property was worth. Japan's manufacturers and retailers have had to adapt and cope with these hard times, and discount stores are the most recent form of their evolution. The gradual shift of the Japanese consumer focus to price awareness is an important change. The shift is driven by the recent economic changes.

The Japanese corporate world, with its well known "lifetime employment" system, seniority based promotion scheme, and enterprise unions, has had to respond. The foreign origin of words such as リストラ, from "restructuring," and ディスカウント・ショップ shows just how new these concepts are to Japan.

There are many questions to consider for the future. Will the Japanese economy become more consumer driven? Will companies try to provide the same services and products for less? Will there be more foreign competition? If consumers shape the economy, will it become less competitive than its international counterparts? How might United States–Japan relations evolve? What about Japan's relations with the European Community and East Asia?

KA-KAKU HA-KAI

KU-SAKA KIMI-NDO

Kono FU-KYOU-KA ni OOkiku URI-AGE o NObashite iru SHOU-BAI ga aru. KOU-GAI o CHUU-SHIN ni TA-TEN-PO TEN-KAI o shite iru OO-GATA no *"disukaun-to shoppu"* ga sore de aru. SHIN-SHI-FUKU ya *sukii*YOU-HIN to it-ta TOKU-TEI BUN-YA ni TOK-KA shita SEN-MON-TEN mo areba, MO-YOri-HIN kara KOU-KYUU *burando* SHOU-HIN made, YASUku Ureru mono nara nan de mo ATSUKAu to iu MISE mo aru.

Korera no *disukaunto shoppu* ni KYOU-TSUU shite iru no wa, RYUU-TSUU–HAN-BAI ni kakaru *kosuto* o KYOKU-GEN made OSAete, KA-NOU na SAI-TEI-GEN no KA-KAKU de SHOU-HIN o TEI-KYOU suru TEN ni aru. JUU-RAI no KAN-KAKU kara suru to GEN-KA o SHITA-MAWAtte iru to shika OMOenai TEI-KA-KAKU de SHOU-HIN ga HAN-BAI sare, KO-JIN SHOU-HI no SHU-RYOKU ga sou shita REN-KA SHOU-HIN e to *shifuto* shite iru GEN-SHOU wa, "KA-KAKU HA-KAI" to YObareru.

KA-KAKU HA-KAI GEN-SHOU no HAI-KEI toshite wa, *ajia* kara no SEI-HIN YU-NYUU ga DAI-ICHI de, SHOU-HI-SHA no SHI-KOU ga KOU-KYUU SHI-KOU kara TEI-KA-KAKU SHI-KOU e to HEN-KA shita koto ga DAI-NI de aru. *Disukaunto* SHOU-BAI wa FU-KYOU da kara koso NObita to iu wake de aru.

Mata, kou shita GEN-SHOU ga, *depaato* mo nakereba EKI-MAE SHOU-TEN-GAI mo nai you na SHIN-KOU no JUU-TAKU-CHI o HIKAeta KOU-GAI de, toku ni KEN-CHO ni mirareru koto kara suru to, *disukaunto shoppu* ga SHIN-

Large discount store, where prices are reduced by 30 to 50 percent.

Price Destruction

Kusaka Kimindo

Under this recession, there is a business which has greatly expanded its sales.
That is the large scale "discount shops" that have opened many stores centered
in the suburbs. If there are specialty shops that specialize in certain
areas like men's clothing and ski goods, there are [also] stores which
handle anything which can be sold cheaply, from daily sundries to high-quality
brand goods.

What these discount shops have in common is the point of holding down the
cost of distribution and marketing to the utmost degree and providing products
at the lowest possible price. Products are sold at low prices that can only be
thought of, from the former sense [of prices], as below cost, and the phenomenon
where the main body of individual consumers shifts to that sort of bargain goods
is called "price destruction."

As the background of the price destruction phenomenon, first there is the import of products
from Asia, and second there is the fact that consumer inclination has shifted from an
inclination for high-quality products to an inclination for low-price products. Thus, it is
exactly because there is a recession that [sales of] discount goods have expanded.

Also, from the fact that this kind of phenomenon is
particularly evident in the suburbs with their new housing
where there are no department stores or station-front shopping

- 地域・ちいき: area; region
- 潜在・せんざい: hidden; latent
- 需要・じゅよう: demand [cf. supply: 供給・きょうきゅう]
- 掘り起す・ほりおこす: "to dig up"; unearth; discover
- 一面・いちめん: one aspect, face, or facet (of a phenomenon)
- 否定(ひてい)する: to deny
- バブル時代(じだい): the "bubble era" [the 80's period of rising land prices, stock markets, and economic growth, which ended in the early 90's. Now one often hears the phrase バブルがはじけてから ("after the bubble burst") to describe the changes when land prices dropped and corporate restructuring began]
- 含める・ふくめる: to include
- 〜年(ねん)ほどのあいだ(間): for a period of about 〜 years
- 物価・ぶっか: prices (of commodities)
- きわめて・極めて: extremely; exceedingly
- 安定(あんてい)する: to stabilize
- 価格帯・かかくたい: a price range
- 意識・いしき: consciousness; awareness
- 同じ・おなじ: the same
- 〜(をする)かぎり: as long as one (does 〜)
- 変わる・かわる: to change
- そこへきて: to this (situation in which awareness of cost has been stable for years) comes (imports cheapened by a strong yen etc.)
- 海外旅行・かいがいりょこう: trips/travel abroad
- 円高・えんだか: the strengthening of the yen [in the ten years after 1985 the yen dropped from over ¥300/$1 to ¥100/$1]
- 大幅・おおはば: greatly; to a great extent [幅: width; breadth]
- 家電製品・かでんせいひん: household electric goods; appliances [short for 家庭電化製品・かていでんかせいひん]
- 技術・ぎじゅつ: technology
- 革新・かくしん: innovation
- 普及効果・ふきゅうこうか: a spreading effect [here, the effect of widespread use of technology which makes goods perform better at a given price]
- 価格パフォーマンス: price performance
- 高める・たかめる: to heighten; improve/raise
- むしろ: rather; if anything
- すくなくない: are not few
- こうなると: when this happens
- 通常・つうじょう: usual; normal
- 設定・せってい: fixing; setting
- 割高感・わりだかかん: a sense of (a price being) comparatively high
- 〜ようになる: to grow to/get so one 〜
- いまどき: at such a time as this; nowadays; these days
- 高(たか)すぎる: to be too high; too expensive
- ビデオ: here, short for ビデオデッキ, a video system/recorder-player
- 沖縄・おきなわ: Okinawa
- グアム: Guam [farther away but cheaper in dollars]
- 当たり前・あたりまえ: "it's only natural" [cf. 当然・とうぜん]
- ありがたい・有り難い: a welcome (thing for consumers); much appreciated
- 経済(けいざい)全体(ぜんたい)からすると: from the perspective of the whole economy
- そう adj.〜くもない: is not such a 〜 (welcome thing)

- 薄利多売・はくりたばい: to sell a lot at a thin profit margin
- モットー: motto
- 伸(の)び: expansion; growth
- かならずしも: (not) necessarily
- つながる: to be connected; tied
- 収益・しゅうえき: profits; revenue; earnings
- verb stem〜にくい: difficult to (〜)
- そうなると: if that is so
- 新規投資・しんきとうし: new investment
- 誘発(ゆうはつ)する: to induce/cause (new investment); bring about
- 従業員・じゅうぎょういん: employee; worker
- 所得・しょとく: income; earnings
- 増加・ぞうか: increase; rise in
- 〜を通(つう)じて: through 〜; by means of
- 増える・ふえる: to increase; rise
- 波及効果・はきゅうこうか: an effect which spreads; a rippling effect like a 波(なみ): wave
- 期待(きたい)する: to expect; hope for
- 他方で・たほうで: on the other hand
- 最盛期・さいせいき: a peak; the height (of the bubble era)
- 〜を追い風に・をおいかぜに: with 〜 as a tail wind
- 着実に・ちゃくじつに: steadily; consistently
- デパート: department store
- いまでこそ: at this time (in particular)
- 深刻・しんこく: serious; grave
- 販売不振・はんばいふしん: poor sales
- 悩む・なやむ: to suffer from
- 衣料品・いりょうひん: clothing
- 品揃え・しなぞろえ: a selection of goods [cf. 揃える・そろえる: to arrange]
- 豊富・ほうふ: rich; abundant
- adj. 〜さ: さ replaces い or な in adj. and nominalizes them
- 売場・うりば: a department or floor in a department store
- 〜自体・じたい: 〜 itself
- 価値・かち: value; worth
- 業態・ぎょうたい: a form of enterprise
- 追随・ついずい: following (in another's wake)
- 許す・ゆるす: to permit; allow
- 追随(ついずい)を許(ゆる)さない: to be peerless; have no equals
- 好機・こうき: a convenient opportunity; a good chance
- リストラ: (corporate) "restructuring"
- (どの)程度・ていど: (what) extent; degree
- 進む・すすむ: to advance; proceed
- 社内(しゃない)コスト: internal costs
- 切り下げ・きりさげ: "cut and lower"; reduction
- 仕入れ先・しいれさき: a supplier; wholesaler
- 転換・てんかん: shifting; converting; changing to
- 立地・りっち: location (of a business)
- 見直し・みなおし: review; reexamination [verb: 見直す]
- 問題・もんだい: problem; trouble; question
- 解決(かいけつ)する: to solve; resolve
- 百貨店・ひゃっかてん: department store
- 復活(ふっかつ)する: to come back; be reborn

出したことで、その地域の潜在需要が掘り起こされたという一面も否定できない。

　バブル時代も含めて、この十年ほどのあいだは物価がきわめて安定していたために、安いとか高いと感じる価格帯についての意識が、同じ商品でみるかぎり、あまり変わっていない。そこへきて、海外旅行や輸入品は円高で大幅に安くなったし、家電製品やハイテク商品のように技術革新とその普及効果で価格パフォーマンスを高めている商品もあり、十年前よりむしろ安くなっている商品も少なくない。こうなると、通常の価格設定では割高感を感じるようになる。「いまどきビデオが十万円は高すぎる」とか、「沖縄よりグアムのほうが安いのは当たり前」といった感覚である。

　しかし、消費者にとってはありがたいこの価格破壊現象も、経済全体からするとそうありがたくもない。

　薄利多売がモットーのこうした販売は、売上の伸びが、かならずしも収益の伸びにはつながりにくい。そうなると、新規投資を誘発したり、従業員の所得の増加を通じて消費が増えるといった波及効果も、あまり期待できないのである。

　他方で、バブルの最盛期には消費者の高級志向を追い風に売上を着実に伸ばしていったデパートは、いまでこそ深刻な販売不振に悩んでいるが、高級衣料品を中心に品揃えの豊富さと売場自体が商品価値をもつという点では他の業態の追随を許さない。この不況を好機に、デパートのリストラがどの程度進むか。社内コストの切り下げ、仕入れ先の転換、立地の見直しなどの問題が解決できれば百貨店も復活するだろう。

慣用句: Idiomatic Expressions

Translate the following into idiomatic English

1. 売上げを伸ばす

不況の波及効果で、薄利多売をモットーとするディスカウント・ショップが大きく
売上げを伸ばしつつある。

2. 〜があれば〜もある

価格破壊現象でありがたいと思っているディスカウント・ショップがあれば、深刻
な販売不振に悩む百貨店もある。

3. コストを抑える

高級品を中心に扱う百貨店もリストラでコストを極限まで抑えねばならないだろう。

4. (〜を) 控える

廉価商品を扱う店をたくさん控えた駅前商店街では高級品を扱う百貨店ほど価格破
壊現象に悩むことがない。

5. そこへ来て

百貨店は販売不振に悩んでいる。そこへ来て郊外を中心とする大型ディスカウン
ト・ショップの増加で、ますます売上が伸びていない。

6. 今でこそ

個人消費の主力は今でこそ廉価商品へとシフトしているが、バブル時代には消費者
の所得も高く、高級志向が主力だった。

7. 他の追随を許さない

薄利多売をモットーとする郊外の新興住宅地のディスカウント・ショップは廉価の
点で他の商店の追随を許さない。

SHUTSU shita koto de, sono CHI-IKI no SEN-ZAI JU-YOU ga HOriOkosareta to i-
u ICHI-MEN mo HI-TEI dekinai.

Baburu JI-DAI mo FUKUmete, kono JUU-NEN hodo no aida wa BUK-KA ga kiwamete AN-TEI shite ita tame ni, YASUi toka TAKAi to KANjiru KA-KAKU-TAI
ni tsuite no I-SHIKI ga ONAji SHOU-HIN de miru kagiri, amari KAwatte inai. Soko e kite, KAI-GAI RYO-KOU ya YU-NYUU-HIN wa EN-DAKA de OO-HABA ni
YASUku natta shi, KA-DEN SEI-HIN ya *haiteku* SHOU-HIN no you ni GI-JUTSU KAKU-SHIN
to sono FU-KYUU KOU-KA de KA-KAKU *pafoomansu* o TAKAmete iru SHOU-HIN mo
ari, JUU-NEN MAE yori mushiro YASUku natte iru SHOU-HIN mo SUKUnaku nai.
Kou naru to, TSUU-JOU no KA-KAKU SET-TEI de wa WARI-DAKA-KAN o KANjiru you ni naru. "Imadoki *bideo* ga JUU-MAN-EN wa TAKAsugiru" toka, "OKI-NAWA yori *guamu* no hou ga YASUi no wa AtariMAE" to itta KAN-KAKU de aru.

Shikashi, SHOU-HI-SHA ni totte wa arigatai kono KA-KAKU HA-KAI GEN-SHOU
mo, KEI-ZAI ZEN-TAI kara suru to sou arigataku mo nai.

HAKU-RI TA-BAI ga *mottoo* no kou shita HAN-BAI wa, URI-AGE no NObi ga,
kanarazushimo SHUU-EKI no NObi ni wa tsunagarinikui. Sou naru to,
SHIN-KI TOU-SHI o YUU-HATSU shitari, JUU-GYOU-IN no SHO-TOKU no ZOU-KA o TSUUjite SHOU-HI
ga FUeru to itta HA-KYUU KOU-KA mo, amari KI-TAI dekinai no de a-
ru.

TA-HOU de, *baburu* no SAI-SEI-KI ni wa SHOU-HI-SHA no KOU-KYUU SHI-KOU o OiKAZE
ni URI-AGE o CHAKU-JITSU ni NObashite itta *depaato* wa, ima de koso SHIN-
KOKU na HAN-BAI FU-SHIN ni NAYAnde iru ga, KOU-KYUU I-RYOU-HIN o CHUU-SHIN ni SHINA-ZOROe
no HOU-FUsa to URI-BA JI-TAI ga SHOU-HIN KA-CHI o motsu to iu TEN de wa HOKA no GYOU-
TAI no TSUI-ZUI o YURUsanai. Kono FU-KYOU o KOU-KI ni, *depaato* no *risu-
tora* ga dono TEI-DO SUSUmu ka. SHA-NAI *kosuto* no KIriSAge, SHI-Ire-SAKI
no TEN-KAN, RIT-CHI no MI-NAOshi nado no MON-DAI ga KAI-KETSU dekireba HYAK-KA-TEN mo
FUK-KATSU suru darou.

内容理解: Comprehension Exercises

Answer in Japanese.

1. ディスカウント・ショップにはどのような種類・タイプのものがありますか。
2. ディスカウント・ショップに共通している点は何でしょうか。
3. 価格破壊の現象にはどのような背景がありますか。
4. ディスカウント・ショップはどのようなところで顕著に見られ、それはどのようなことを意味するのでしょうか。
5. この十年ほどの間に商品の価格に対する消費者の感覚はどのように変わってきましたか。またそれはどうしてでしょう。
6. 筆者はどうして「価格破壊現象は経済全体から見るとありがたくない」と考えていますか。またそのような考え方についてどう思いますか。
7. デパートはどのような点で他の業態の追随を許さないのでしょうか。
8. デパートの復活にはまずどのような問題を解決すべきでしょうか。

練習問題: Exercises

True or False ?

1. 不況のため大型ディスカウント・ショップが販売不振に悩んでいる。
2. 価格破壊の現象によって最も潜在需要が掘り起こされたのは近くに駅を控えた商店街、つまり「駅前商店街」である。
3. 価格破壊で深刻な販売不振に悩むデパートの復活にはまず高級品売場を廉価商品売場に変えることである。
4. ディスカウント・ショップなどの薄利多売によって消費が増えるから、価格破壊現象は経済全体から見てありがたい。

areas, one cannot deny the aspect that those area's latent
demand has been aroused by the advance of the discount stores.

Including the "Bubble Era," because prices have been extremely stable for these [past] ten years, the awareness concerning the price range where one feels [something is] expensive or cheap, as long as one looks at the same goods, hasn't changed much. Furthermore, things such as foreign travel and imports have grown cheaper to a large extent with the yen's strength; there are goods such as household appliances and high tech goods that have higher price performance through technological discovery and the effect of diffusion; and there are not a few goods that have, if anything, gotten cheaper than ten years before. When this occurs, one grows to feel things are rather expensive at the usual price settings. There is the sense that "These days a hundred thousand yen is too much for a VCR," or "Its natural that [to travel to] Guam is cheaper than Okinawa."

But even this price destruction phenomenon, which is so welcome for consumers, is not so welcome from the [point of view] of the whole economy.

With these sorts of sales which hold "selling more at a thin margin" as their motto, it is not easy for expansion of sales always to be tied to expansions of revenue. When that occurs, the spreading effect of inducing new investments and increasing consumption by increasing employee income cannot really be expected.

On the other hand, department stores, which steadily expanded sales during the height of the Bubble Era backed by consumer inclination for high-quality goods, are presently suffering from a serious inactivity in sales, but on the point of abundance of selection, with high-quality clothing at its center, and the value of the sales floor itself [as a] commodity, they are unmatched by any other form of marketing. With the recession as a golden opportunity, to what extent will department store restructuring proceed? If problems such as cutting internal costs, the changing of suppliers, and the reconsideration of location can be solved, perhaps even department stores will come back.

語句と語法: Phrases and Usage

- お土産・おみやげ: a gift bought on one's travels for members of one's family, club, group (fellow workers, especially)
- 文化・ぶんか: culture
- 京都・きょうと: Kyoto; Japan's capital 794–1868
- 新幹線・しんかんせん: "New Trunk Line"; a passenger railroad system opened in 1964 and known for its high speed and punctuality; also called "the bullet train"
- しばしば: often; frequently
- 新婚旅行・しんこんりょこう: "newlywed trip"; a honeymoon
- 二人連れ・ふたりづれ: a couple
- いっしょ(一緒)になる: to come together
- 何日間か・なんにちかんか: for a number of days
- ～にわたる旅(たび): a trip spanning (several days)
- 終える・おえる: to end; finish
- ～とみ(見)える: to look (appear) as if ～
- 風情・ふぜい: appearance; air
- たのしい・楽しい: fun; enjoyable; pleasant
- ～げ: = ～そうに: "appears/seem(s) ～" [with adj. stems]
- 見知らぬ・みしらぬ: unknown (on sight)
- 第三者・だいさんしゃ: a third person (stranger)
- 心・こころ: heart [indicates one's (inner) feelings]
- おめでとう: "congratulations"
- 気持ち・きもち: a feeling
- もつ・持つ: to have; hold
- 同時(どうじ)に: at the same time
- なんとも: quite; indescribable
- かわいそう(可哀そう)な: pitiable; pathetic
- 感(かん)になる: to have a feeling; receive an impression
- といのは: that is; which is to say
- ほとんど: almost completely
- 例外・れいがい: an exception
- ～なしに: without ～
- 若い・わかい: young; youthful
- 新婚夫婦・しんこんふうふ: a newlywed couple
- 紙袋・かみぶくろ: a paper (shopping) bag
- 重い・おもい: heavy; weighty
- ～そうに: attached to the stem of い and な adjectives, means "appears" or "seems"

- ぶらさげる: to dangle; carry (suspended from a hand)
- かれら・彼ら: they [彼 is "he," but 彼ら can include women as well]
- さっそうと: smartly; dashingly; valiantly
- おおむね・概ね: largely; for the most part [= だいたい]
- 仕立ておろし・したておろし: newly tailored
- 服・ふく: clothing
- 身(み)をつつむ: "to wrap one's body (in)"; be clothed; dressed in
- 真っ白・まっしろ: pure white
- スーツケース: a suitcase
- 軽装・けいそう: with little baggage
- 同一人物・どういつじんぶつ: "(those) very same people" [同一: one and the same; 人物: person]
- 帰(かえ)りがけに: on the way home; when leaving for home
- 大荷物・おおにもつ: great amount of baggage
- 両手・りょうて: both hands
- アゴを出(だ)す: to be incredibly tired/fatigued [顎(あご): the chin, jaw]
- 花(はな)ムコ・花婿: the "flower groom"; bridegroom
- なかには: among them
- 荷物(にもつ)はこび: carrying luggage [cf. 運ぶ・はこぶ: to carry]
- イライラ: irritation; frustration [cf. 苛立つ(いらだつ): to get vexed; irritated]
- 原因・げんいん: a cause
- さっそく・早速: at once; right away
- 夫婦喧嘩・ふうふげんか: a "couple quarrel"
- 第一号・だいいちごう: number one; the first (of many)
- おっぱじめる: "launch right into" [coll. for はじめる: to start]
- スマート: not "smart" in the sense of "intelligent," but slim, well proportioned (body); chic; stylish
- わずか: a small amount; a short time
- ぐったり: slumping over; being dead-tired
- くたびれる: to be tired out; done in
- そもそも: what on earth ["to begin with"; "in the first place"]
- いうまでもない: needless to say

お土産文化

加藤秀俊

　京都から新幹線にのると、しばしば、新婚旅行の二人連れといっしょになる。何日間かにわたる旅行を終えたところとみえて、風情はたのしげであり、私も見知らぬ第三者として、心のなかで、おめでとう、という気持ちをもつのだが、同時に、なんともかわいそうな感じになる。というのは、ほとんど例外なしに、この若い新婚夫婦たちは大きな紙袋を重そうにぶらさげているからだ。

　旅行に出るときのかれらは、さっそうとしており、おおむね仕立ておろしの服に身をつつみ、まっ白なスーツケースひとつ、という軽装なのだけれど、その同一人物が、帰りがけには大荷物で両手がいっぱい。アゴを出している花ムコもいるし、なかには、荷物はこびのイライラが原因でさっそく夫婦喧嘩の第一号をおっぱじめているのもいる。あのスマートな二人連れが、わずか三、四日のあいだにぐったりとくたびれてしまっているのである。

　かれらを、こんなふうにくたびれさせてしまうあの大荷物は、そもそもなんであるのか。いうまでも

GIFT GIVING IN JAPAN 1

Gift giving in Japan follows a long tradition and has become an entire industry. Part of this is giving *omiyage* ("souvenirs") to one's co-workers and superiors when returning from a business trip. Going on a private pleasure trip is likely to require taking paid leave. This requires notifying the office. Thus, everyone at work may know that you are going skiing in Nagano. This, too, may require gifts to appease those who stay back in the office. Such gifts may consist of a box of chocolates or a local delicacy of the place visited, to be shared by one and all. Or they may encompass that and include as well a little something for a select few.

There are two main gift giving seasons. The seasons roughly coincide with the bi-annual bonuses most workers receive, making it easier to afford the expense. In mid-July is お中元 (*ochūgen*). *Ochūgen* gifts are given to superiors, good customers, or to people to whom one feels particularly obligated. They are given individually and professionally by people of all walks of life. As with most gifts, the value itself is probably not as important as letting someone know you have not forgotten your co-worker.

The other main gift or gift season is お歳暮 (*oseibo*). These are given at year's end to one's superiors at work, or to people towards whom one feels a special obligation. Year's end is traditionally a time to end one's indebtedness to others and to pay off old debts, both monetary and otherwise. To repay with gifts allows two people to head into the new year with a "clean slate" and improved relations.

Gifts are also made to colleagues at a new work place to or to neighbors in a new neighborhood. What is given must suit the nature of the relationship; an expensive gift is not always best. What matters is to give in order to smoothly enter into good relations with those in one's community.

In addition, there is a whole world of ritual accompanying the proper way to give cash, which is rather common. Money is given in envelopes, usually ones which have special decorations varying according to the occasion. Money is given at wakes and funerals, weddings, to children at New Year's, and even to those in the hospital.

It is commonly said that "money makes the world go round." In Japan, gifts are possibly the most common social lubricant.

OMIYAGE BUN-KA

KA-TOU HIDE-TOSHI

KYOU-TO kara SHIN-KAN-SEN ni noru to, shibashiba, SHIN-KON RYO-KOU no
FUTA-RI-ZUre to issho ni naru. NAN-NICHI-KAN ka ni wataru RYO-KOU
o Oeta tokoro to miete, FU-ZEI wa tanoshige de ari,
WATASHI mo MISHIranu DAI-SAN-SHA toshite, KOKORO no naka de, omedeto-
u, to iu KI-MOchi o motsu no da ga, DOU-JI ni, nan to mo
kawaisou na KANji ni naru. To iu no wa, hotondo REI-
GAI nashi ni, kono WAKAi SHIN-KON FUU-FUtachi wa OOkina KAMI-BUKURO o OMO-
sou ni burasagete iru kara da.

RYO-KOU ni DEru toki no karera wa, sassou to shite ori,
oomune SHI-TAteoroshi no FUKU ni MI o tsutsumi, masSHIRO na
suutsukeesu hitotsu, to iu KEI-SOU na no da keredo, so-
no DOU-ITSU JIN-BUTSU ga, KAErigake ni wa OO-NI-MOTSU de RYOU-TE ga ippa-
i. *Ago* o DAshite iru HANA*muko* mo iru shi, naka ni wa,
NI-MOTSUhakobi no *iraira* ga GEN-IN de sassoku FUU-FU GEN-KA no
DAI-ICHI-GOU o oppajimete iru no mo iru. Ano *sumaato*
na FUTA-RI-ZUre ga, wazuka SAN, YOK-KA no aida ni guttari
to kutabirete shimatte iru no de aru.

Karera o, konna fuu ni kutabiresasete shimau a-
no OO-NI-MOTSU wa, somosomo nan de aru no ka. Iu made mo

GIFT GIVING IN JAPAN II

S ometimes gifts can be troublesome, as indicated in this piece on *omiyage*. For example, people who receive *ochūgen* and *oseibo* gifts often re-give them to others. One common theme, which appears in television dramas, is the person who received the very same gift from two different people. Some department stores now wrap gifts with the card from the sender inside the wrapping paper. The receiver of the gift must unwrap it in order to send a proper thank-you note. To send a proper note and also re-give the gift, some have developed the art of unwrapping, removing the card, and re-wrapping the gift into a well-honed skill.

The selected piece is an excerpt from Katō Hidetoshi's 「日本人の周辺」 (The Surroundings of the Japanese), Tokyo: Kodansha Ltd., 1975.

Omiyage Culture

Katō Hidetoshi

When I get on the bullet train from Kyoto, I occasionally find myself together with a pair on their honeymoon. Apparently just having finished a trip spanning several days, they seem to be enjoying themselves, and as an unknown third person I have the sentiment in my heart, "congratulations," but at the same time I get the impression that [they are] indescribably pathetic. By which I mean, almost without exception, that these young newlywed couples are heavily hung with large paper bags.

When departing on their trip, they look dashing, usually dressed in newly tailored clothes, and traveling lightly with one perfectly white suitcase, but on their return those same people have both hands full with large [amounts of] baggage. There are exhausted bridegrooms, and among them, with the frustration of carrying baggage as the cause, some even get right to their first fight as husband and wife. That stylish couple has gotten completely tired out in the brief span of three or four days.

What, in the first place, is that huge [amount of] baggage which has tired them out in this way? Needless to

- 披露宴・ひろうえん: a wedding reception
- だの…だの: or [presents a non-inclusive list of items]
- 駅・えき: train station
- 見送り・みおくり: seeing (someone) off
- 親類・しんるい: relatives; relations
- 縁者・えんじゃ: relatives (often used in the form 親類縁者)
- 友人・ゆうじん: friends
- 知己・ちき: acquaintances
- 好意・こうい: goodwill; kindness
- 報いる・むくいる: to repay; return (a favor)
- べく: having to [infinitive form of べし, expressing obligation]
- 新婚さんたち: newlyweds (in general) [a slightly affectionate term, not detached, with the addition of さんたち]
- 旅行先・りょこうさき: a travel destination [〜先 describes a place at which action or things are directed]
- どっさり: lots of; plenty of
- 買い込む・かいこむ: to buy in great quantity
- 方・かた: honorific for 人 [perhaps a boss or other superior]
- 人・ひと: person
- かぞえあげる: to count up (the people needing gifts)
- 配布先・はいふさき: places to distribute (gifts to)
- ほう大(だい)・膨大: huge; enormous
- 数・かず: number; figure
- (かず)にのぼる: "to climb (to a huge number)"; rise
- となると: "if/when it gets to (this point)"; and so
- 値段・ねだん: price
- 制約・せいやく: limitation; constriction
- まず・先ず: probably; most likely ["first and foremost"]
- 〜包(つつ)み: a package (a counter)
- 菓子折・かしおり: a box of Japanese confections/sweets
- 数が数だから: because it is such a huge number
- テレビ: television
- 受像機・じゅぞうき: "receiver"; (TV) set
- 一台・いちだい: one unit [台 is a counter for large items]
- 〜ぶん・分: a portion; amount
- 重さ・おもさ: weight [〜さ nominalizes adj.]
- かんが(考)えてみれば: if (when) you think (about it)
- あたりまえ・当たり前: only to be expected
- 餞別・せんべつ: a traditional gift or money given to someone traveling far away
- 反対給付・はんたいきゅうふ: "supply in the opposite direction"; reimbursement; compensation
- むかし・昔: the old days; long ago
- 講・こう: association organized for a pilgrimage
- 組織(そしき)する: to organize
- それぞれ: each; respective
- 交替・こうたい: in turn; alternation
- 代表者・だいひょうしゃ: a representative; delegate
- たとえば・例えば: for example
- 伊勢・いせ: Ise [site of the famous Ise Shrine, Mie Prefecture]
- とか…とか: or [presents a non-inclusive list of items]
- 熊野・くまの: Kumano [site of three famous shrines in Wakayama Prefecture]
- 参詣・さんけい: a pilgrimage; visit to a shrine/temple
- 送る・おくる: to send
- 参詣先・さんけいさき: shrine to be visited
- ないし: or

- 信仰・しんこう: faith; belief (religious)
- 対象・たいしょう: subject (of belief); object (of study)
- 白山・はくさん: an extinct volcano in central Honshu
- 名前・なまえ: names (given the groups traveling to shrines)
- ぞくする・属する: to belong to
- 代参者・だいさんしゃ: proxy for a pilgrim
- しかも: moreover; on top of that
- 旅費・りょひ: travel expenses
- 無尽・むじん: mutual financing
- 方式・ほうしき: system; method
- メンバー: member (of a group)
- 全員・ぜんいん: all members
- 負担(ふたん)する: to bear; carry (an expense)
- 代参・だいさん: to go (on a pilgrimage) in place of another
- 済ませる・すませる: to finish; get through with
- 神社・じんじゃ: Shinto shrine
- 仏閣・ぶっかく: Buddhist temple
- 故郷・こきょう: one's hometown [where one was raised]
- 待つ・まつ: to wait
- 仲間・なかま: a fellow member
- 持って帰る・もって かえる: "carry and return"; to take back
- 買い求める・かいもとめる: to buy; obtain
- お守り・おまもり: a "protective amulet" or charm obtained at a shrine [these days they exist for "traffic safety" (交通安全), "successful study" (学業成就), and other purposes]
- 〜をはじめとする: beginning with 〜
- 宗教的・しゅうきょうてき: religious
- 色彩・しきさい: tint; color (quality/character)
- おびる・帯びる: to take on (a meaning); be tinged with
- 多い・おおい: many
- したがって・従って: accordingly
- 意味・いみ: meaning; [〜といういみで: "in the sense that/of 〜"]
- 宮笥・みやけ: a shrine box
- 字・じ: a character (letter) [cf. 文字, 漢字]
- 語源・ごげん: "a word('s) source"; etymology
- 〜らしい: "it seems that 〜"
- 土産・みやげ: something like "local (土: ground) product (産: product)"
- 後世・こうせい: later times
- アテ字(じ)・当て字: characters used for their reading, regardless of meaning [当(あ)てる: to assign]
- そうした: that kind (sort) of [= のような, そういう]
- 共同体・きょうどうたい: communal group [indicates the 講]
- 制度・せいど: (social, legal) system
- 習慣・しゅうかん: a custom; practice; habit
- 奥ゆかしい・おくゆかしい: refined; elegant
- 人間らしい・にんげんらしい: characteristic of human beings; humane; human
- たいへんに・大変に: extremely
- うつくしい・美しい: beautiful
- われわれ・我々: we [我々日本人: "we Japanese"]
- 付随(ふずい)する: to accompany; be attendant on
- すくなくとも・少なくとも: at least
- 歴史的・れきしてき: historical
- 理由・りゆう: a reason
- 伝統・でんとう: tradition

なく、おみやげである。披露宴だの、駅での見送りだのにきてくれた親類・縁者・友人知己——そうしたすべての人びとの好意に報いるべく、新婚さんたちは旅行先でおみやげをどっさり買いこんでゆくのだ。あの方にも、この人にも、とかぞえあげてゆくと、おみやげの配布先は三十とか五十とかいったぼう大な数にのぼることになる。となると、値段の制約から、まず、ひと包み五百円の菓子折、というようなことになるのだが、数が数だから、テレビ受像機一台ぶんぐらいの大きさと重さになってしまう。新婚さんたちが、これでぐったりするのは、かんがえてみればあたりまえのことといわなければならないだろう。

　おみやげというのはドライにいえば、お餞別にたいする反対給付である。むかし「講」というものが組織され、それぞれの講は交替で代表者をたとえば伊勢だの熊野だのの参詣に送った。参詣先、ないし信仰の対象によって、講には伊勢講だとか白山講だとかいった名前がつけられた。代表者はそのぞくする講を代表する代参者であり、しかもその旅費などは、無尽方式で講のメンバーが全員で負担してくれたわけだから、代参を済ませた代表者は、行った先の神社・仏閣で、故郷に待つ講の仲間に持って帰るものを買い求めた。それは、お守りをはじめとする宗教的色彩をおびたものであることが多く、したがって、神社で求めた、という意味で「宮笥」という字がその語源になっているらしい。「土産」というのは後世のアテ字である。

　そうした共同体の制度、ないし習慣には奥ゆかしさと、人間らしさがあって、たいへんにうつくしいことだ、とわたしは思う。われわれ日本人の旅行に、おみやげというものが付随していることには、すくなくとも歴史的理由がある。そして、その伝統の継

Window display of お中元（おちゅうげん）at a department store.

naku, omiyage de aru. HI-ROU-EN dano, EKI de no MI-OKUri

dano ni kite kureta SHIN-RUI–EN-JA–YUU-JIN-CHI-KI ——sou shi-

ta subete no HITObito no KOU-I ni MUKUiru beku, SHIN-KON-santa-

chi wa RYO-KOU-SAKI de omiyage o dossari KAikonde yuku no

da. Ano KATA ni mo, kono HITO ni mo, to kazoeagete yuku

to, omiyage no HAI-FU-SAKI wa SAN-JUU toka GO-JUU toka itta bo-

uDAI na KAZU ni noboru koto ni naru. To naru to, NE-DAN no SEI-

YAKU kara, mazu, hitoTSUTSUmi GO-HYAKU-EN no KA-SHI-ORI, to iu yo-

u na koto ni naru no da ga, KAZU ga KAZU da kara, *terebi* JU-ZOU-

KI ICHI-DAI bun gurai no OOkisa to OMOsa ni natte shimau.

SHIN-KON-santachi ga, kore de guttari suru no wa, kanga-

ete mireba atarimae no koto to iwanakereba narana-

i darou.

Omiyage to iu no wa *dorai* ni ieba, oSEN-BETSU ni ta-

isuru HAN-TAI KYUU-FU de aru. Mukashi "KOU" to iu mono ga

SO-SHIKI sare, sorezore no KOU wa KOU-TAI de DAI-HYOU-SHA o tatoeba

I-SE dano KUMA-NO dano no SAN-KEI ni OKUtta. SAN-KEI-SAKI, naishi

SHIN-KOU no TAI-SHOU ni yotte, KOU ni wa I-SE KOU da toka HAKU-SAN KOU da

toka itta NA-MAE ga tsukerareta. DAI-HYOU-SHA wa sono zokusu-

ru KOU o DAI-HYOU suru DAI-SAN-SHA de ari, shikamo sono RYO-HI nado

wa, MU-JIN HOU-SHIKI de KOU no *menbaa* ga ZEN-IN de FU-TAN shite kure-

ta wake da kara, DAI-SAN o SUmaseta DAI-HYOU-SHA wa, Itta SAKI

no JIN-JA–BUK-KAKU de, KO-KYOU ni MAtsu KOU no NAKA-MA ni MOtte KAEru

mono o KAiMOTOmeta. Sore wa, oMAMOri o hajime to suru

SHUU-KYOU-TEKI SHIKI-SAI o obita mono de aru koto ga OOku, shitaga-

tte, JIN-JA de MOTOmeta, to iu I-MI de "MIYA-KE" to iu

JI ga sono GO-GEN ni natte iru rashii. "MIYAGE" to iu

no wa KOU-SEI no *ate*JI de aru.

Sou shita KYOU-DOU-TAI no SEI-DO, naishi SHUU-KAN ni wa OKUyukashi-

sa to, NIN-GEN rashisa ga atte, taihen ni utsukushii

koto da, to watashi wa OMOu. Wareware NI-HON-JIN no RYO-KOU ni,

omiyage to iu mono ga FU-ZUI shite iru koto ni wa, suku-

nakutomo REKI-SHI-TEKI RI-YUU ga aru. Soshite, sono DEN-TOU no KEI-

慣用句: Idiomatic Expressions I

Translate the following into idiomatic English

1. 何とも～のような（そうな）

肩を寄せあっておみやげの持参先のリストをつくっている新婚の二人連れは何とも楽しそうだ。

2. そもそも

そもそもおみやげの習慣には宗教的・歴史的理由があるらしい。

3. ～だの～だの

むかしの「講」の組織には参詣先や信仰の対象によって伊勢講だの白山講だのといった名前がつけられた。

4. ～（に報いる）べく

故郷で待つ「講」の仲間たちの好意に報いるべく代参者たちは神社、仏閣でいろいろな「みやげ」を買い求めていた。

5. 数が数だから

おみやげの数が数だし、重さが重さだから新幹線の若い新婚夫婦たちはぐったりとくたびれてしまっていた。

6. ～をおびる

おみやげなどの日本の古い習慣には宗教的・歴史的色彩をおびたものがおおい。

7. ～（て）しかたない

おみやげの精神を虚礼としてしりぞけるよりも「物質的なおみやげ」の習慣をまず考えなおすべきだと思えてしかたない。

say, it is omiyage. Relatives, relations, and friends
at the reception or who came to see them off at the station, [for]
all those people who should have their well wishing rewarded, the newlyweds
go on buying up tons of omiyage wherever they
visit. If one counts them up, for this very important person, and for that guy, too,
the places to receive omiyage can climb to huge
numbers such as thirty or fifty. When it gets like this,
from constraints of price, probably the gift will be something like
a single 500 yen box of sweets, but because the numbers are what they are,
they get to be the size and weight of a television set.
That the newlyweds tire out because of this,
when one thinks about it, must be said to be only
natural.

    Omiyage, to put it in a hard-boiled way, is a reimbursement for
parting gifts. Long ago, things called "Koh"
were organized, and the respective Koh sent delegates in turn on pilgrimages to, for
example, Ise or Kumano. Depending on the site of the pilgrimage
or the object of faith, names were given to the Koh, such as the Ise
Koh or the Hakusan Koh. The delegates were the representative pilgrims visiting
for the Koh they belonged to, and moreover, because the trip expenses
were borne by all the members of the Koh on a mutual system,
the delegates who had visited [the shrine] on behalf of the others bought something at the
shrine or temple to take home for their fellow Koh members waiting
in their hometown. Many of the items were things with religious color,
starting with protective amulets, and accordingly,
it seems the characters "shrine box" are the
etymology from the sense that they were bought at a shrine. "Local product" are
arbitrary characters from later times.

    This kind of communal body system, or custom, has an
elegance and human quality, and is a very beautiful
thing, I think. In the fact that these things called omiyage
are attendant on the trips of us Japanese, there is at least a historical reason. And I will

- 継承者・けいしょうしゃ: a successor (of a skill or tradition)
- 現代・げんだい: "modern," meaning "the world now"
- その他・そのほか or そのた: things other than ~ (boxes of sweets)
- 持ち帰る・もちかえる: to bring back
- けっして・決して: certainly (not); definitely (not); by no means
- 反対(はんたい)する: to oppose
- なんだか: somehow; in some vague way
- ノイローゼ: neurosis; overanxiety; neurotic behavior
- 名づける・なづける: to name
- ~verbべき: one should/must/ought to ~
- とりつかれる・とり憑かれる: to be possessed by
- ようにおもえる: to seem to be (when one thinks about it)
- しかた(が)ない: "one cannot help but ~" [with おもえて: it just seems to me that …]
- じっさい・実際: actually
- 列車・れっしゃ: a train [cf. 電車・でんしゃ an electric train (passenger, cargo, etc.)]
- ~さえ: even (inside the train)
- 手帳・てちょう: a notebook (for addresses etc.)
- ひろげる・広げる: to open up
- 肩(かた)を寄(よ)せあう: "to put (their) shoulders together"; lean together
- 土産持参先・みやげじさんさき: places to which gifts will be taken
- リスト: a list
- つくる・作る: to make; draw up
- カップル: a couple
- せっかく: implies deliberate or special effort for a particular purpose; here, a one-time honeymoon (ruined by gift buying)
- たのしかる・楽しかる: to enjoy [literary form of 楽しい used before べき; contraction of 楽しくある]
- たのしかるべき: which should be enjoyed
- Aという名(な)のB: a B called/named A
- 幽霊・ゆうれい: a ghost; phantom
- verb~てしまう: to ~ completely [also indicates a bad result]
- われわれにとって: for us
- 必要・ひつよう: necessary; needed
- 虚礼・きょれい: an empty gesture; a meaningless formality
- しりぞける・しり退ける: to reject; turn away
- むしろ・寧ろ: rather; if anything
- あたらしい・新しい: new
- 品目・ひんもく: "list of articles"; items; types of items
- ~や~や: when listing a category of items which is not exhaustive or all inclusive

- 作法・さほう: etiquette; manners
- 展開(てんかい)する: to develop; unfold
- ~のではあるまいか: =~のではないでしょう／だろうか
- ある・或る: a certain
- 海外旅行・かいがいりょこう: a trip abroad
- いっさい・一切: (not) at all
- そのかわり・その代わり: instead; in place of that
- 旅先・たびさき: destination
- ほんの~: just a little ~
- 走り書き・はしりがき: something hurriedly written
- 程度・ていど: extent; degree
- 簡単・かんたん: simple; uncomplicated
- 絵(え)ハガキ(葉書): a [picture] postcard
- もともと・元元: originally
- 経験・けいけん: experience
- わかちあう・分かち合う: to share; divide among
- 精神・せいしん: spirit
- 大いに・おおいに: largely; greatly
- 理(り)にかなう: to be logical; consistent with reason or logic
- 方法・ほうほう: method; means
- おみやげ品(ひん): souvenir items (goods)
- 物質・ぶっしつ: physical material; substance
- ~によって: by means of ~
- 情報・じょうほう: information
- かかえる・抱える: to hold in one's arms; carry
- 汗(あせ)をかく: to sweat
- ポスト: a postbox; mailbox
- 投げこむ・なげこむ: to toss into
- 身軽・みがる: light (of body); nimble; (travel) light
- 旅(たび)をする: to travel; take a trip
- ずっと: much more; far and away
- 気が利く・きがきく: to be sensible; be intelligent
- のん気・のんき: carefree; easygoing
- 問題・もんだい: a problem; question
- 解決・かいけつ: solution
- 文化的・ぶんかてき: cultural
- 緊急事・きんきゅうじ: an urgent matter; matter deserving immediate attention
- 開発・かいはつ: development; innovation; cultivation
- 可能性・かのうせい: possibility; potential
- 洋々たる・ようようたる: boundless (possibilities)

承者としての現代の新婚旅行が菓子折その他のおみ
やげを持ち帰ることに、わたしはけっして反対はし
ない。
　しかし、あの大荷物をぶらさげた二人連れをみる
と、なんだか、かれらが「おみやげノイローゼ」と
でも名づけるべきものにとりつかれているように思
えてしかたないのである。じっさい、行きがけの列
車のなかでさえ手帳をひろげ、肩を寄せあっておみ
やげ持参先のリストをつくっているカップルもいる
のだ。せっかくのたのしかるべき新婚旅行が、はじ
めからおみやげという名の幽霊にとりつかれてしま
っているのである。

　われわれにとっていま必要なのは、おみやげを虚
礼としてしりぞけることではなく、むしろ、あたら
しいおみやげの品目や作法を展開することなのでは
あるまいか。わたしの知っているある人は、海外旅
行でいっさいおみやげを持ち帰らない。そのかわり、
旅先から、ほんの走り書き程度の簡単な絵ハガキを
たくさんの友人たちに出すことを習慣にしている。
もともと旅先での経験をわかちあうのがおみやげの
精神なのだから、これは、大いに理にかなった方法
だと思う。経験は、おみやげ品という物質によって
だけわかちあうことができるのではなく、絵ハガキ
という情報によってもわかちあえるものだからであ
る。すくなくとも、あの大荷物をかかえて汗をかく
よりも、絵ハガキをポストに投げこんで身軽な旅を
するほうが、ずっと気が利いている。旅は、のん気
に、身軽でありたい。われわれ日本人にとって、お
みやげ問題の解決は文化的緊急事であり、しかもそ
の開発の可能性は洋々たるものがあるとわたしはか
んがえている。

慣用句: Idiomatic Expressions II

Translate the following into idiomatic English

8. せっかくのたのしかるべき〜

軽装で身軽な旅をしないとせっかくのたのしかるべき旅がだめになってしまいますよ。

9. ほんの〜程度の

ほんのちょっと旅行した程度のことで、日本人の習慣・作法はよくわからない。

10. 理にかなう

奥ゆかしさ、人間らしさのある「お土産文化」だが旅先から大荷物を持ち帰る「伝統文化の継承」は理にかなったことではない。

11. 気が利く

現代の若者はとても気が利いていて新婚旅行先から友人知己に絵ハガキを出し、おみやげの大荷物で汗をかいたりしない。

SHOU-SHA toshite no GEN-DAI no SHIN-KON RYO-KOU ga KA-SHI-ORI sono HOKA no omiyage o MOchiKAEru koto ni, watashi wa kesshite HAN-TAI wa shinai.

Shikashi, ano OO-NI-MOTSU o burasageta FUTA-RI-ZUre o miru
to, nandaka, karera ga "omiyage *noirooze*" to
de mo NAzukeru beki mono ni toritsukarete iru you ni OMO-
ete shikata nai no de aru. Jissai, Ikigake no RES-
SHA no naka de sae TE-CHOU o hiroge, KATA o YOseatte omiyage JI-SAN-SAKI no *risuto* o tsukuttte iru *kappuru* mo iru
no da. Sekkaku no tanoshikaru beki SHIN-KON RYO-KOU ga, hajime kara omiyage to iu NA no YUU-REI ni toritsukarete shimatte iru no de aru.

Wareware ni totte ima HITSU-YOU na no wa, omiyage o KYO-
REI toshite shirizokeru koto de wa naku, mushiro, atarashii omiyage no HIN-MOKU ya SA-HOU o TEN-KAI suru koto na no de wa
arumai ka. Watashi no SHItte iru aru HITO wa, KAI-GAI RYO-
KOU de issai omiyage o MOchiKAEranai. Sono kawari,
TABI-SAKI kara, hon no HASHIriGAki TEI-DO no KAN-TAN na E*hagaki* o
takusan no YUU-JINtachi ni DAsu koto o SHUU-KAN ni shite iru.
Motomoto TABI-SAKI de no KEI-KEN o wakachiau no ga omiyage no SEI-SHIN na no
da kara, kore wa, OOini RI ni kanatta HOU-HOU
da to OMOu. KEI-KEN wa, omiyage HIN to iu BUS-SHITSU ni yotte
dake wakachiau koto ga dekiru no de wa naku, E*hagaki*
to iu JOU-HOU ni yotte mo wakachiaeru mono da kara de a-
ru. Sukunakutomo, ano OO-NI-MOTSU o kakaete ASE o kaku
yori mo, E*hagaki* o *posuto* ni NAgekonde MI-GARU na TABI o
suru hou ga, zutto KI ga KIite iru. TABI wa, nonKI
ni, MI-GARU de aritai. Wareware NI-HON-JIN ni totte, o-
miyage MON-DAI no KAI-KETSU wa BUN-KA-TEKI KIN-KYUU-JI de ari, shikamo sono KAI-HATSU no KA-NOU-SEI wa YOU-YOUtaru mono ga aru to watashi wa kangaete iru.

内容理解: Comprehension Exercises

Answer in Japanese

1. 京都からの新幹線にのると、どんな人たちとよくいっしょになりますか。
2. このような人たちを見て筆者はどんな気持になりますか。どうしてでしょうか。
3. 新婚旅行に出る時の若い二人連れの風情はどうでしょうか。
4. 新婚さんたちが旅行先でおみやげをどっさり買いこんでゆくのはどうしてでしょうか。
5. おみやげの習慣にはどのような歴史的理由がありますか。
6. おみやげの習慣についていま必要なのはどんなことでしょうか。
7. 筆者の知っている人はどのような「気の利いたこと」をしていますか。
8. 筆者の知っているその人の方法はどうして「理にかなったこと」でしょうか。
9. 筆者はおみやげ問題の解決の可能性についてどう考えていますか。

練習問題: Exercises

True or False?

1. おみやげの習慣には宗教的・歴史的理由がある。
2. おみやげの習慣は宗教的色彩をおびた奥ゆかしいものだから、新婚さんたちは必ず神社・仏閣でおみやげを買って帰らなければならない。
3. 「おみやげノイローゼ」にならないためにもおみやげの習慣は「虚礼」としてしりぞける必要がある。
4. 大荷物になるおみやげのかわりに旅先から簡単な絵ハガキを送ったりすることはたしかに「気が利いている」だろうが、伝統的な習慣ではないからおみやげ問題の解決にはならない。

absolutely not object to modern honeymoon[ers]
bringing home boxes of sweets and other omiyage as the successors to that
tradition.

But when I see couples carrying all that baggage, I
cannot but be left with the feeling that it seems somehow
they have been possessed by something which might even
be called "omiyage neurosis." Actually, there are even
couples who, inside the departing train, spread open their
notebooks and are, shoulder to shoulder, making lists of to
whom to bring omiyage. Their once in a lifetime honeymoon, which
should be something to enjoy, is, from the start,
haunted by a ghost called omiyage.

What is necessary for us is not to reject omiyage
as a meaningless gesture, but rather isn't it to
develop new categories and rules of etiquette for
omiyage? A certain person I know brings absolutely no
omiyage home from trips abroad. Instead of that,
she has decided on the custom of sending simple postcards
from her destination with just a little bit of hurried writing to many friends.
Originally, the spirit of omiyage was to share the
experience of one's travels, so I think this is a very reasonable
method. This is because the experience can be shared not
only through the physical substance of omiyage goods, but
can also be shared through information on a postcard.
At the very least, more than sweating from carrying that huge
[amount of] baggage, the alternative of traveling lightly and throwing
postcards into the postbox is far more sensible. We want travel
to be carefree and unencumbered. For us Japanese,
finding the solution to the problem of omiyage is an urgent
cultural matter, and I think, moreover, that there are boundless possibilities
for innovation.

語句と語法: Phrases and Usage

- リサイクル: recycling
- 社会・しゃかい: society
- 構築・こうちく: building; construction
- ～に向(む)ける: to direct toward ～; toward ～
- さまざま・様々: various; many different
- 環境・かんきょう: environment
- 問題・もんだい: problem; question; issue
- 廃棄物・はいきぶつ: waste; refuse; disposed-of items
- いわば: so to speak; as it were
- トランプ: playing cards [from "trump"]
- ババ: a joker (in a deck of cards)
- といえる: can be called
- 大気・たいき: atmosphere; air
- 水質・すいしつ: water quality
- 浄化(じょうか)する: to purify; clean
- ツケ: "a bill (to be paid at a later date)"; penalty for being negligent
- 集まる・あつまる: to collect; gather
- 誰も・だれも: nobody
- verb stem + たがる: to want ～ [not used in reference to oneself]
- ジョーカー: a joker (in a deck of cards)
- 処理(しょり)する: to get rid of; dispose of
- ゴミ: garbage; trash; refuse
- 量・りょう: an amount; quantity
- 減らす・へらす: to decrease; make less; reduce
- 方策・ほうさく: a plan or scheme; measures
- 1950年代(ねんだい): the 1950's
- 後半・こうはん: the latter half (of a period)
- 高度・こうど: a high level or degree
- 成長・せいちょう: growth; expansion
- 期・き: a period
- 迎える・むかえる: to enter (a certain period); reach
- 反動・はんどう: a reaction; recoil
- 公害・こうがい: pollution
- 噴出(ふんしゅつ)する: to erupt; spurt out; shoot out
- 多く・おおく: a large number [noun]
- 解決・かいけつ: a solution; settlement

- 近づく・ちかづく: to approach; get closer to; draw near
- ～に関(かん)する: concerning ～
- 今(いま)なお: even now
- 大量・たいりょう: mass/large amounts
- 生産・せいさん: production [大量～: mass production]
- 消費・しょうひ: consumption (of products) [大量～: mass consumption]
- 流れ・ながれ: the flow; current; trend
- 続く・つづく: to continue
- 断ち切る・たちきる: to cut off; sever
- 手段・しゅだん: means; a measure
- ここ～年(ねん): these past ～ years
- 間(あいだ)に: during
- 特に・とくに: particularly; especially
- 関心・かんしん: interest; concern
- 高まる・たかまる: to heighten; rise
- 必要性・ひつようせい: necessity; need
- 叫ぶ・さけぶ: to shout; appeal for; clamor for
- 第一(だいいち)に: firstly
- 増加(ぞうか)する: to increase; rise
- 一方(いっぽう): for an action to continue exclusively in one direction
- ますます: increasingly; more and more
- 最終 ・さいしゅう: final; ultimate
- 処分場・しょぶんじょう: disposal site; dump site
- 確保(かくほ)する: to secure; guarantee; ensure
- 難しい・むずかしい: difficult; hard
- 逼迫(ひっぱく)した: urgent; compelling; pressing
- データ: data; information
- 一般・いっぱん: general; ordinary
- 残余量・ざんよりょう: the amount left over; excess
- ～年分・ねんぶん: ～ year's equivalent (of garbage)
- 産業・さんぎょう: industry
- わずかに・僅かに: merely; slightly; just
- 対応(たいおう)する: to cope with; deal with
- 新(あら)たな: new; renewed
- 中間・ちゅうかん: intermediate; in-between

リサイクル社会の構築に向けて

小柳秀明

　さまざまな環境問題の中で、廃棄物問題はいわばトランプのババといえます。大気や水質を浄化してもそこからまた廃棄物は出るわけで、すべてのツケがここに集まってきます。誰も取りたがらないそのジョーカーをどう処理するか、というのが廃棄物問題。そしてリサイクルは、ゴミの量を減らすための方策の一つです。

　日本は1950年代後半に高度成長期を迎え、その反動として1970年代にさまざまな公害問題が噴出しました。その多くは解決に近づいていますが、廃棄物問題に関しては、今なお大量生産、大量消費、大量廃棄の流れが続いています。その流れを断ち切る手段の一つがリサイクルで、ここ5年ほどの間に特に関心が高まっています。

　日本でなぜ今リサイクルの必要性が叫ばれているのでしょうか。第一に廃棄物が増加する一方で、ますます処分場の確保が難しくなってきているという逼迫した問題があります。1993年のデータでは一般廃棄物の最終処分場の残余量は8.2年分、産業廃棄物についてはわずか2.3年分しか確保されていません。しかし、このような逼迫した状況に対応するため、新たな最終処分場や中間処理

ECOLOGICAL MILESTONES I

In early Japanese culture, the indigenous religion seemed to have had a fairly positive attitude toward nature. According to this tradition, the entire natural world is pervaded by *kami*—divine spirits which inhabit mountains, springs, rivers, trees, and other natural phenomena. Willful exploitation of the natural world would be desecration. In particular, Kūkai (774–835) developed a philosophy according to which natural phenomena are not only sacred but also a source of wisdom in that they expound the teachings of Buddhism, though not in human language. A similar world view is to be found in the teachings of the Sōtō Zen master Dōgen (1200–1253). Although Kūkai and Dōgen are to this day regarded as two of the greatest cultural figures in Japan, their conceptions have not had much effect in the modern period. Other realities had to be faced. It should perhaps be added that the ecological interpretation of their thought might be a modern one, because the balance of man vs. nature has changed drastically since then.

The "religion" of modern Japan's quest for security and equality, from the Meiji period (1868–1912) to the 1960s, was industrial growth. In the second half of the Showa period (1926–89), nothing more vividly symbolized the dark side of this high growth than Minamata disease, the tragic mercury poisoning of thousands of people who consumed fish and shellfish contaminated by organic mercury discharged into the sea from 1932 to 1968 by the Chisso chemical factory in Minamata. Small animals such as cats felt the symptoms first. The high mercury levels caused permanent nerve damage to people in the area, who then had to suffer further from ostracism. For the Japanese, the "Minamata disease incident" (*Minamatabyō jiken* 水俣病事件) also symbolizes the "citizen's group movement" (*shimin undō* 市民運動) that flowered in the 1960s and 1970s in response to Japan's Cold War alliance with the United States and to the many environmental problems (*kankyō mondai* 環境問題).

In 1959, after protracted negotiations that minimally compensated the victims of Minamata disease, the Chisso company installed pollution control facilities that failed to remove the mercury. Another outbreak of Minamata disease occurred in 1965 in Niigata Prefecture, which prompted the government to announce officially that Chisso was the culprit. After an initial victory for the victims in 1973, the legal battle continued well into the mid 90s, with an out-of-court settlement (*wakai* 和解) in 1996 that was not sufficiently satisfactory to the victims.

Risaikuru SHA-KAI no KOU-CHIKU ni MUkete

KO-YANAGI HIDE-AKI

Samazama na KAN-KYOU MON-DAI no NAKA de, HAI-KI-BUTSU MON-DAI wa iwaba *toranpu* no *baba* to iemasu. TAI-KI ya SUI-SHITSU o JOU-KA shite mo soko kara mata HAI-KI-BUTSU wa DEru wake de, subete no *tsuke* ga koko ni ATSUmatte kimasu. DARE mo TOritagaranai sono *jookaa* o dou SHO-RI suru ka, to iu no ga HAI-KI-BUTSU MON-DAI. Soshite *risaikuru* wa, *gomi* no RYOU o HErasu tame no HOU-SAKU no HITOtsu desu.

NI-HON wa SEN-KYUU-[HYAKU]-GO-[JUU]-NEN-DAI KOU-HAN ni KOU-DO SEI-CHOU-KI o MUKAe, sono HAN-DOU toshite SEN-KYUU-[HYAKU]-NANA-[JUU]-NEN-DAI ni samazama na KOU-GAI MON-DAI ga FUN-SHUTSU shimashita. Sono OOku wa KAI-KETSU ni CHIKAzuite imasu ga, HAI-KI-BUTSU MON-DAI ni KANshite wa, IMA nao TAI-RYOU SEI-SAN, TAI-RYOU SHOU-HI, TAI-RYOU HAI-KI no NAGAre ga TSUZUite imasu. Sono NAGAre o TAchiKIru SHU-DAN no HITOtsu ga *risaikuru* de, koko GO-NEN hodo no AIDA ni TOKU ni KAN-SHIN ga TAKAmatte imasu.

NI-HON de naze IMA *risaikuru* no HITSU-YOU-SEI ga SAKEbarete iru no deshou ka. DAI-ICHI ni HAI-KI-BUTSU ga ZOU-KA suru IP-POU de, masumasu SHO-BUN-JOU no KAKU-HO ga MUZUKAshiku natte kite iru to iu HIP-PAKU shita MON-DAI ga arimasu. SEN-KYUU-[HYAKU] KYUU-[JUU]-SAN-NEN no *deeta* de wa IP-PAN HAI-KI-BUTSU no SAI-SHUU SHO-BUN-JOU no ZAN-YO-RYOU wa HACHI-TEN-NI-NEN-BUN, SAN-GYOU HAI-KI-BUTSU ni tsuite wa wazuka NI-TEN-SAN NEN-BUN shika KAKU-HO sarete imasen. Shikashi, kono you na HIP-PAKU shita JOU-KYOU ni TAI-OU suru tame, ARAta na SAI-SHUU SHO-BUN-JOU ya CHUU-KAN SHO-RI

ECOLOGICAL MILESTONES II

On other issues, most notably air pollution, Japan acted rapidly and effectively after a late start in dealing with the problem. The "pollution Diet" (*kōgai kokkai* 公害国会) of 1970 enacted a number of pollution control laws and established the Environment Agency (*kankyō-chō* 環境庁). Soon, Mount Fuji was once again visible from Tokyo on a fine day. Yet, the 1973 oil shock ended Japan's period of "miraculous" high growth, bringing economic uncertainties that lowered the priority of dealing with pollution. This, along with the weakening of the citizens group movement and the widespread belief that pollution problems had been solved, slowed progress. However, awareness remained focused on cases such as Minamata, thus equating ecology with human health. (The term *kōgai* 公害 literally means "public harm." A more direct equivalent of "pollution" is *osen* 汚染).

It was only at the end of the next period of high growth, the "bubble economy," that the public became aware of persistent domestic environmental problems such as ground water pollution and the importance of global issues such as acid rain and deforestation.

Pollution is a great problem for Japan because of its high population density coupled with a high standard of living. Japan has done better in the area of recycling than many other countries because it is aware of its limitations. Environmental awareness is regaining strength in Japan, as exemplified by the International Convention on Climate Change of 1997 that was held in Kyoto.

Can you cite other examples where Japan tries to preserve its natural heritage?

Additional Reading:

Miyamoto Ken'ichi 宮本憲一. *Kankyō to Kaihatsu* 環境と開発. Tokyo: Iwanami Shoten, 1992.

Frank K. Upham. *Law and Social Change in Postwar Japan.* Cambridge, Mass.: Harvard University Press, 1987.

Towards the Building of a Recycling Society

Koyanagi Hideaki

Among the various environmental problems, the waste product problem can be called the joker in the deck. Even if one cleans the air and water, from there waste will be produced again, and this is where all the debt collects. How to handle that joker that nobody wants to draw is the waste product problem. And recycling is one strategy in order to reduce the amount of garbage.

Japan, in the latter half of the 1950's, entered a long period of high growth, and as a reaction to that, in the 1970's various pollution problems erupted. Many of those are getting closer to resolution, but as far as waste goes, even to this day, the current of mass production, mass consumption, and mass waste continues. One means of cutting off that current is recycling, and particularly in the past five years interest in it has risen.

Why is there such a clamoring for recycling in Japan now? First, with waste ever on the increase, there is the pressing problem of dumping space, the securing of which is growing more and more difficult. According to 1993 data, for general waste disposal, the amount of final dump space remaining is 8.2 years' worth, and as far as industrial waste, only a tiny 2.3 years' worth [of space] has been secured. But, in order to respond to these sorts of strained conditions, even if plans are made for the construction of new final waste disposal sites and intermediate

- 施設・しせつ: a (processing) facility
- 建設・けんせつ: construction; erection
- 計画(けいかく)する: to plan; project
- 計画地・けいかくち: planned site
- 周辺住民・しゅうへんじゅうみん: residents in surrounding area
- 反発・はんぱつ: resistance; opposition
- ～にあう: to meet with ～
- 難航(なんこう)する: to have a rough passage; encounter trouble, difficulty
- 現状・げんじょう: the actual situation; the present situation
- 第二・だいに: second
- 地球サミット: the Earth Summit, held in 1992 in Rio de Janeiro to resolve global environmental issues
- 契機・けいき: an opportunity; chance; turning point
- 資源・しげん: natural resources
- 枯渇・こかつ: drying up; exhaustion [from 枯(か)れる: to wither, and 渇(かわ)く: to dry up]
- 規模・きぼ: scale; dimension
- 認識(にんしき)する: to be aware of; take cognizance of
- (～する)ようになる: to grow/get to the point where one (does ～)
- 未来・みらい: the future
- 世代・せだい: a generation
- 預(あず)かりもの: something entrusted, held in trust
- 残(のこ)す: to leave behind
- 何回でも・なんかいでも: many times; over and over
- 気運・きうん: a trend; a tendency
- 高まり・たかまり: a build-up; a rise
- 推進(すいしん)する: to promote; be a driving force
- 力・ちから: force; power; strength
- 企業・きぎょう: corporations; firms; businesses
- 動かす・うごかす: to move; cause to move; cause to take action
- 力(ちから)を入(い)れる: to make a serious effort; work hard at
- 企業道徳・きぎょうどうとく: corporate morals
- (～に)欠(か)ける: to be lacking in ～
- (～と)見(み)られる: to appear as ～
- 現在・げんざい: the present time; currently
- システム: a system
- 確立(かくりつ)する: to establish
- 我々・われわれ: us, we ["々" repeats the kanji before it]
- 家庭・かてい: home; family; household
- 発生(はっせい)する: to be produced; be generated
- 古紙・こし: old paper
- ガラスびん(瓶): glass jars; bottles
- 缶・かん: cans
- アルミ: aluminum (in full, アルミニウム)
- 上(あ)げる: to give as examples
- この他(ほか): other than this
- 産業系・さんぎょうけい: industrial type (of waste)
- 高炉・こうろ: a blast furnace
- スラグ: slag; molten leftovers
- 石炭灰・せきたんばい: coal ash
- ペットボトル: a PET bottle; polyethylene terephthalate resin bottle [commonly used as containers for chilled drinks]

- プラスチック: plastic
- 製品・せいひん: product(s)
- 再資源化(さいしげんか)する: to recycle; reprocess
- 即ち・すなわち: namely; that is
- 今後・こんご: from now on; henceforth
- 大型・おおがた: large scale/size
- 家電製品・かでんせいひん: electric appliances/products [usually denotes televisions, washing machines, refrigerators, etc.]
- 近い・ちかい: close; near
- 将来・しょうらい: future
- 予想(よそう)する: to expect; anticipate
- 家電・かでん: = 家電製品, above
- 構造・こうぞう: structure; construction
- 複雑・ふくざつ: complex; complicated; intricate
- ～(な)だけに: simply/if only because of ～
- 自治体・じちたい: local governments
- 従来・じゅうらい: up to this point; hitherto
- 枠(わく)を超(こ)える: to go beyond a certain framework (枠)
- 早急に・さっきゅうに: immediately; promptly
- 法整備・ほうせいび: legal preparation; legislation
- 徐々に・じょじょに: gradually
- 整う・ととのう: to make ready; prepare for use
- verb stem + つつある: =～ている [progressive form]
- 制定(せいてい)する: to enact (a law)
- 再生資源・さいせいしげん: recycled resources
- 利用・りよう: utilization
- 促進・そくしん: promotion; hastening; acceleration
- 法律・ほうりつ: law
- 節目・ふしめ: a milestone; something representing a turning point
- さらに・更に: furthermore; moreover
- 容器・ようき: a container
- 包装・ほうそう: wrapping; packaging
- 本格的・ほんかくてき: regular; full-scale; full-blown
- 施行(しこう)する: to put into effect
- ～のうち: among (several) ～
- 割合・わりあい: share; percentage
- 占める・しめる: to make up; account for
- 動き・うごき: movement
- 一層・いっそう: a level (higher); still more; even more
- 期待(きたい)する: to expect; anticipate
- 発想・はっそう: a concept; idea; way of thinking
- 視点・してん: a viewpoint; a perspective
- 立(た)つ: "to stand"; to take (a view, perspective)
- 必要・ひつよう: a necessity; a requirement
- 設計・せっけい: plan; design
- 段階・だんかい: a stage (in a process)
- 部品・ぶひん: a part; a component
- 材質・ざいしつ: the nature of a material (used in a product)
- 単純化(たんじゅんか)する: to simplify
- 配慮(はいりょ)する: to take into consideration
- 製品(せいひん)アセスメント: product assessment

施設の建設を計画しても、計画地の周辺住民の反発にあって難航しているのが現状です。

　第二は、1992年の地球サミットなどが契機となり、地球資源の枯渇が地球規模で認識されるようになったこと。「地球は未来の世代からの預かりもの」と言われます。使える物は何回でも使い、残せる資源を残していこう、という気運の高まりは、リサイクルを推進する力になっています。それは企業をも動かしました。今ではリサイクルに力を入れないと企業道徳に欠ける、と見られるのです。

　現在、日本でリサイクルのシステムが確立されているものとして、我々の家庭から発生するものでは、古紙、ガラスびん、スチール缶、アルミ缶を上げることができます。この他、産業系から発生するものとして、高炉スラグ、石炭灰などが上げられます。ペットボトルやプラスチック製品をどう再資源化、即ちリサイクルするかは今後の問題です。大型の家電製品については、近い将来大量に廃棄されることが予想されます。家電は構造が複雑なだけに、自治体やメーカーという従来の枠を超えた処理・リサイクルのシステムを早急に作らなくてはなりません。

　法整備は徐々に整いつつあります。1991年に制定された「再生資源の利用の促進に関する法律（リサイクル法）」は一つの節目でした。さらに1997年4月には容器包装リサイクル法という新しい法律が本格的に施行されます。容器包装廃棄物は一般廃棄物のうち大きな割合を占めており、この法律が再資源化への動きを一層推進すると期待されています。

　これまでの廃棄物処理は「発生したゴミをどう処理するか」という発想でしたが、これからは「ゴミを出さない」、「ゴミになったとき処理しやすい」という視点に立つことが必要です。リサイクルしやすいように、設計段階から部品の材質や構造を単純化するように配慮する製

Two housewives demonstrating on behalf of a short-lived recycling "deposit system," according to which customers were reimbursed for bottles and cans returned to the store of purchase.

SHI-SETSU no KEN-SETSU o KEI-KAKU shite mo, KEI-KAKU-CHI no SHUU-HEN JUU-MIN no HAN-PATSU ni a-tte NAN-KOU shite iru no ga GEN-JOU desu.

DAI-NI wa, SEN-KYUU-[HYAKU] KYUU-[JUU]-NI-NEN no CHI-KYUU *samitto* nado ga KEI-KI to nari, CHI-KYUU SHI-GEN no KO-KATSU ga CHI-KYUU KI-BO de NIN-SHIKI sareru you ni natta ko-to. "CHI-KYUU wa MI-RAI no SE-DAI kara no AZUkarimono" to Iwarema-su. TSUKAeru MONO wa NAN-KAI de mo TSUKAi, NOKOseru SHI-GEN o NOKOshite iko-u, to iu KI-UN no TAKAmari wa, *risaikuru* o SUI-SHIN suru CHIKARA ni natte imasu. Sore wa KI-GYOU o mo UGOkashimashita. IMA de wa *ri-saikuru* ni CHIKARA o Irenai to KI-GYOU DOU-TOKU ni KAkeru, to MIrare-ru no desu.

GEN-ZAI, NI-HON de *risaikuru* no *shisutemu* ga KAKU-RITSU sarete iru mono toshite, WARE-WARE no KA-TEI kara HAS-SEI suru mono de wa, KO-SHI, *garasu*bin, *suchiiru*KAN, *arumi*KAN o Ageru koto ga deki-masu. Kono HOKA, SAN-GYOU-KEI kara HAS-SEI suru mono toshite, KOU-RO*su-ragu*, SEKI-TAN-BAI nado ga Ageraremasu. *Pettobotoru* ya *pura-suchikku* SEI-HIN o dou SAI-SHI-GEN-KA, SUNAWAchi *risaikuru* suru ka wa KON-GO no MON-DAI desu. OO-GATA no KA-DEN SEI-HIN ni tsuite wa, CHIKAi SHOU-RAI TAI-RYOU ni HAI-KI sareru koto ga YO-SOU saremasu. KA-DEN wa KOU-ZOU ga FUKU-ZATSU na dake ni, JI-CHI-TAI ya *meekaa* to iu JUU-RAI no WAKU o KOeta SHO-RI—*risaikuru* no *shisutemu* o SAK-KYUU ni TSUKUranakute wa nari-masen.

HOU SEI-BI wa JO-JO ni TOTONOitsutsu arimasu. SEN-KYUU-[HYAKU]-KYUU-[JUU]-ICHI-NEN ni SEI-TEI sare-ta "SAI-SEI SHI-GEN no RI-YOU no SOKU-SHIN ni KANsuru HOU-RITSU (*risaikuru* HOU)" wa HITOtsu no FUSHI-ME deshita. Sara ni SEN-KYUU-[HYAKU]-KYUU-[JUU]-SHICHI-NEN SHI-GATSU ni wa YOU-KI HOU-SOU *ri-saikuru* HOU to iu ATARAshii HOU-RITSU ga HON-KAKU-TEKI ni SHI-KOU saremasu. YOU-KI HOU-SOU HAI-KI-BUTSU wa IP-PAN HAI-KI-BUTSU no uchi OOkina WARI-AI o SHImete ori, kono HOU-RITSU ga SAI-SHI-GEN-KA e no UGOki o IS-SOU SUI-SHIN suru to KI-TAI sarete imasu.

Kore made no HAI-KI-BUTSU SHO-RI wa "HAS-SEI shita *gomi* o dou SHO-RI su-ru ka" to iu HAS-SOU deshita ga, kore kara wa "*gomi* o DAsana-i," "*gomi* ni natta toki SHO-RI shiyasui" to iu SHI-TEN ni TA-tsu koto ga HITSU-YOU desu. *Risaikuru* shiyasui you ni, SEK-KEI DAN-KAI kara BU-HIN no ZAI-SHITSU ya KOU-ZOU o TAN-JUN-KA suru you ni HAI-RYO suru SEI-

Empty cans and bottles set out for garbage collectors to pick up on the day stipulated for this type of refuse.

A receptacle for the exclusive disposal of cans located within a public housing project.

disposal facilities, the fact is that, meeting with local resident's opposition, they are facing difficulties.

Second, with things like the 1992 [Rio] Earth Summit as a turning point, is the fact that the withering of the earth's resources has come to be realized on a global scale. It is said that "the earth is something entrusted to us by future generations." The increasing trend of using usable things many times, and saving resources that can be saved, is a force that promotes recycling. That has even put corporations in motion. Nowadays if no effort is put into recycling, it is seen as a lacking in corporate morals.

At present, as to items for which there is an established recycling system, one can list, among items which our households produce, old paper, glass jars, steel cans, and aluminum cans. Other than these, as to items which are produced by industry, one can list blast furnace slag, coal ash, and so forth. How to turn polyethylene bottles or plastic products back into natural resources, or namely, to recycle [them] is the next problem. For large electric appliances, we can expect that large volumes will be disposed of in the near future. If only because of the complex construction of electric appliances, a disposal/recycling system that goes beyond the conventional framework of localities and manufacturers must be created immediately.

Legislation is also gradually being set up. The "Law for Promotion of Utilization of Recycleable Resources (Recycling Law)" established in 1991 is one milestone. In addition, in April of 1997, a new law called the law on the recycling of containers and packaging will also come fully into effect. Containers and packaging make up a large portion of general waste, and this law is expected to press the movement to recycle them to the next level.

Up to now waste disposal was the concept of "how to dispose of the refuse produced," but from this point on it is necessary to take the viewpoints of "don't make refuse" and "when something becomes waste, make it easy to dispose of." In order to make things easy to recycle, product assessment from the design stage with consideration for the nature of materials used in parts and simplification

- 流(なが)れを汲(く)む: to descend from; follow in the wake of [汲む = to draw (water)]
- 取り組み・とりくみ: tackling or grappling with (a problem)
- 車(くるま)の両輪(りょうりん): to be inseparable (as a cart needs both wheels to work)
- 取(と)り組(く)む: to tackle or grapple with (a problem)
- 消費者・しょうひしゃ: consumer
- 意識・いしき: consciousness; awareness
- 改革・かいかく: reform
- 国内・こくない: domestic
- 限る・かぎる: to limit
- 〜のみならず: not only [=だけじゃなくて]
- バーゼル条約(じょうやく): the Basel Convention on the Control of Transboundary Movements of Hazardous Wastes and their Disposal [条約 = treaty, convention]
- 国際・こくさい: international
- ISO 14000シリーズ: ISO 14000 series [standards set by the International Organization for environmental management systems]
- 規格・きかく: a standard
- 進める・すすめる: to advance (a cause)
- 遡る・さかのぼる: to trace back
- 実(じつ)は: in fact; in reality
- リサイクル国(こく): a country that practices recycling
- 戦後・せんご: after the war (WWII)
- しばらくの間(あいだ): for a while
- 服・ふく: clothing
- 自転車・じてんしゃ: a bicycle
- 古物商・こぶつしょう: a second-hand shop
- 介(かい)する: to go through; use as a medium for
- 循環・じゅんかん: circulation
- 還元・かんげん: restoration
- それが: but
- いつのま(間)にか: before one knows it
- 豊か・ゆたか: abundant; plentiful
- 新品・しんぴん: a new item; new goods
- 時代・じだい: a period; an age

- 今や・いまや: but now
- 仕組み・しくみ: construction; a mechanism
- 裏返し・うらがえし: the other side of something
- 浸透(しんとう)する: to seep into; permeate; penetrate
- 捨てる・すてる: to abandon; discard
- 困る・こまる: to be troublesome; be troubled
- 進めつつ・すすめつつ: while promoting
- 転換(てんかん)する: to make a change; transform
- 最終的・さいしゅうてき: in the end
- 理解(りかい)する: to understand
- 再生品・さいせいひん: recycled goods
- 積極的・せっきょくてき: positive; active [cf. 消極的(しょうきょくてき): passive]
- 成立(せいりつ)する: to come into being; be realized
- 比べる・くらべる: to compare; contrast
- 質・しつ: quality (of a product)
- 劣る・おとる: to be inferior [cf. 優る(まさる): to be superior]
- 値段・ねだん: price
- せめて: at least
- 下(さ)げる: to lower
- 購買量・こうばいりょう: quantities purchased
- 増やす・ふやす: to increase; raise (the number of)
- 保全・ほぜん: preservation
- 環境保全型製品・かんきょうほぜんがたせいひん: products of the type that preserve the environment
- 優先的・ゆうせんてき: primarily; preferentially
- 購入(こうにゅう)する: to buy; purchase
- 活動・かつどう: activities
- 地方自治体・ちほうじちたい: local government
- NGOら: NGO; nongovernmental organizations [ら here means "and so on"]
- 団体・だんたい: group; organization; association
- 加わる・くわわる: to join in; participate in
- 本格化(ほんかくか)する: to become serious; become full-scale
- 世紀・せいき: century
- 力(ちから)となる: become a [driving] force [for recycling]

品アセスメントもその流れを汲んでいます。また、企業の取り組みだけでなく、それをバックアップするシステムを作り、車の両輪として取り組んでいかなければなりません。消費者の意識改革も必要です。さらに、これからは国内の廃棄物処理・リサイクルといった限られた視点のみならず地球規模の視点で考えていくことも必要です。バーゼル条約など廃棄物処理に関する国際ルールやISO14000シリーズでリサイクル等に関する国際規格作りも進められつつあります。

　遡れば、日本も実はリサイクル国だったのです。戦後しばらくの間は、服でも自転車でも使える物は古物商などを介してどこかで循環していました。それが、いつのまにか物が豊かになり、古い物より新品を買うほうがいい、という時代に変わってしまいました。今や社会そのものがゴミを出しやすい仕組みになっています。それは豊かさの裏返しと言えるでしょう。

　今後リサイクルが浸透しても、リサイクルするから捨ててもいい、と考えてもらっては困ります。リサイクルを進めつつ、ゴミを出さないようにライフスタイルを転換していくことが必要です。リサイクルをしても最終的にはゴミは出る、このことを我々は理解しなければなりません。

　また、リサイクルというのは再生品を積極的に利用することによって初めて成立するものです。ただ現状では、再生品は新品と比べて質が劣り、値段も高い。せめて少しでも値段を下げるためにも、再生品の購買量を増やす必要があります。1996年2月、リサイクル製品などの環境保全型製品を優先的に購入しようというグループ（グリーン購入ネットワーク）が活動を始めました。企業、地方自治体、NGOらがメンバーとして加わっています。こうした動きが本格化すれば、21世紀のリサイクル社会の構築に大きな力となるでしょう。

慣用句: Idiomatic Expressions

Translate the following into idiomatic English.

1. (〜の)反発にあう

「グリーン購入ネットワーク」グループなどの反発にあって、設計段階からリサイクルしやすい製品の開発をする企業体が多くなった。

2. 難航する

大型家電製品の廃棄物問題はプラスチック製品の処理問題とともに今後もその解決は難航するだろう。

3. (〜が)契機となる / (〜を)契機として

「リサイクル法」が契機となって、企業体も一層製品の再資源化に配慮するようになった。

4. (〜に)欠ける

公害問題の多くは解決されつつあるが、まだまだ企業体の枠を超えた地球規模での認識に欠けると言っていいだろう。

5. 視点に立つ

21世紀のリサイクル社会の構築には「地球規模でのリサイクル、再資源化」という視点に立った取り組み、意識改革が必要だ。

6. (〜の)流れを汲む

「グリーン購入ネットワーク」グループの動きは地球サミットを契機とする諸団体の活動の流れを汲むものだ。

7. (〜を)介する

21世紀には法整備だけでなく、地球規模の諸団体を介した再資源化への動きが一層促進されるだろう。

8. 力となる

地球サミットが力となって、地球規模での再資源化の動きが本格化するようになった。

HIN *asesumento* mo sono NAGAre o KUnde imasu. Mata, KI-GYOU
no TOriKUmi dake de naku, sore o *bakkuappu* suru *shisute-*
mu o TSUKUri, KURUMA no RYOU-RIN toshite TOriKUnde ikanakereba nari-
masen. SHOU-HI-SHA no I-SHIKI KAI-KAKU mo HITSU-YOU desu. Sara ni, kore kara wa KOKU-NAI no HAI-KI-BUTSU SHO-RI—*risaikuru* to itta KAGIrareta SHI-
TEN nominarazu CHI-KYUU KI-BO no SHI-TEN de KANGAete iku koto mo HITSU-YOU desu. *Baazeru* JOU-YAKU nado HAI-KI-BUTSU SHO-RI ni KANsuru KOKU-SAI *ruuru* ya
AI-ESU-OO ICHI-[MAN]-YON-[SEN] *shiriizu* de *risaikuru* NADO ni KANsuru KOKU-SAI KI-KAKU-ZUKUri
mo SUSUmeraretsutsu arimasu.

SAKANOBOreba, NI-HON mo JITSU wa *risaikuru*KOKU datta no desu. SEN-GO
shibaraku no AIDA wa, FUKU de mo JI-TEN-SHA de mo TSUKAeru MONO wa KO-BUTSU-SHOU nado o KAIshite doko ka de JUN-KAN shite imashita. Sore ga, itsu no
ma ni ka MONO ga YUTAka ni nari, FURUi MONO yori SHIN-PIN o KAu hou ga i-
i, to iu JI-DAI ni KAwatte shimaimashita. IMA ya SHA-KAI sono
mono ga *gomi* o DAshiyasui SHI-KUmi ni natte imasu. Sore wa
YUTAkasa no URA-GAEshi to Ieru deshou.

KON-GO *risaikuru* ga SHIN-TOU shite mo, *risaikuru* suru kara SU-
tete mo ii, to KANGAete moratte wa KOMArimasu. *Risaikuru*
o SUSUmetsutsu, *gomi* o DAsanai you ni *raifusutairu* o TEN-
KAN shite iku koto ga HITSU-YOU desu. *Risaikuru* o shite mo SAI-SHUU-TEKI
ni wa *gomi* wa DEru, kono koto o WARE-WARE wa RI-KAI shinakereba nari-
masen.

Mata, *risaikuru* to iu no wa SAI-SEI-HIN o SEK-KYOKU-TEKI ni RI-YOU su-
ru koto ni yotte HAJImete SEI-RITSU suru mono desu. Tada GEN-JOU de wa,
SAI-SEI-HIN wa SHIN-PIN to KURAbete SHITSU ga OTOri, NE-DAN mo TAKAi. Semete SUKO-
shi de mo NE-DAN o SAgeru tame ni mo, SAI-SEI-HIN no KOU-BAI-RYOU o FUyasu
HITSU-YOU ga arimasu. SEN-KYUU-[HYAKU]-KYUU-[JUU]-ROKU-NEN NI-GATSU, *risaikuru* SEI-HIN nado no KAN-
KYOU-HO-ZEN-GATA SEI-HIN o YUU-SEN-TEKI ni KOU-NYUU shiyou to iu *guruupu* (*gu-*
riin KOU-NYUU *nettowaaku*) ga KATSU-DOU o HAJImemashita. KI-GYOU,
CHI-HOU JI-CHI-TAI, ENU-GII-OO ra ga *menbaa* toshite KUWAwatte imasu.
Koushita UGOki ga HON-KAKU-KA sureba, NI-[JUU]-IS-SEI-KI no *risaikuru* SHA-KAI
no KOU-CHIKU ni OOkina CHIKARA to naru deshou.

内容理解: Comprehension Exercises

Answer in Japanese

1. 「廃棄物問題はいわばトランプのババ」という筆者のことばを説明しましょう。
2. 廃棄物処理について今日本で大きな問題となっているのは何でしょうか。
3. 地球サミットを契機として、どのようなことが認識され、どのような気運の高まりが見られるようになりましたか。
4. 大型家電製品の廃棄物処理のほかにどのような製品の再資源化が今後の課題としてあげられますか。
5. リサイクル問題については、どのような法律が制定され、また施行されようとしていますか。
6. リサイクルについて企業体はどのようなことに配慮するようになりましたか。
7. 消費者としてはどのような意識改革、ライフスタイルの転換が必要でしょうか。
8. 再生品の質や値段についてはどのような改革、努力が必要ですか。
9. 21世紀のリサイクル社会に今一番必要なことはどのようなことでしょうか。本文をまとめながら話し合いましょう。

練習問題: Exercises

True or False ?

1. 高度成長による消費量の増加は廃棄物の量に反比例する。
2. 環境問題は企業道徳の問題でもある。
3. 今のところ再生品は新品に比べて質が劣るが値段は安い。
4. ゴミを出さないようにするには消費者の意識改革、ライフスタイルの転換が必要だ。

of construction also follows this trend. Not only [must the] corporations [be] tackling this, but the making of a system to back up that effort must be tackled as an inseparable part [of the process]. There is also a need for a reform in consumer consciousness. In addition, thinking in a global-scale perspective, not only from a limited domestic-disposal and recycling point of view, is also necessary. The international rules for waste disposal such as the Basel Convention and, with the ISO 1400 series, the creation of international standards for things such as recycling are now being advanced.

Looking back in time, Japan, too, was actually a recycling country. For a brief period after the war, usable things, whether clothes or bicycles, were recycled and restored through second-hand shops. But, before you knew it, things became abundant, and it became an age when, rather than old things, it was better to buy something new. Now society itself has grown into a structure which makes it easy to produce garbage. That can be said to be the reverse side of affluence.

Even if recycling spreads from this point on, things will not work out if one thinks that it is alright to throw things away because they will be recycled. While advancing recycling, altering one's lifestyle so that garbage is not produced is what is necessary. Even if one recycles, in the end garbage will be produced, and this is the fact that we must understand.

Also, recycling is something which will only be realized when recycled products are actively used. However, at present, recycled goods are of inferior quality compared to new items, and their price is higher. At the very least, there is the need to increase the amount of recycled goods purchased in order to lower the price. In February of 1996, a group (Green Purchase Network) which seeks primarily to buy environmentally safe products such as recycled goods has started into action. Corporations, local governments, and NGOs have become members. If that type of movement becomes full-scale, it will likely be a great force in building the recycling society of the 21st century.

語句と語法: Phrases and Usage

- フクロウ: owl [animal names are often rendered in katakana]
- 谷・たに: valley; glen; gorge
- 日記・にっき: a (daily) diary
- 南・みなみ: south
- アルプス: the Japan Alps
- 幾重にも・いくえにも: in many folds or layers; repeated several times over
- つらなる・連なる: to range; lie in a row
- 端山・はやま: "outer mountains"; foothills [端(はし) = edge]
- 最終人家・さいしゅうじんか: last house (habitation)
- 林道・りんどう: a forestry road; mountain road
- およそ: about; around
- 登りつめる・のぼりつめる: to climb to the top of/to the highest point of
- ～ところ: a place; "just at (the end of the mountain road)"
- 周囲・しゅうい: surroundings; periphery
- 赤松・あかまつ: red pine
- 雑木・ぞうき: miscellaneous trees
- ～に囲まれる・かこまれる: to be surrounded by ～
- 静か・しずか: quiet; still
- 昔・むかし: long ago; the old days
- 棲む・すむ: to live; inhabit [this kanji used for animals; cf. 住む for human beings]
- 巣・す: a nest
- 頂き・いただき: the summit; the top
- 樹齢・じゅれい: a tree's age
- たつ・経つ: (time) passes
- 周辺・しゅうへん: periphery; vicinity
- 林・はやし: woods
- 樹木・じゅもく: trees
- ～たち・達: primarily used to indicate a plurality of human beings; in reference to flora and fauna, it adds an element of personification and intimacy
- ひときわ・一際: remarkably; strikingly; still more; further
- ぬきんでる・抜きんでる: to be prominent
- ～本・～ほん: a counter for long, thin items and round items (such as trees)
- こんもり: thick (woods)
- 杜・もり: a forest; (sacred) grove/woods [= 森]
- あいている・開いている: to be open [開く・あく: to open]
- 樹洞・じゅどう: a cavity (洞・ほら) in a tree
- 毎年・まいとし: every year
- 春・はる: spring (the season)
- 営む・いとなむ: to carry on (a business or activity)
- 僕・ぼく: I [more informal than 私 and used by men]
- 巣穴・すあな: a "nest hole"
- 知る・しる: to learn of; know of (for the first time)
- 後半・こうはん: the latter half
- 以来・いらい: since then; thereafter
- 幾代・いくだい: many generations
- 世代・せだい: a generation
- 交代・こうたい: alternation
- 繰り返す・くりかえす: to repeat
- 毎年(まいとし)のように: almost evey year
- 繁殖・はんしょく: breeding; reproduction
- 子育て・こそだて: raising offspring
- いったい・一体: in heaven's name; what (how) on earth [also, 一体全体・いったいぜんたい]
- 何年前・なんねんまえ: how many (previous) years
- ～年近く・～ねんちかく: close to ～ years
- 見(み)つづける: to continue to watch
- ようす・様子: the appearance; looks
- ほとんど(殆ど) … ない: hardly (any)
- 何も・なにも: nothing; no; not … any; at all
- 変化(へんか)する: to change; transform
- 一世紀・いっせいき: one century
- ～以上・いじょう: more than ～
- ～にもわたって: across ～ (years)
- かもしれない: may; might; perhaps
- ある: a certain; one
- 年・とし: year
- 残す・のこす: to leave (behind)
- あたり・辺り: vicinity
- 一面・いちめん: a surface; the whole surface/area
- 広大・こうだい: expansive; vast
- 面積・めんせき: area; size of a flat surface
- 伐採(ばっさい)する: to fell/cut trees
- 現場・げんば: a site
- 撮影・さつえい: photography; taking pictures
- 観察・かんさつ: observation; watching
- 思い立つ・おもいたつ: to think of; decide to do
- 跡地・あとち: land (after cleared of buildings, trees)
- 若い・わかい: young; new
- 芽・め: buds; sprouts
- いっせいに: in unison; all at once
- 生える・はえる: to grow (plants, hair, etc.)

フクロウ谷日記(抄)

宮崎学

　フクロウ谷は、南アルプスから幾重にもつらなる端山のなかにある。長野県上伊那郡中川村の最終人家から、林道をおよそ一・五キロメートル登りつめたところ、周囲を赤松と雑木に囲まれた、静かな谷である。

　ここには昔からフクロウが棲んでいた。

　フクロウ谷のフクロウが巣にしている木は、谷からおよそ百六十メートルほど登った山の頂きにある。樹齢が二百～三百年はたっている松の木だ。周辺で林をつくっている樹木たちよりも、ひときわぬきんでた大きな赤松が三本だけあって、こんもりと一つの杜をつくっている。その赤松の一本にあいている樹洞に、フクロウは毎年春になると巣を営んでいた。

　僕がこの巣穴を知ったのが一九六〇年代の後半だった。以来フクロウは幾代にもわたって世代交代を繰り返しながら、毎年のように繁殖と子育てを繰り返している。いったい僕が知る何年前からこの樹洞で子育てをしてきたのだろう。三十年近く同じ巣穴を見つづけていても、樹洞のようすはほとんど何も変化していないのだ。一世紀以上にもわたって使われているかもしれない。

　ある年、フクロウ谷の赤松周辺の林を残して、あたり一面が広大な面積で伐採された。その伐採現場を見て、僕はフクロウの撮影と観察を思い立った。

Miyazaki Manabu

Miyazaki Manabu was born in Nagano Prefecture in 1949. After working on various assignments, he became a free-lance professional photographer in 1972. In 1990 he published an award-winning photo-journal, *Fukurō*, exclusively devoted to owls and their behavior throughout the four seasons. He has also published works on eagles, hawks, and animals in their natural winter habitat. Miyazaki is known in Japan as one of today's foremost nature photographers.

The excerpts here are from *Mori no sanbyaku-rokujūgo-nichi*, a 158-page book in diary form with beautiful photographs of owls and other woodland creatures, as well as their natural surroundings. While writing the diary, Miyazaki lived in a small hut for one year in the mountains. In the book he writes about owls and their nesting and feeding habits, their adaptability to urban sprawl, their interaction with him as an intruder, and about the woodlands where they live.

*Fukurou*DANI NIK-KI (SHOU)

MIYA-ZAKI MANABU

*Fukurou*DANI wa, MINAMI *arupusu* kara IKU-E ni mo tsuranaru HA-YAMA no naka ni aru. NAGA-NO-KEN KAMI-INA-GUN NAKA-KAWA-MURA no SAI-SHUU JIN-KA kara, RIN-DOU o oyoso IT-TEN-GO *kiromeetoru* NOBO-ritsumeta tokoro, SHUU-I o AKA-MATSU to ZOU-KI ni KAKOmareta, SHIZUka na TANI de aru.

Koko ni wa MUKASHI kara *fukurou* ga SUnde ita.

*Fukurou*DANI no *fukurou* ga SU ni shite iru KI wa, TANI kara oyoso HYAKU-ROKU-JUU *meeto-ru* hodo NOBOtta YAMA no ITADAki ni aru. JU-REI ga NI-HYAKU ~ SAN-BYAKU-NEN wa tatte iru MATSU no KI da. SHUU-HEN de HAYASHI o tsukutte iru JU-MOKUtachi yori mo, hitokiwa nukindeta OOkina AKA-MATSU ga SAN-BON dake atte, konmori to HITOtsu no MORI o tsukutte iru. Sono AKA-MATSU no IP-PON ni aite iru JU-DOU ni, *fukurou* wa MAI-TOSHI HARU ni naru to SU o ITONANde ita.

BOKU ga kono SU-ANA o SHItta no ga SEN-KYUU-[HYAKU]-ROKU-[JUU]-NEN-DAI no KOU-HAN datta. I-RAI *fukurou* wa IKU-DAI ni mo watatte SE-DAI KOU-TAI o KUriKAEshinagara, MAI-TOSHI no you ni HAN-SHOKU to KO-SODAte o KUriKAEshite iru. Ittai BOKU ga SHIru NAN-NEN MAE kara kono JU-DOU de KO-SODAte o shite kita no darou. SAN-JUU-NEN CHIKAku ONAji SU-ANA o MItsuzukete ite mo, JU-DOU no yousu wa hotondo NANI mo HEN-KA shite inai no da. IS-SEI-KI I-JOU ni mo watatte TSUKAwarete iru kamo SHIrenai.

Aru TOSHI, *fukurou*DANI no AKA-MATSU SHUU-HEN no HAYASHI o NOKOshite, atari ICHI-MEN ga KOU-DAI na MEN-SEKI de BAS-SAI sareta. Sono BAS-SAI GEN-BA o MIte, BOKU wa *fukurou* no SATSU-EI to KAN-SATSU o OMOiTAtta.

An owl in Owl Valley photographed by Miyazaki Manabu.

Owl Valley Diary (An Excerpt)

Miyazaki Manabu

Owl valley is in the foothills of the many-layered ranges of the Southern Alps. From the
last house in Nakagawa town, Kami-Ina County, Nagano Prefecture, just when one has climbed up a forestry road
about 1.5 kilometers, there is a quiet valley surrounded all around by red pines and a variety of other trees.

Here, owls have been living from long ago.

The trees in which the owls of owl valley make their nests are at the summit of a mountain about
a 160-meter climb from the valley. They are pine trees whose age spans 200 to 300 years.
There are three huge red pines which, more so than the trees making up the surrounding forest, cut a strikingly
prominent figure, and make their own luxuriant grove. In a hollow opened in one of the red pines,
every year when it becomes spring, the owls open their nest for business.

When I first learned of this nest-hole, it was the latter half of the 1960's. Since then, across several
generations, while repeating the alternation of generations, the owls have reproduced and raised their
young every year. From how many years since before I knew of it have they been raising their young in the hollow
in this tree? Though I have continued to watch the same nest-hole for close to thirty years, the hollow's appearance
has hardly changed at all. It has perhaps been in use for even more
than a century.

One year, leaving the surrounding forest of the owl valley uncut, the whole area was forested over
a wide area. Looking at that forested site, I hit upon the idea of photographing and observing the owls.

- 植物・しょくぶつ: plants; vegetation
- 〜同士・どうし: fellow 〜; 〜 of the same kind
- 競争・きょうそう: competition
- 始まる・はじまる: to begin; start
- 主食・しゅしょく: main food source; staple
- ノネズミ: field mouse/mice
- まちがいなく・間違いなく: without mistake; for certain
- 増える・ふえる: to increase (in number)
- しかも: moreover
- 全体・ぜんたい: the whole; entirety
- 見渡す・みわたす: to look across (a large area)
- 止まり木・とまりぎ: a tree to stop/perch on
- 〜となる: to become; be transformed into
- 枯れ木・かれき: a dead, withered tree
- 立てる・たてる: to erect; stand something up
- 必ず・かならず: without fail
- 利用(りよう)する: to use; utilize
- 野外・やがい: outdoors; open-air
- スタジオ: a studio
- 建設・けんせつ: construction; building
- 沿う・そう: to run parallel to
- 電柱・でんちゅう: a telephone pole; pole with electric wires
- 電気・でんき: electricity; electric power
- 引く・ひく: to draw; install
- 夜間・やかん: nighttime
- 照明・しょうめい: illumination; lighting
- 施設・しせつ: facilities; equipment
- 小屋・こや: a hut; shack
- 掘っ立て小屋・ほったてごや: a temporary shack or hut
- 建てる・たてる: to build (a building); put up; erect
- 長期間・ちょうきかん: a long period
- そなえる・備える: to prepare for
- プロパンガス: propane (gas)
- 炊事道具・すいじどうぐ: cooking utensils; kitchenware
- …から…い(至)たるまで: from … to
- 生活・せいかつ: life; living
- 用具・ようぐ: equipment; tools; instruments
- そろえる・揃える: to assemble; equip; outfit
- なかなか: quite; pretty
- 快適・かいてき: comfortable; pleasant
- なるべく: as much as possible [= できるだけ]
- 形・かたち: form; shape
- 幾人・いくにん: several/many people
- 人手・ひとで: "people's hands"; workers; people
- かりる・借りる: to borrow
- 運ぶ・はこぶ: to carry; transport
- てっぺん: the top (of something); the highest point
- やって来(く)る: to come (here); turn up
- それなら: if so; if that's the case
- 教える・おしえる: to teach; inform
- センサー: a sensor
- 取り付ける・とりつける: to install
- ハイテク: high tech

- 装置・そうち: a device; an apparatus
- ほどこす・施す: to carry out; equip; furnish
- 見極め・みきわめ: an insight; foresight
- 思わぬ・おもわぬ: unexpected [ぬ = ない]
- 出遭う・であう: to meet; run into
- 街はずれ・まちはずれ: the outskirts of town
- 養鶏場・ようけいじょう: a poultry farm
- 建物・たてもの: a building; structure
- 横・よこ: the side
- 車・くるま: a car; automobile
- 通(とお)りかかる: to be about to pass by; be just passing by
- 前方・ぜんぽう: ahead; in front of
- 〜羽・わ: a counter for birds
- 鳥・とり: a bird
- 飛び立つ・とびたつ: to take flight
- ライト: a light; headlight
- 照らす・てらす: to shine upon; illuminate something
- 姿・すがた: a form; shape (usually of a body)
- 飛翔・ひしょう: flight; flying
- ぐあい・具合: condition; manner; way
- まぎれもなく・紛れも無く: without mistake
- 森・もり: a forest
- 暮らす・くらす: to live; make a living
- 夜行性・やこうせい: "night-roaming nature"; nocturnal
- 人里・ひとざと: human habitation; village
- こうこうと: brightly
- 明かり・あかり: light
- 驚き・おどろき: a surprise; shock
- 考える・かんがえる: to think; consider [考えてみれば = come to think of it]
- ニワトリ: chickens
- 餌・えさ: (chicken) feed; food
- 狙う・ねらう: to go after; aim for
- すみつく: to settle in (an area to live)
- 捕らえる・とらえる: to catch; seize
- 生きもの・いきもの: living things; animals; creatures
- たえず・絶えず: without stopping; endlessly
- 環境・かんきょう: environment; surroundings
- 適応(てきおう)する: to adapt to; respond to
- 生きる・いきる: to live
- たとえ〜であろうと: even if (something) is a 〜
- 人工物・じんこうぶつ: "man-made thing"; artificial thing
- 獲物・えもの: prey; quarry; game
- 野生・やせい: wild; untamed
- 遠慮(えんりょ)する: to hold back; refrain [せずに = しないで]
- 安心(あんしん)する: to be at ease; relax
- 来(き)やすい: easy to come
- ようにすれば: if (this) is done
- 自由に・じゆうに: freely
- 行動(こうどう)する: to act; behave
- 〜にちがいない・〜に違いない: there is no doubt that 〜
- こうして: in this way
- 構想・こうそう: a concept; idea; plan

　大きな木が伐採された跡地には、雑木の若い芽がいっせいに生えてきて植物同士の競争が始まり、フクロウの主食であるノネズミが、まちがいなく増えてくる。

　しかも、伐採でフクロウ谷全体を見渡すこともできるようになった。このようなところに、フクロウの止まり木となる枯れ木を立てれば、必ず利用するであろう。

　そう思ったときから、フクロウ谷の「野外スタジオ建設」が、始まった。

　林道に沿って電柱を立て、電気を引き、フクロウ谷全体を夜間でも見られるように、照明施設もつくった。フクロウを観察するための観察小屋も二つ建てた。小屋といっても名ばかりの小さな掘っ立て小屋だが、長期間の観察にそなえて、プロパンガスから炊事道具にいたるまで生活用具をそろえたなかなか快適な小屋でもある。

　なるべく形のよい木を見つけてきて、幾人もの人手をかりてフクロウ谷まで運んだ。枯れ木のてっぺんには、フクロウがやって来たことを教えてくれるセンサーを取り付けた。

　フクロウ谷に、こうしたハイテク撮影装置をほどこしたのには、一つの見極めがあった。

　今から十年以上前、僕は思わぬところでフクロウと出逢った。

　伊那谷のとある街はずれの、養鶏場の大きな建物の横を車で通りかかったときのことだ。前方の電柱の上から一羽の鳥が飛び立った。車のライトに照らされた姿は、大きさといい飛翔のぐあいといい、まぎれもなくフクロウのものだった。

　森で暮らす夜行性の鳥フクロウが、こんな人里の、しかもこうこうと明かりをともした養鶏場に来ているとは驚きだった。考えてみれば、ここにはニワトリたちの餌を狙ってたくさんのネズミたちがすみついている。それをフクロウは捕らえに来ていたのだ。

　生きものたちは、たえず変化する環境に適応しながら生きている。たとえ人工物であろうと、そこに獲物がたくさんいるのであれば、野生のフクロウも遠慮せずにやって来るのだ。

　それなら、観察のために建物を建て、照明で山ひとつ照らしてみても、フクロウは、安心して来やすいようにすれば、自由に行動してくれるにちがいない。

　こうして「フクロウ谷構想」は始まったのだ。

THE KAMIOKA NEUTRINO OBSERVATORY

Japan is also very active in the study of the fundamental natural phenomena that shape the universe. Thus, the Institute of Cosmic Ray Research of the University of Tokyo has been operating for over fifteen years a special observatory in an old zinc mine near the town of Kamioka in Gifu Prefecture, in the Japanese Alps. In this mine, a specially excavated cathedral-size cave was lined with over ten thousand large photoelectric sensors, filled with ultra-pure water, and thus converted into a huge volume capable of detecting the passage of neutrinos. These elusive elementary particles bring us information on the life cycle of stars, including our sun, and other mysteries of the universe. The Kamioka scientists, a team consisting of a hundred physicists from Japan and the United States, have recently made the momentous discovery that the neutrinos possess a mass. Although the neutrino mass is very small, their prevalence can solve what is known as the puzzle of the missing mass in the universe. The balance of mass and radiation is of paramount importance for understanding the nature, history, and future of the universe.

The Kamioka Neutrino Observatory is also helping to study the processes going on in our sun, and to detect supernovae—stars which suddenly flash with great brilliance in the deep reaches of space. Eventually, it may also answer the question for which it was built in the first place: is the proton, a primary constituent of all matter in the world, stable?

As is always the case with pure research at the frontiers of science, the technological by-products of the Kamioka experiment, as well as of other fundamental research in physics carried out in Japan, are also of great benefit to the high-technology sector of Japanese industry.

The Kamioka Neutrino Observatory under construction.

OOkina KI ga BAS-SAI sareta ATO-CHI ni wa, ZOU-KI no WAKAi ME ga issei ni HAete kite SHOKU-BUTSU DOU-SHI no KYOU-SOU ga HAJImari, *fukurou* no SHU-SHOKU de aru *nonezumi* ga, machigai naku FUete kuru.

Shikamo, BAS-SAI de *fukurou*DANI ZEN-TAI o MI-WATAsu koto mo dekiru you ni natta. Kono you na tokoro ni, *fukuruo* no TOmariGI to naru KAreKI o TAtereba, KANARAzu RI-YOU suru de arou.

Sou OMOtta toki kara, *fukurou*DANI no "YA-GAI *sutajio* KEN-SETSU" ga, HAJImatta.

RIN-DOU ni SOtte DEN-CHUU o TAte, DEN-KI o HIki, *fukurou*DANI ZEN-TAI o YA-KAN de mo MIrareru you ni, SHOU-MEI SHI-SETSU mo tsukutta. *Fukurou* o KAN-SATSU suru tame no KAN-SATSU GO-YA mo FUTAtsu TAteta. KO-YA to itte mo NA bakari no CHIIsana HOtTAte-GO-YA da ga, CHOU-KI-KAN no KAN-SATSU ni sonaete, *puropangasu* kara SUI-JI DOU-GU ni itaru made SEI-KATSU YOU-GU o soroeta nakanaka KAI-TEKI na KO-YA de mo aru.

Narubeku KATACHI no yoi KI o MItsukete kite, IKU-NIN mo no HITO-DE o karite *fukurou*DANI made HAKOnda. KAreKI no teppen ni wa, *fukurou* ga yatte KIta koto o OSHIete kureru *sensaa* o TOriTSUketa.

*Fukurou*DANI ni, koushita *haiteku* SATSU-EI SOU-CHI o hodokoshita no ni wa, HITOtsu no MI-KIWAme ga atta.

IMA kara JUU-NEN I-JOU MAE, BOKU wa OMOwanu tokoro de *fukurou* to DE-Atta.

I-NA-DANI no to aru MACHIhazure no, YOU-KEI-JOU no OOkina TATE-MONO no YOKO o KURUMA de TOOrikakatta toki no koto da. ZEN-POU no DEN-CHUU no UE kara ICHI-WA no TORI ga TObiTAtta. KURUMA no *raito* ni TErasareta SUGATA wa, OOkisa to ii HI-SHOU no guai to ii, magiremonaku *fukurou* no mono datta.

MORI de KUrasu YA-KOU-SEI no TORI *fukurou* ga, konna HITO-ZATO no, shikamo koukou to Akari o tomoshita YOU-KEI-JOU ni KIte iru to wa ODOROki datta. KANGAete mireba, koko ni wa *niwatori*tachi no ESA o NERAtte takusan no *nezumi*tachi ga sumitsuite iru. Sore o *fukurou* wa TOrae ni KIte ita no da.

Ikimonotachi wa, taezu HEN-KA suru KAN-KYOU ni TEKI-OU shinagara Ikite iru. Tatoe JIN-KOU-BUTSU de arou to, soko ni E-MONO ga takusan iru no de areba, YA-SEI no *fukurou* mo EN-RYO sezu ni yatte KUru no da.

Sore nara, KAN-SATSU no tame ni TATE-MONO o TAte, SHOU-MEI de YAMA hitotsu TErashite mite mo, *fukurou* wa, AN-SHIN shite KIyasui you ni sureba, JI-YUU ni KOU-DOU shite kureru ni chigainai.

Koushite "*fukurou*DANI KOU-SOU" wa HAJImatta no da.

慣用句: Idiomatic Expressions I

Translate the following into idiomatic English

1. 巣を営む

母フクロウは胸の羽毛をふっくらと毛布のようにふくらませてヒナを守りながら赤松の中で<u>巣を営んでいる</u>。

2. (〜と)思い立つ

毎日フクロウの生活を観察しているうちに僕はその観察を「フクロウ谷日記」にしょうと<u>思い立った</u>。

3. 名ばかりの〜

「フクロウ谷構想」といってもはじめは<u>名ばかりの</u>もので、山の掘っ立て小屋からフクロウを観察するだけだった。

4. (〜に)そなえる

<u>寒さにそなえて</u>母フクロウは、生まれたばかりのヒナの保温には卵のとき以上に神経を使っている。

5. 人手をかりる

名ばかりの「野外スタジオ」ではあったが、ハイテク照明装置をほどこすには幾人かの<u>人手をかり</u>なければならなかった。

6. まぎれもなく

親鳥が食べている小さい塊は<u>まぎれもなく</u>ヒナの糞だった。

In the area where large trees were cut down, the many different trees' young buds had all grown at once and the competition among plants had begun, and the [number of] field mice, the staple of the owls' diet, would doubtless increase.

Moreover, with the foresting it had become possible to look across the entire owl valley. In this kind of place, if one stood up a withered tree for owls to perch on, they would certainly use it.

From the time I though of that, the "outdoor studio construction" of the owl valley began.

Along the forestry road I put up poles for power lines, drew electricity, and made a lighting set-up so that I could see the whole of the owl valley even at night. In order to observe the owls I built two observation huts. Even calling it a "hut," it is only a small make-shift hovel, but it is also a comfortable hut prepared for long periods of observation, set up with a variety of tools for living.

I found a large dead tree with the best shape possible, and, borrowing hands of several others, carried it to owl valley. On top of the dead tree I installed a sensor which would tell me that an owl had come.

Behind putting up these kinds of high-tech devices in owl valley, there was a single bit of foresight.

It was more than ten years before now that I had a meeting with an owl in an unexpected place.

It happened on the outskirts of Inadani Valley just as I passed along the side of a large building of a poultry farm in my car. From the top of a telephone pole ahead, a single bird took off in flight. The figure illuminated by the car lights was, from the size and manner of flight, without mistake that of an owl.

That an owl, a nocturnal bird living in the forest, would be coming to this sort of human habitation, and moreover to a brightly lit poultry farm, was a surprise. I realized that there were many mice living here who were after the feed of the chickens. That is what the owl had come to catch.

Animals live while responding to an endlessly changing environment. Even if something is man-made, if there is a lot of prey there, even wild owls will come without any reservation.

In that case, even if I built buildings for observation purposes, even if I lit up the entire mountain with lights, the owls, as long as I made it easy for them to be at ease coming [to the area], would without a doubt freely go about their business for me.

In this way, the "owl valley plan" was started.

- 晴れ・はれ: clear; sunny
- のち・後: afterwards; and then
- 雪・ゆき: snow
- (三日)かける(掛ける): to take (three days' time)
- ヒナ: a chick; newly hatched bird
- 全員・ぜんいん: all; everyone (of a group)
- 生(う)まれる: to be born; be hatched
- 卵・たまご: an egg [as food, often written 玉子]
- 〜とはいえ: "even if/though one says 〜"; although; but
- とても: very
- か弱い・かよわい: delicate; fragile [the prefix か adds emphasis to adjs.]
- 以上・いじょう: more than
- 母親・ははおや: "mother parent"; a mother
- 神経(しんけい)をつかう: "to use one's nerves"; worry about; be on edge; be on pins and needles over
- まるで: "entirely"; as if [followed by a figure of speech]
- 腫(は)れもの: a swelling; an inflammation
- さわる(触る): to touch
- 扱う・あつかう: to deal with; treat
- 鋭い・するどい: sharp; pointy
- 爪・つめ: claws: nails
- 傷(きず)つける: to injure; harm; wound [ぬ = ない]
- よう: so as to [= ように]
- 歩く・あるく: to walk
- きわめて・極めて: extremely
- 慎重・しんちょう: careful; cautious
- 胸・むね: chest; breast
- いつも: always
- 温める・あたためる: to warm; heat
- 親鳥・おやどり: parent bird
- 保温・ほおん: keeping heat in; retaining warmth
- 凍え死ぬ・こごえしぬ: to freeze to death
- むしろ: rather; if anything
- 殻・から: a shell
- ガード: a guard; protection
- ぶん: proportion; extent
- 寒さ・さむさ: the cold [〜さ in place of い nominalizes adjs.]
- だから: that's why; so
- 羽毛・うもう: feathers; down
- ふっくらと: describes something full or plump
- 毛布・もうふ: a blanket
- ふくらます・膨ます: to puff up; swell
- 守り続ける・まもりつづける: to continue to protect/guard
- そんな: such; that sort [= そのような]
- 糞・ふん: dung; droppings
- すべて・全て: all; everything
- 自分・じぶん: self; oneself
- 処理(しょり)する: to dispose of
- 不潔・ふけつ: unclean; dirty; filthy
- 病原菌・びょうげんきん: disease-causing bacteria [菌・きん = bacteria]
- 発生(はっせい)する: to be produced; break out
- 〜ともかぎらない: it is not always the case that 〜
- 生きる知恵・いきるちえ: wisdom for living (survival)

- そのために: for that purpose; to that end
- 塊・かたまり: a lump; pellet
- 食(た)べやすい: easy to eat
- 排泄(はいせつ)する: to excrete
- 猛禽類・もうきんるい: order Raptores; birds of prey
- ワシ・鷲: eagle
- タカ・鷹: hawk
- ペンキ: house paint
- 水溶性・すいようせい: water-soluble
- 根本的・こんぽんてき: fundamental
- ちがう: to be different
- それぞれ: respective; each
- 〜にまで: even (including) 〜
- 理由(りゆう)づけをする: to provide a reason
- してある: there is (a reason)
- 〜みたいだ: there seems 〜
- 雨・あめ: rain
- 曇り・くもり: cloudy
- 巣立つ・すだつ: to leave the nest
- かえる: to hatch
- 一ヵ月・いっかげつ: one month
- ほぼ: almost; nearly
- 翼・つばさ: wings
- バランスをとる: to keep balance
- 内側・うちがわ: the inside (of 〜)
- よじ登る・よじのぼる: to crawl/clamber up
- 足指・あしゆび: toes
- 幹・みき: a (tree) trunk
- 飛ぶ・とぶ: to fly
- 〜だけの: here, (just) enough (strength to fly)
- 飛翔力・ひしょうりょく: strength to fly
- そのぶん: to that degree; in that extent
- 相当・そうとう: considerable
- 一夜・いちや: one night
- 〜のうちに: during 〜
- 移動(いどう)する: to move; travel
- だって: even
- 枝・えだ: a branch
- 気に入る・きにいる: to take a liking to
- 陣どる・じんどる: to take up position; encamp
- めがける・目掛ける: to set one's sights on; aim at
- 進入(しんにゅう)する: to advance into
- コース: a course; path
- 集まる・あつまる: to come together; assemble (at a place)
- 少しでも・すこしでも: even a little
- 多く・おおく: more; a lot [noun]
- ありつく: to get; come by
- 啼く・なく: to cry [cf. 泣く・なく in reference to human beings]
- 位置・いち: a place; position
- 声・こえ: a voice; cry
- 知らせる・しらせる: to inform; tell of
- にわかに: suddenly; unexpectedly; abruptly
- 騒がしい・さわがしい: noisy; boisterous

4月5日 晴れのち雪

　三日かけて、ヒナは全員生まれてきた。卵ではなくなったとはいえ、このころのヒナはとてもか弱い。卵のとき以上に、母親は神経を使っている。まるで腫（は）れものにさわるように扱う。鋭い爪でヒナを傷つけぬよう、歩くときなどはきわめて慎重だ。

　ヒナは母親の胸のなかでいつも温められている。親鳥からの保温がなければ、凍（こご）え死んでしまう。むしろ卵の殻というガードがなくなったぶん寒さには弱い。だから母親は胸の羽毛をふっくらと毛布のようにふくらませて、ヒナたちを守り続ける。

　そんな母親だから、ヒナの糞などはすべて自分が食べて処理してしまう。巣のなかが不潔になると、思わぬ病原菌が発生しないともかぎらない。だれが教えたわけでもない、母フクロウの生きる知恵である。そのために、ヒナも考えてそうしているわけではないが、糞は小さな塊（かたまり）として、母親が食べやすいように排泄（はいせつ）されてくる。

　これは、同じ猛禽類（もうきんるい）のワシやタカたちがする、ペンキのような水溶性の糞とは根本的にちがっている。それぞれの生き方に合わせて、糞にまで理由づけをしてあるみたいだ。

5月7日 雨のち曇り

　今日、フクロウのヒナが巣立った。卵からかえって、ほぼ一ヵ月である。

　翼でバランスをとりながら樹洞の内側をよじ登り、巣穴を出てから、足指を使って木の幹をよじ登っていく。ヒナにはまだ飛べるだけの飛翔（ひしょう）力はないが、そのぶん足の力は相当あるようだ。一夜のうちに五十〜百メートルも移動してしまうことだってある。

　巣立ったヒナは高い木の枝の、それぞれ気に入ったところに陣どる。といっても獲物を運んで帰ってくる親が、フクロウ谷めがけて進入してくるコースに集まることになる。だから、少しでも多くの獲物にありつきたいために、ヒナはよく啼（な）く。自分のいる位置を、その声で親に知らせているのだ。フクロウ谷は、にわかに騒がしくなった。

慣用句: Idiomatic Expressions II
Translate the following into idiomatic English

7. こうこうと明かりをともす

電柱を立て、電気を引き、<u>こうこうと明かりをともす</u>と夜間でもフクロウ谷全体の撮影ができるようになった。

8. 棲みつく

フクロウは一世紀以上も、このフクロウ谷に<u>棲みついて</u>繁殖を繰り返しているようだ。

9. たとえ〜であろうと

巣の中に病原菌が発生しないように、<u>たとえ</u>ヒナの糞<u>であろうと</u>親鳥はそれを食べて処理してしまう。

10. まるで腫れ物にさわるように

卵からかえったばかりのヒナを母フクロウは<u>まるで腫れ物にさわるように</u>慎重に扱い育てる。

11. (〜しない)ともかぎらない

鋭い爪を持つ親フクロウが生まれたばかりのヒナを傷つけない<u>ともかぎらない</u>だろうと、僕は親鳥の行動を慎重に観察しつづけた。

12. 獲物にありつく

フクロウは<u>獲物にありつこう</u>と、人里に近い養鶏場にまでやって来ていた。

SHI-GATSU ITSU-KA HAre nochi YUKI

MIK-KA kakete, *hina* wa ZEN-IN Umarete kita. TAMAGO de wa naku natta to wa ie, kono koro no *hina* wa totemo kaYOWAi. TAMAGO no toki I-JOU ni, HAHA-OYA wa SHIN-KEI o TSUKAtte iru.
Marude HAremono ni sawaru you ni ATSUKAu. SURUDOi TSUME de *hina* o KIZUtsukenu you, ARUku
toki nado wa kiwamete SHIN-CHOU da.

Hina wa HAHA-OYA no MUNE no naka de itsumo ATATAmerarete iru. OYA-DORI kara no HO-ON ga nakereba, KOGOeSHInde shimau. Mushiro TAMAGO no KARA to iu *gaado* ga nakunatta bun SAMU-
sa ni wa YOWAi. Dakara HAHA-OYA wa MUNE no U-MOU o fukkura to MOU-FU no you ni fukuramase-
te, *hina*tachi o MAMOriTSUZUkeru.

Sonna HAHA-OYA da kara, *hina* no FUN nado wa subete JI-BUN ga TAbete SHO-RI shite shimau.
SU no naka ga FU-KETSU ni naru to, OMOwanu BYOU-GEN-KIN ga HAS-SEI shinai to mo kagiranai. Dare ga OSHIeta wake de mo nai, HAHA *fukurou* no Ikiru CHI-E de aru. Sono tame ni,
hina mo KANGAete sou shite iru wake de wa nai ga, FUN wa CHIIsana KATAMARI toshite, HAHA-OYA ga
TAbeyasui you ni HAI-SETSU sarete kuru.

Kore wa, ONAji MOU-KIN-RUI no *washi* ya *taka* tachi ga suru, *penki* no you na SUI-YOU-SEI no
FUN to wa KON-PON-TEKI ni chigatte iru. Sorezore no IkiKATA ni Awasete, FUN ni made RI-
YUUzuke o shite aru mitai da.

GO-GATSU NANO-KA AME nochi KUMOri

KYOU, *fukurou* no *hina* ga SU-DAtta. TAMAGO kara kaette, hobo IK-KA-GETSU de aru.

TSUBASA de *baransu* o torinagara JU-DOU no UCHI-GAWA o yojiNOBOri, SU-ANA o DEte kara, ASHI-
YUBI o TSUKAtte KI no MIKI o yojiNOBOtte iku. *Hina* ni wa mada TOberu dake no HI-SHOU-RYOKU wa
nai ga, sono bun ASHI no CHIKARA wa SOU-TOU aru you da. ICHI-YA no uchi ni GO-JUU ~ HYAKU *meeto-
ru* mo I-DOU shite shimau koto datte aru.

SU-DAtta *hina* wa TAKAi KI no EDA no, sorezore KI ni Itta tokoro ni JINdoru. To
itte mo E-MONO o HAKOnde KAEtte kuru OYA ga, *fukurou*DANI megakete SHIN-NYUU shite kuru
koosu ni ATSUmaru koto ni naru. Dakara, SUKOshi de mo OOku no E-MONO ni aritsukitai
tame ni, *hina* wa yoku NAku. JI-BUN no iru I-CHI o, sono KOE de OYA ni SHIrasete iru
no da. *Fukurou* DANI wa, niwaka ni SAWAgashiku natta.

━━∿━━

内容理解: Comprehension Exercises

Answer in Japanese

1. フクロウ谷はどんなところにありますか。
2. フクロウはいつ、どんなところで巣を営むのですか。
3. フクロウの撮影と観察のためにどのような「野外スタジオ」が建設されましたか。
4. 筆者が夜行性のフクロウの観察と撮影にハイテク照明装置をほどこしてもいいだろうと考えたのはどうしてですか。
5. ヒナを守る母フクロウの「知恵」について筆者はどのような観察をしていますか。
6. フクロウのヒナが卵からかえって巣立つまでにはどのぐらいかかりますか。
7. まだ飛翔力のない、巣立ったばかりのヒナはどのようにして木や林の中を移動するのですか。
8. 巣立ったヒナたちはどんなところに陣どって騒がしく啼くのでしょうか。それはどうしてですか。

練習問題: Exercises

True or False ?

1. フクロウ谷のフクロウが毎年巣を営み、子育てをするようになったのは1960年代の後半からである。
2. 夜行性のフクロウは、こうこうと明かりをともした人里にはやって来ない。
3. 生まれたばかりのヒナたちは、巣の中が不潔にならないように自分たちの排泄物を自分たちで処理するという生きる知恵を持っている。
4. 巣立ったヒナたちは、母親の運んでくる獲物にありつくために自分のいる位置を親に知らせようと、よく啼く。

April 5: Clear, later snow

In three days the chicks have all been born. Though they are no longer eggs, the chicks at this period are very weak. Even more than when in the egg, the mother uses painstaking care. She treats them [tenderly] as if she were touching a swollen area. When she walks about in such a way so as to not wound the chicks with her sharp talons, she is extremely cautious.

The chicks are always being kept warm in their mother's breast. Without the warmth from the mother bird they will freeze and die. If anything, they are weaker against the cold to the extent that they have lost the protection of the shell of their eggs. Thus, the mother puffs up the feathers of her breast like a blanket and continues to protect the chicks.

Being that kind of mother, she disposes of all the chicks' droppings and such by eating them herself. If the inside of the nest grows unclean, unexpected bacterial sources of disease may be produced. It is not that anyone taught her. It is the wisdom for living of the mother owl. For that reason, though the chicks are not doing so because they have thought about it, the droppings are small lumps, excreted so that they are easy for the mother to consume.

This is fundamentally different from the paint-like watery dung made by other raptors such as eagles and hawks. In accordance with each way of living, even droppings seem to have a reason [for being as they are].

May 7: Rain, later cloudy

Today the owl chicks have left their nest. From their hatching from their eggs, about a month has passed.

While keeping their balance with their wings, they scale the inside of the tree hollow, and after they emerge from the nest-hole, they clamber up the tree trunk using their talons. The chicks still do not have enough strength to fly, but to make up for that the strength of their feet seems considerable. During a night they even move around some fifty to one hundred meters.

Chicks that have left the nest position themselves on high tree branches in various places they take a liking to. But even having said this, they end up gathering on the course taken by the parent carrying back the spoils when entering the area coming toward owl valley. Thus, in order to come by even a little more of the spoils, the chicks often cry out. With that voice they inform the parent of their position. Suddenly owl valley has become clamorous.

語句と語法: Phrases and Usage

- 夏・なつ: summer
- 花・はな: a flower
- 抄・しょう: excerpt
- 私・わたし: I
- 街・まち: town [in contrast to 町, which is also read まち and means "town," 街 tends to connote the hustle and bustle of town life]
- 街に出て花を買うと…: と here has the meaning of "upon"; i.e., "upon going to town and buying some flowers…."
- 妻・つま: wife [one's own or used objectively of wives in general]
- 墓・はか: a grave; tomb
- 訪れる・おとずれる: to visit
- 訪(おとず)れようと思(おも)った: I thought I would visit
- ポケット: a pocket
- 仏壇・ぶつだん: a small Buddhist altar in the home, gilded or lacquered. Food, incense and candles are offered to the ancestral dead whose names are written on small wooden plaques placed in the altar.
- 線香・せんこう: small incense sticks for use at funerals, graves, and in the 仏壇.
- 一束・ひとたば: one packet [束 is a counter for bundles of long slender objects]
- にとって: for (my wife)
- 初盆・はつぼん: first Obon following a person's death [お盆・おぼん is the (religious) Festival of Lanterns, usually from the thirteenth to the fifteenth of July (in August in some areas). Prayers and lights guide the spirits of the family dead back to their homes. Hara's wife died of illness in the fall of the previous year, 1944.
- 〜に当たる・あたる: to correspond to; fall on
- それまで: until then
- ふるさと・古里: one's home town; place where one's roots are
- 無事・ぶじ: safe; safe and sound
- かどうか: whether or not
- 疑わしい・うたがわしい: doubtful; questionable
- ちょうど: exactly; precisely [modifying あった]
- 休電日・きゅうでんび: "electricty intermission day" [from the middle to the end of WWII limits were set on electricity use in order to cope with power shortages, especially in industrial areas]
- ではあったが: は approximates "admittedly"; "although 〜" [puts emphasis on the verb "to be": "it was a day when …"]
- 朝から・あさから: "from the morning"; in the morning (with emphasis on the earliness of the hour)
- 持つ・もつ: to carry
- 街を歩く・まちをあるく: to walk around town [を indicates the location where an action is carried out]
- 男・おとこ: a man
- 〜のほかに: other than 〜
- 見(み)あたる: to see; come across; find [usually in the negative]
- 何という名称か・なんというめいしょうか: what their name was
- 黄色・きいろ: yellow
- 小弁・こべん: a small petal
- 可憐・かれん: cute, pretty, or lovely with a touching quality
- 野趣・やしゅ: a rural, natural, simple character or flavor

- 帯びる・おびる: to possess a certain characteristic, trait, or atmosphere
- いかにも: truly; just (like)
- noun らしい: typically; a true 〜; worthy of being (called) [らしい often describes things or conditions that are apparently true, but here it describes something that is an ideal of its kind]
- 炎天・えんてん: burning sun [炎: flame; 天: heaven, sky]
- にさらす: to expose to
- 墓石・ぼせき: a gravestone [usually upright and narrow, sometimes like small pillars, with etched characters that read from top to bottom]
- 水を打つ・みずをうつ: to pour water over [here 打つ is used instead of the more banal かける]
- 二つに分ける・ふたつにわける: to divide into two portions
- 左右・さゆう: left and right
- 花立て・はなだて: a container for holding flowers; loosely, flower vase
- 挿す・さす: to insert; put into [note that there are many verbs read さす that are written with different characters, each with a different meaning or nuance (cf. 挿, 刺, 差, 指)]
- 面・おもて: (front) surface
- なんとなく: somehow; in some vague way
- すがすがしい: refreshing
- しばらく: for a while
- 石・いし: stone [i.e., the gravestone]
- 見入る・みいる: to stare at intently; gaze at
- 墓の下・はかのした: "below the grave" [i.e., below the gravestone]
- ばかりか: not only
- 父母・ふぼ: father and mother; one's parents
- 骨・ほね: bones, remains
- 納まる・おさまる: to lie; rest; be ensconced
- マッチをつける: to light a match
- 黙礼・もくれい: a silent bow showing respect
- 済ます・すます: to finish; complete
- かたわら: (located) at one side; nearby
- 井戸・いど: a well
- 飲む・のむ: to drink
- それから: after that
- 饒津公園・にぎつこうえん: a park containing Nigitsu Shrine; destroyed during the war and never rebuilt due to urbanization
- ほう・方: direction; in the direction (of); toward
- を回る・まわる: to go around [the particle を is used here to mark a place traveled or walked through]
- 家・いえ: home
- 戻る・もどる: to return
- その日(ひ)もその翌日(よくじつ)も: both that day and the following day, too
- におい: a smell
- しみ込(こ)む・染み込む: to sink into; permeate
- 原子・げんし: atom
- 爆弾・ばくだん: bomb
- 襲う・おそう: to attack; assault; assail

夏の花 (抄)

原民喜

　私は街に出て花を買うと、妻の墓を訪れようと思った。ポケットには仏壇から取り出した線香が一束あった。八月十五日は妻にとって初盆に当たるのだが、それまでこのふるさとの街が無事かどうかは疑わしかった。ちょうど、休電日ではあったが、朝から花を持って街を歩いている男は、私のほかに見あたらなかった。その花はなんという名称なのか知らないが、黄色の小弁の可憐な野趣を帯び、いかにも夏の花らしかった。

　炎天にさらされている墓石に水を打ち、その花を二つに分けて左右の花立てに挿すと、墓の面がなんとなくすがすがしくなったようで、私はしばらく花と石に見入った。この墓の下には、妻ばかりか、父母の骨も納まっているのだった。持ってきた線香にマッチをつけ、黙礼を済ますと、私はかたわらの井戸で水を飲んだ。それから、饒津公園のほうを回って家に戻ったのであるが、その日も、その翌日も、私のポケットは線香のにおいがしみ込んでいた。原子爆弾に襲われたのは、その

Hara Tamiki

Hara Tamiki was born in Hiroshima in 1905. He attended the prestigious Keio University and graduated with a degree in English literature. He was influenced by Dadaism and Marxism in the early 1930s and published short stories and poems in the college literary magazines. By 1936 he was a regular contributor to the journal *Mita Bungaku*. From 1942 to 1944 he taught English in Chiba Prefecture. On August 6th he was in Hiroshima at his brother's house when the atomic bomb was dropped. He was a witness to the horrors of "that day." His friends noted that he rarely ever spoke of what he had seen. He committed suicide in 1951, haunted by the fear of war in Korea and the recurring visions of the hell he was caught in during the bombing of Hiroshima.

Hara Tamiki wrote *Natsu no Hana* in 1947, at a time when the people of Hiroshima were still numbed and disoriented. His legacy is to have broken that silence through lucid writing.

Natsu no Hana won him the first Minakami Takitarō Prize. The juxtaposition of peaceful images from everyday life—flowers and incense—with the destruction that follows is particularly chilling. In 1951, just before his suicide, he completed *Shingan no Kuni* ("The Land of One's Desire"). Hara is most remembered as a "writer of the atomic bomb."

Natsu no Hana, as presented here, is an excerpt of a version that appears in high school textbooks, in which the second paragraph from the bottom of page 245 was abridged. This paragraph was printed in slightly smaller type in the textbook version.

NATSU no HANA (SHOU)

HARA TAMI-KI

WATASHI wa MACHI ni DEte HANA o KAu to, TSUMA no HAKA o OTOZUreyou to

OMOtta. *Poketto* ni wa BUTSU-DAN kara TOriDAshita SEN-KOU ga

HITO-TABA atta. HACHI-GATSU JUU-GO-NICHI wa TSUMA ni totte HATSU-BON ni Ata-

ru no da ga, sore made kono furusato no MACHI ga BU-JI ka do-

u ka wa UTAGAwashikatta. Choudo, KYUU-DEN-BI de wa at-

ta ga, ASA kara HANA o MOtte MACHI o ARUite iru OTOKO wa, WATASHI

no hoka ni MIataranakatta. Sono HANA wa nan to iu

MEI-SHOU na no ka SHIranai ga, KI-IRO no KO-BEN no KA-REN na YA-SHU

o Obi, ikanimo NATSU no HANA rashikatta.

EN-TEN ni sarasarete iru BO-SEKI ni MIZU o Uchi, sono HANA

o FUTAtsu ni WAkete SA-YUU no HANA-TAte ni SAsu to, HAKA no OMOTE ga

nan to naku sugasugashiku natta you de, WATASHI wa shiba-

raku HANA to ISHI ni MI-Itta. Kono HAKA no SHITA ni wa, TSUMA baka-

ri ka, FU-BO no HONE mo OSAmatte iru no datta. MOtte

kita SEN-KOU ni *matchi* o tsuke, MOKU-REI o SUmasu to, WATASHI wa

katawara no I-DO de MIZU o NOnda. Sore kara, NIGI-TSU-KOU-

EN no hou o MAWAtte IE ni MODOtta no de aru ga, sono HI

mo, sono YOKU-JITSU mo, WATASHI no *poketto* wa SEN-KOU no nioi ga

shimiKOnde ita. GEN-SHI-BAKU-DAN ni OSOwareta no wa, sono

Gravestones and memorial staves at a Buddhist temple.

Flowers of Summer (An Excerpt)

Hara Tamiki

Having gone to town and bought some flowers, I thought I'd visit my wife's
grave. I had a packet of incense in my pocket which I had taken from our Buddhist altar. August fifteenth would be the first Bon festival since my wife's
passing, but whether or not this town of her birth would remain unscathed
until then was uncertain. Though it happened to be a day when the power was being
rationed, other than myself I didn't see any men with flowers out walking about
town that morning. I don't know what the names of those
flowers were, but they had small yellow petals with a sweet rural beauty
to them, and were as flowers of summer should be.

I poured some water on the gravestone, which stood exposed to the scorching sun and,
dividing the flowers into two bunches, put them in the flower holders on the right and left. The face
of the grave seemed somehow to have become refreshed, and for a while I
gazed intently at the flowers and the stone. Below the gravestone were the remains
of not only my wife but also of my parents. I set
a match to the incense I had brought, and after a silent bow I
drank some water from the nearby well. After that, I
returned home by way of Nigitsu park. That day
and the next day, the scent of the incense
permeated my pocket. The day we were hit by the atomic bomb

- 翌々日・よくよくじつ: the day after next
- 厠・かわや: (archaic) a toilet
- 一命を拾う・いちめいをひろう: to escape with one's life
- ごろ: about
- 床を離れる・とこをはなれる: "to leave one's place of sleep"; to get out of bed
- 前の晩・まえのばん: the night before
- 二回・にかい: two times; twice
- 空襲警報・くうしゅうけいほう: an air-raid siren ["warning"]
- 出・で: stem of the verb 出る (to go forth; be issued)
- 何事(なにごと)も～ない: there is nothing eventful
- 夜明け前・よあけまえ: dawn
- 服・ふく: clothing
- 全部・ぜんぶ: all; completely
- 脱ぐ・ぬぐ: to take off (clothing)
- 久(ひさ)しぶりに: (for the first time) in quite a while
- 寝巻き・ねまき: light gown-like nightclothes secured loosely around the waist with a sash
- 着替える・きがえる: to change clothes
- 眠る・ねむる: to sleep; go to sleep
- それで: and so
- 起き出す・おきだす: to get up (out of bed)
- パンツ: underpants
- 一つ・ひとつ: "one"; only [here, 一つ is used to indicate that he was *only* in his underpants, having taken off his 寝巻き]
- 妹・いもうと: a younger sister
- 姿・すがた: form; appearance; the way one looks
- 見る・みる: to see
- ぶつぶつ: muttering, grumbling; under one's breath [onomatopoeia]
- 難じる・なんじる: to criticize; find fault with
- 黙る・だまる: to keep quiet; not say anything
- 便所・べんじょ: toilet; privy
- 入る・はいる: to go into
- 何秒後・なんびょうご: after how many seconds
- こと: happening; event
- はっきりする: to be clear; certain
- 突然・とつぜん: suddenly; all of a sudden
- 頭上・ずじょう: one's head [also, overhead]
- 一撃を加える・いちげきをくわえる: to deal a blow
- 目(め)の前(まえ)に: before one's (very) eyes
- 暗闇・くらやみ: darkness
- 滑り落ちる・すべりおちる: to slide down; come sliding down
- 思わず・おもわず: "without thinking"; unconsciously
- うわあ: uwaah [his scream; a more realistic variation of the standard わあ, which the author emphasizes by superior dots]
- わめく・喚く: to shriek; scream; cry out
- 頭・あたま: head
- 手(て)をやる: to place one's hand on
- 立(た)ち上(あ)がる: to stand up; get up
- 嵐・あらし: storm
- ～のようなもの: something like a ～
- 墜落(ついらく)する: to fall from the sky; crash (often in reference to airplanes)
- 音・おと: sound
- ～のほか: other than ～

- 真っ暗・まっくら: pitch dark [cf. 真っ赤(まっか) bright red]
- 何も・なにも: nothing; nothing at all
- わかる: to know; tell; make out
- 手探り・てさぐり: searching with one's hand; groping
- 扉・とびら: a door
- 縁側・えんがわ: loosely translated as "veranda" [often enclosed with glass doors and sliding doors which, when closed, create a hallway and, when opened, a neutral space between inside and outside where, for example, people can sit and chat without actually coming into the privacy of the home]
- そのときまで: until that time
- 自分・じぶん: oneself; one's self
- 声・こえ: voice
- ザアー: a rushing or roaring sound
- 物音・ものおと: "sound of an object"; sound [usually refers to the sound of objects that are out of eyesight]
- はっきり: clearly [could also have been written はっきりと]
- 耳に聞く・みみにきく: "to hear with the ears": to hear [the seeming redundancy of "hear" and "ears" is a form of emphasis]
- 目(め)が見(み)える: to be able to see
- もだえる・悶える: to be in agony; writhe in agony
- しかし: but, however
- まもなく・間もなく: soon; before long
- 薄ら明かり・うすらあかり: a faint light [薄ら is attached to a number of words to add the meaning of "slight" or "faint"]
- 破壊(はかい)する: to destroy; demolish
- 家屋・かおく: house(s)
- 浮(う)かび出(だ)す: "to float forth"; rise up; emerge
- 気持ち・きもち: feelings; emotional and mental state of being
- はっきりする: to clear up; become lucid
- それは: that [referring to the whole situation just described]
- ひどい: terrible
- 嫌・いや: awful
- 夢・ゆめ: a dream
- 出来事・できごと: happening; event
- 似る・にる: to resemble
- 最初・さいしょ: at first
- 倒れる・たおれる: to fall down
- 知る・しる: to know; realize; find out
- 面倒・めんどう: bothersome; irksome; tedious
- 思う・おもう: to think
- 腹立たしい・はらだたしい: exasperating; annoying
- そして: and
- 叫ぶ・さけぶ: to shout out; yell
- なんだか: somehow
- 別人・べつじん: someone else; another person
- 聞(き)こえる: to sound (like)
- 辺り・あたり: surroundings; area around one
- 様子・ようす: appearance; condition
- おぼろげながら: "while in a haze"; dimly; vaguely
- 目(め)に見(み)えだす: to become visible; come to view [verb + だす(出す) = to begin/start to (verb)]
- 今度・こんど: this time
- 惨劇・さんげき: a tragedy; disastrous event
- 舞台・ぶたい: stage; scene
- 立(た)つ: to stand

翌々日のことであった。

　私は厠にいたため一命を拾った。八月六日の朝、私は八時ごろ床を離れた。前の晩二回も空襲警報が出、何事もなかったので、夜明け前には服を全部脱いで、久しぶりに寝巻きに着替えて眠った。それで、起き出したときもパンツ一つであった。妹はこの姿を見ると、朝寝したことをぶつぶつ難じていたが、私は黙って便所へ入った。

　それから何秒後のことかはっきりしないが、突然、私の頭上に一撃が加えられ、目の前に暗闇が滑り落ちた。私は思わずうわあとわめき、頭に手をやって立ち上がった。嵐のようなものの墜落する音のほかは真っ暗で何もわからない。手探りで扉を開けると、縁側があった。そのときまで、私はうわあという自分の声を、ザアーという物音の中にはっきり耳に聞き、目が見えないのでもだえていた。しかし、縁側に出ると、まもなく薄ら明かりの中に破壊された家屋が浮かび出し、気持ちもはっきりしてきた。

　それはひどく嫌な夢の中の出来事に似ていた。最初、私の頭に一撃が加えられ目が見えなくなったとき、私は自分が倒れてはいないことを知った。それから、ひどく面倒なことになったと思い腹立たしかった。そして、うわあと叫んでいる自分の声が、なんだか別人の声のように耳に聞こえた。しかし、辺りの様子がおぼろながら目に見えだしてくると、今度は惨劇の舞台の中に立っているよ

"JO"—TŌGE SANKICHI

The short poem "Jo" ("Prelude") draws us into the world of the *Gembaku Shishū* (1952), a collection of twenty-four free verse poems and two prose passages written by Hiroshima native and atomic-bomb survivor Tōge Sankichi (1917–53). He died at the age of 36 from illness and radiation-related complications. To survive the aftermath of the bomb and re-enter normal life, "Give me back myself" was perhaps Tōge's most elemental statement. It seems that the poet has expressed the pain and anguish of the survivors with the simplest choice of words, so that the rest of the world can understand. His other poems are far more complex descriptions of the explosion and the resulting horrors. He tells how people attempted to help each other on "that day" as long as a spark of life remained in their eyes.

He understood the plight of the *hibakusha*, the A-bomb survivors, all too well. In his poetry, Tōge Sankichi expresses the survivors' deep anguish and resolve to regain dignity amidst countrymen who would rather ignore them than face their illnesses and deformities. These were times when everyone in Japan was trying to rise from the ashes and rebuild the country.

Out of this destruction, action for the common good must come forth. Tōge Sankichi urges everyone to rise in protest against the spread of nuclear weapons. His poetry became a rallying cry for the non-proliferation movement in which Kenzaburo Oe—winner of the 1994 Nobel Prize for literature—was an active participant.

Tōge Sankichi is today recognized not only as a poet but also as a folk hero. A monument to the survivors of Hiroshima bears an inscription of the poem "Jo" in Japanese and in English. The Japanese non-proliferation movement was very vocal during the cold war when the threat of nuclear weapons was real. Today, various peace movements in Japan, especially those involving women, continue to call for world peace and a world free of nuclear weapons.

Following is a translation of "Jo" by Ohara Miyao, as it appears on the Hiroshima Peace Memorial Park's monument:

Give back my father, give back my mother; ちちをかえせ　ははをかえせ
Give grandpa back, grandma back; としよりをかえせ
Give me my sons and daugthers back. こどもをかえせ

Give me back myself. わたしをかえせ　わたしにつながる
Give back the human race. にんげんをかえせ

As long as this life lasts, this life, にんげんの　にんげんのよのあるかぎり
Give back peace くずれぬへいわを
That will never end. へいわをかえせ

Additional Reading:
 Oe Kenzaburo et al. *Hiroshima Notes*. New York: Grove / Atlantic Publishers, 1996.

Gembaku

YOKU-YOKU-JITSU no koto de atta.

WATASHI wa KAWAYA ni ita tame ICHI-MEI o HIROtta. HACHI-GATSU MUI-KA no ASA, WATASHI wa HACHI-JI goro TOKO o HANAreta. MAE no BAN NI-KAI mo KUU-SHUU KEI-HOU ga DE, NANI-GOTO mo nakatta no de, YO-Ake-MAE ni wa FUKU o ZEN-BU NUide, HISAshiburi ni NE-MAki ni KI-GAete NEMUtta.

Sore de, OkiDAshita toki mo *pantsu* HITOtsu de atta.

IMOUTO wa kono SUGATA o MIru to, ASA-NE shita koto o butsubutsu NAN-jite ita ga, WATASHI wa DAMAtte BEN-JO e HAItta.

Sore kara NAN-BYOU-GO no koto ka hakkiri shinai ga, TOTSU-ZEN, WATASHI no ZU-JOU ni ICHI-GEKI ga KUWAerare, ME no MAE ni KURA-YAMI ga SUBEriOchita. WATASHI wa OMOwazu <u>uwaa</u> to wameki, ATAMA ni TE o yatte TAchiAgatta. ARASHI no you na mono no TSUI-RAKU su-ru OTO no hoka wa MAK-KURA de NANI mo wakaranai. TE-SAGUri de TOBIRA o Akeru to, EN-GAWA ga atta. Sono toki made, WATASHI wa <u>uwaa</u> to iu JI-BUN no KOE o, *zaa* to iu MONO-OTO no NAKA ni hakkiri MIMI ni KIki, ME ga MIenai no de modae-te ita. Shikashi, EN-GAWA ni DEru to, mamonaku USUraA-kari no NAKA ni HA-KAI sareta KA-OKU ga UkabiDAshi, KI-MOchi mo hakkiri shite kita.

Sore wa hidoku IYA na YUME no NAKA no DE-KI-GOTO ni NIte ita. SAI-SHO, WATASHI no ATAMA ni ICHI-GEKI ga KUWAerare ME ga MIenaku nat-ta toki, WATASHI wa JI-BUN ga TAOrete wa inai koto o SHItta. Sore kara, hidoku MEN-DOU na koto ni natta to OMOi HARA-DA-tashikatta. Soshite, <u>uwaa</u> to SAKEnde iru JI-BUN no KOE ga, nan da ka BETSU-JIN no KOE no you ni MIMI ni KIkoeta. Shikashi, ATAri no YOU-SU ga oboronagara ME ni MIedashi-te kuru to, KON-DO wa SAN-GEKI no BU-TAI no NAKA ni TAtte iru yo-

Atomic Bomb Dome in Hiroshima, left unreconstructed as a memorial site.

Gembaku

was two days later.

It was because I was in the toilet that my life was spared. On the morning
of August sixth I got up at about eight. The previous night the air raid sirens
had sounded twice, but since nothing had happened I undressed before
dawn, changed into my sleeping gown for the first time in a long while, and slept.
So when I got up, I was in only my underpants.
Upon seeing me like that, my younger sister took me to task for it, grumbling about
my sleeping late. I, saying nothing, went into the toilet.
How many seconds passed after that is unclear, but suddenly
I was dealt a blow on top of my head and darkness descended
before my eyes. I unconsciously screamed out "uwaaah!," put my hands to my head
and stood up. Aside from the sound of something like a storm crashing
about, everything was pitch-dark and I had no idea what was happening. Upon groping
for and opening the door I found the verandah. Until then I was
clearly hearing my own voice screaming, backed by a rushing noise,
and as I was unable to see, I was incredibly distraught.
But when I went out onto the verandah, the vision of the
destroyed houses soon floated into view inside a faint brightness,
and I became lucid again.
That [experience] resembled events as in an incredibly horrible dream.
First, when I received a blow on the head and became unable to
see, I knew that I hadn't been knocked down.
After that, I felt infuriated when I thought about what a horribly distressing situation
this had become. Also, my own voice screaming "uwaaah!"
somehow sounded like a different person's voice.
But when I became able to see things around me again, albeit indistinctly,
I felt now as if I were standing in the middle of a stage of

- たしか: fairly sure; if I remember correctly
- 光景・こうけい: a scene; sight
- 映画・えいが: a movie
- など: or elsewhere (e.g., in a book or painting)
- 濛々・もうもう: the billowing or massing of mist, smoke, dust, or steam
- 煙る・けむる: to smoke; rise up like smoke
- 砂塵・さじん: "sand and dust"; dust [often a cloud of dust]
- 向(む)こうに: beyond; on the other side of
- 青い・あおい: blue
- 空間・くうかん: space
- 見(み)える: to be visible; can be seen
- 続く・つづく: to follow immediately; come one after another [here, modifying 増えた]
- 数・かず: number; numerical quantity
- 増(ふ)える: to increase (in quantity)
- 壁・かべ: a wall
- 脱落(だつらく)する: to come loose and drop off; be missing
- 所・ところ: place; part; section
- や: and also (among other places) [a list of places from which light appeared is given]
- 思(おも)いがけない: unexpected [this is an adjective and appears only in the negative form]
- 方向・ほうこう: direction
- 明(あ)かり: light
- さす・差す: to shine (on or through)
- 畳・たたみ: a mat [made of straw covered with woven rush; about 6 cm thick with the area varying by region (176 x 0.88 meters in Tokyo)]
- 飛(と)び散(ち)る: to fly here and there; scatter about [the subject of this verb is 畳]
- 座板・ざいた: floorboards on which the tatami normally rest [now, more commonly called 床板・ゆかいた]
- そろそろ: gingerly; cautiously
- ゆく・行く: to go [synonymous with いく・行く]
- すさまじい: tremendous; terrific
- 勢い・いきおい: energy; vigor; intensity
- 駆(かけ)けつける: to rush up; hurry (in a certain direction)
- やられる: to be injured; be hurt; suffer damage
- 大丈夫・だいじょうぶ: safe; all right
- 血が出る・ちがでる: "blood comes out"; to bleed
- 速い・はやい: quick; fast
- 洗う・あらう: to wash: rinse
- 台所・だいどころ: a kitchen
- 流し・ながし: a kitchen sink
- 水道・すいどう: tap water
- 出(で)る: to run [of water]
- 教える・おしえる: to inform; tell
- 散乱(さんらん)する: to be (lie) scattered about
- ふすま・襖: paper sliding doors between rooms
- 上・うえ: over; over the top of
- 踏み越える・ふみこえる: "to step and go over"; to step over
- 身に着ける・みにつける: to put on [of clothing]
- 探す・さがす: to search for; look for
- 一面・いちめん: the whole surface; all around; all over the place
- 崩れ落ちる・くずれおちる: to collapse
- 塊・かたまり: "lump"; a mass; heap; pile

- やや: slightly
- かなた・彼方: in the distance; far away
- 鉄筋(てっきん)コンクリート: reinforced concrete
- 建物・たてもの: a building [distinguished from the earlier mentioned 家屋・かおく: houses]
- 残る・のこる: to remain; be intact
- ほか: other than [modified by preceding clause]
- 目標・もくひょう: "target; goal"; a landmark
- そのうちに: before long
- 隣・となり: nextdoor
- 製薬会社・せいやくがいしゃ: a pharmaceutical company
- 倉庫・そうこ: a warehouse
- 赤い・あかい: red
- 小(ちい)さな: small
- 炎・ほのお: a flame
- 見(み)えだす: to begin to be seen; show itself
- 打ち倒す・うちたおす: to knock down
- 土塀・どべい: an earthen wall
- わき・脇: at the side of; next to [わきの modifies 木]
- ぽっくり: describes a snapping sound or action
- 折(お)れ曲(ま)がる: to be bent
- かえで・楓: maple
- 木・き: a tree
- 乗(の)り越(こ)える: to climb over
- 家・いえ: home
- 出る・でる: to leave
- 栄橋・さかえばし: a bridge over the Kyobashi river
- たもと・袂: foot (of the bridge)
- 避難者・ひなんしゃ: people seeking refuge or shelter
- 続々・ぞくぞく: one after another [続・つづく: continue; 々 indicates a repeated character]
- 集まる・あつまる: to gather
- 泉邸・せんてい: the ruins of Hiroshima's feudal lord Asano's second home; also called Shukukeien (縮景園). An emergency shelter upstream from the Sakae bridge
- やぶ・藪: a thicket; grove of shrubs or bamboo
- ほう・方: a direction; the direction toward; way
- 道・みち: road
- とる・採る: to take (one alternative)
- 竹やぶ・たけやぶ: a bamboo grove
- なぎ倒す・なぎたおす: to mow down; cut down
- 逃(に)げる: to flee; run away; escape
- 自然と・しぜんと: naturally; as a matter of course
- 開く・ひらく: to open up
- 見上げる・みあげる: to look up at
- 樹木・じゅもく: trees (both kanji mean "tree")
- おおかた・大方: almost all; nearly all
- 中空・ちゅうくう: mid-air
- そぎ取る・削ぎ取る: to scrape off; shave off; stip bare
- に沿(そ)う: to be alongside; run parallel to
- 由緒(ゆいしょ)ある: having a history; historic
- 名園・めいえん: a famous or celebrated garden
- 今・いま: now
- 傷(きず)だらけ: "covered with wounds"; having received many telling blows [だらけ is attached to nouns and means "covered with" or "filled with," with negative connotations]

うな気持ちであった。たしか、こういう光景は映画などで見たことがある。濛々と煙る砂塵の向こうに青い空間が見え、続いてその空間の数が増えた。壁の脱落した所や、思いがけない方向から明かりがさしてくる。畳の飛び散った座板の上をそろそろ歩いてゆくと、向こうからすさまじい勢いで妹が駆けつけてきた。

　「やられなかった、やられなかったの、大丈夫？」と妹は叫び、「目から血が出ている、早く洗いなさい。」と台所の流しに水道が出ていることを教えてくれた。

　私は散乱した畳やふすまの上を踏み越えて、身に着けるものを探した。縁側から見ると、一面に崩れ落ちた家屋の塊があり、ややかなたの鉄筋コンクリートの建物が残っているほか、目標になるものもない。そのうちに、隣の製薬会社の倉庫から赤い小さな炎が見えだした。私は、打ち倒された土塀のわきの、ぽっくり折れ曲がったかえでの木を乗り越えて、家を出た。——栄橋のたもとまで来ると、そこには避難者が続々と集まってきていた。私は、そこから泉邸のやぶのほうへ道をとった。

　その竹やぶはなぎ倒され、逃げてゆく人の勢いで、道が自然と開かれていた。見上げる樹木もおおかた中空でそぎ取られており、川に沿った、この由緒ある名園も、今は傷だらけの姿であった。

BRIEF POST-WAR HISTORICAL BACKGROUND

The nuclear attacks on Hiroshima and Nagasaki on August 6 and 9, 1945, caused a death toll of over 200,000 within four months. This number increased to 340,000 within five years, due to the delayed effects of radiation. A few days later, on August 15, Japan laid down its arms and, on September 2, formally surrendered to the Allies. General MacArthur, the Supreme Commander of the Allied Powers, represented the Allies. Thereafter the wartime government leaders were removed and political parties were created. The new constitution, based on a model drawn up by a consortium of scholars, the military, and administrators from the United States, went into effect in 1947. It spelled out a parliamentary system where the emperor became the ceremonial head of state. Emperor Hirohito himself renounced all of the prerogatives of "divinity." Only the Diet, the Japanese parliament, had the right to write the laws of the land. The occupation of Japan by the United States lasted until 1952, during which Japan was subjected to a democratization and demilitarization process. The reforms, among them partial freedom of the press and a new style of politics, were the direct results of General MacArthur's policies.

The Constitution's Article Nine prohibits Japan from holding or maintaining the means to wage war. Pacifist attitudes grew to be very strong among the population. Attempts by the United States to have the Japanese government reconsider Article Nine during the Korean war were unsuccessful.

On September, 8, 1951, a formal peace treaty was signed with Japan at the San Francisco Conference. Forty-nine nations cosigned the treaty. Prime Minister Yoshida Shigeru apologized for Japan's militaristic actions that took place after 1937. According to the peace treaty, Japan was not given the right to intervene militarily in international affairs. Only self-defense was permissible and nuclear weapons were banned. Unlimited rights to trade, however, were granted to Japan. The population embraced wholeheartedly the demilitarization clause.

In 1952 Japan regained its full independence. The stage was set for Japan's entry into the world as a major economic power, slowly at first, then at an accelerating pace. Not being able to exert any military power, Japan focused its energies on commercial success.

Barred from international arms negotiations and participation in international military conflicts, Japan has played a negligible role in these matters. However, in that it did not participate in the United Nations peacekeeping forces, Japan has been expected to make large financial contributions to those activities. Today, Japan's presence in the United Nations forces, albeit in a non-military capacity, is increasingly felt. Japanese mediators have been instrumental in helping to resolve several international conflicts.

u na KI-MOchi de atta. Tashika, kou iu KOU-KEI wa EI-
GA nado de MIta koto ga aru. MOU-MOU to KEMUru SA-JIN no MUko-
u ni AOi KUU-KAN ga MIe, TSUZUite sono KUU-KAN no KAZU ga FUe-
ta. KABE no DATSU-RAKU shita TOKORO ya, OMOigakenai HOU-KOU kara A-
kari ga sashite kuru. TATAMI no TObiCHItta ZA-ITA no UE o so-
rosoro ARUite yuku to, MUkou kara susamajii IKIOi
de IMOUTO ga KAketsukete kita.

"Yararenakatta, yararenakatta no, DAI-JOU-
BU?" to IMOUTO wa SAKEbi, "ME kara CHI ga DEte iru, HAYAku ARA-
inasai." to DAI-DOKORO no NAGAshi ni SUI-DOU ga DEte iru koto o
OSHIete kureta.

WATASHI wa SAN-RAN shita TATAMI ya fusuma no UE o FUmiKOete, MI
ni TSUkeru mono o SAGAshita. EN-GAWA kara MIru to, ICHI-MEN ni
KUZUreOchita KA-OKU no KATAMARI ga ari, yaya kanata no TEK-KIN *ko-
nkuriito* no TATE-MONO ga NOKOtte iru hoka, MOKU-HYOU ni naru
mono mo nai. Sono uchi ni, TONARI no SEI-YAKU-GAI-SHA no SOU-KO kara AKAi CHIIsana HONOO ga MIedashita. WATASHI wa, UchiTAOsare-
ta DO-BEI no waki no, pokkuri OreMAgatta kaede no
KI o NOriKOete, IE o DEta. —SAKAE-BASHI no tamoto made KUru to, soko ni wa HI-NAN-SHA ga ZOKU-ZOKU to ATSUmatte kite
ita. WATASHI wa, soko kara SEN-TEI no yabu no hou e MICHI o to-
tta.

Sono TAKEyabu wa nagiTAOsare, NIgete yuku HITO no IKIOi
de, MICHI ga SHI-ZEN to HIRAkarete ita. MI-Ageru JU-MOKU mo o-
okata CHUU-KUU de sogiTOrarete ori, KAWA ni SOtta, kono YUI-SHO aru MEI-EN mo, IMA wa KIZU darake no SUGATA de atta.

Article 9 of the Japanese Constitution reads:

"Aspiring sincerely to an international peace based on justice and order, the Japanese people forever renounce war as a sovereign right of the nation and the threat or use of force as a means of settling international disputes.

(2) In order to accomplish the aim of the preceding paragraph, land, sea, and air forces, as well as other war potential, will never be maintained. The right of belligerency of the state will not be recognized."

a tragedy. Surely I had seen this scene

before in a movie or something. Beyond the dark

swirling clouds of dust I could see spaces of blue. The number of spaces was continually

increasing. Light shone from where the wall had dropped away and from other

unexpected directions. As I walked slowly over the floorboards strewn

with the blown-about reed mats, my sister came running up to me at a fierce pace

from the other side [of the house].

"Did anything hit you? Did you get hurt? Are you OK?"

she yelled. "There's blood coming from your eye. Go and wash

it quickly," and she told me that water was [still] coming from

the kitchen sink.

I walked over the scattered tatami mats and fusuma, and looked for

something to wear. Looking from the verandah, everywhere there were

piles of houses which had crumbled and fallen flat, and aside from the slightly distant reinforced

concrete buildings which still remained, there was nothing to serve as a landmark.

Soon I saw a small red flame from the drug company's

warehouse next door. I climbed over

the bent snapped maple tree at the side of the knocked-over

clay wall, and exited the house.... When I came to the foot

of the Sakae bridge, evacuees were coming to gather in a steady

stream. From there I took the road to the Sentei

grove.

The bamboo thicket had been flattened, and under the force of the people

fleeing, a road through it had been opened naturally. The trees I saw

upon looking up were cut off in midair, and the famous garden along the river

now appeared terribly scarred.

- ふと: unexpectedly; suddenly
- 灌木・かんぼく: a shrub; bush
- そば・側: beside; by the side of
- だらりと: languidly; limply
- 豊か・ゆたか: full; voluptuous
- 肢体・したい: limbs; body
- 投げ出す・なげだす: to fling out; abandon in disarray
- うずくまる: to crouch; squat
- 中年・ちゅうねん: middle-aged
- 婦人・ふじん: a woman; mature woman; married woman
- 顔・かお: a face
- 魂・たましい: spirit
- 抜(ぬ)けはてる: to lose utterly; be devoid of
- 見ているうちに: as I was looking
- 何か・なにか: for some reason
- 感染(かんせん)する: to infect
- ～そうになる: to seem as if ~ might happen [verb stem + そう]
- こんな: this kind of; this type of
- 出(で)くわす: to run into
- 初めて・はじめて: the first time
- が: but
- それより: even more than that
- もっと: more; to a greater degree
- 奇怪・きかい: strange; weird
- その後(ご): thereafter; after that
- 限りない・かぎりない: limitless; infinite [adj.]
- ～ねばならない: must do ~; have to do ~
- 川岸・かわぎし: the bank/shore of a river
- 出る・でる: to protrude; come out to
- 学徒・がくと: students [at this time students from junior high school and above were required to work in factories]
- ひとかたまり: "one lump"; a group; a band
- 出会う・であう: to meet by accident
- 工場・こうじょう: a factory [here, one where students were working]
- 逃げ出す・にげだす: to run away; escape from [here, 出す means "to leave"]
- 彼女(かのじょ)たち: plural of "she" [all the students were girls]
- 一様に・いちように: equally; uniformly
- 軽い・かるい: light; minor
- 負傷(ふしょう)をする: to be wounded; be injured
- 出現(しゅつげん)する: to appear; materialize
- 出来事・できごと: a happening; event
- 新鮮・しんせん: freshness; newness; novelty
- ～さ: added to the end of an adjective in place of the い or な, changes the adjective into a noun
- おののく: to tremble; quaver
- ～ながら: while ~ [added to the verb stem]
- かえって: on the contrary; instead
- 元気そうに・げんきそうに: cheerfully
- しゃべり会(あ)う: to talk (chat) together
- そこへ: at that juncture
- 長兄・ちょうけい: one's oldest brother
- 姿があらわれる(現れる): "a form appears"; to show up
- シャツ: an undershirt
- 一枚・いちまい: one; only [枚 is a counter for flat objects; here, the word emphasizes that the brother was wearing nothing more on his upper body, not that he was naked]
- 片手・かたて: one hand
- ビール瓶(びん): a beer bottle
- まず: "first of all"; at least; at any rate
- 異状・いじょう: irregularity; abnormality
- ～なさそう: "didn't seem ~" [ない becomes なさ with the そう suffix]
- 向こう岸・むこうぎし: opposite shore
- 見わたす(渡す): to look out (over an expanse)
- verb + 限り(かぎり): as far as; as long as
- 崩れる・くずれる: to fall; collapse
- 電柱・でんちゅう: a telephone pole; pole with power lines
- もう: already
- 火の手・ひので: flames; fire
- 回る・まわる: to move from one place to another; spread
- 狭い・せまい: narrow
- 腰を下ろす・こしをおろす: to sit down
- 気持(きも)ちがする: to feel
- 長い間・ながいあいだ: for a long time
- おびやかす・脅かす: to threaten
- ついに: at long last; finally
- 来(き)たる: to be coming; be awaited
- verb + べき: to be expected to + verb [in modern Japanese, べき in this formula most often express obligation, "should"]
- さばさばする: to feel relieved
- 生きながらえる・生き長らえる: "to live long"; be alive; survive
- 顧みる・かえりみる: to reflect on
- かねて: for some time
- 二つに一つ・ふたつにひとつ: a one in two, or 50%, chance (of surviving)
- 助かる・たすかる: to be saved; emerge alive
- かもしれない・かも知れない: maybe; perhaps; may; might [following either positive or negative verbs]
- 己・おのれ: oneself
- 意味・いみ: meaning; significance
- はっと: describes surprise or a sudden realization
- 弾く・はじく: to be struck; be hit [commonly, to snap, flick with the finger]
- 書き残す・かきのこす: to put down in writing
- 心に・こころに: "to one's heart"; to oneself
- つぶやく: to murmur
- けれども: however
- まだ: as yet
- 空襲・くうしゅう: an air raid
- 真相・しんそう: the truth, the real nature of something
- ほとんど: almost all

ふと、灌木(かんぼく)のそばにだらりと豊かな肢体を投げ出してうずくまっている中年の婦人の顔があった。魂の抜けはてたその顔は、見ているうちに何か感染しそうになるのであった。こんな顔に出くわしたのは、これが初めてであった。が、それよりもっと奇怪な顔に、その後私は限りなく出くわさねばならなかった。

　川岸に出るやぶのところで、私は学徒のひとかたまりと出会った。工場から逃げ出した彼女たちは、一様に軽い負傷をしていたが、今、目の前に出現した出来事の新鮮さにおののきながら、かえって元気そうにしゃべり合っていた。そこへ長兄の姿があらわれた。シャツ一枚で、片手にビール瓶を持ち、まず異状なさそうであった。向こう岸も見わたす限り建物は崩れ、電柱の残っているほか、もう火の手が回っていた。私は狭い川岸の道へ腰を下ろすと、しかし、もう大丈夫だという気持ちがした。長い間おびやかされていたものが、ついに来るべきものが、来たのだった。さばさばした気持ちで、私は自分が生きながらえていることを顧みた。かねて、二つに一つは助からないかもしれないと思っていたのだが、今、ふと己が生きていることと、その意味が、はっと私を弾(はじ)いた。

　このことを書き残さねばならない、と、私は心につぶやいた。けれども、そのときはまだ、私はこの空襲の真相をほとんど知ってはいなかったのである。

——〜——

慣用句: Idiomatic Expressions

Translate the following into idiomatic English.

1. いかにも～らしい

シャツ一枚、そして片手にビール瓶というのはいかにも長兄らしい姿だった。

2. なんとなく

これはなんとなく映画などで見たことがある光景だと思った。

3. 一命を拾う

その橋のたもとには、一命を拾った避難者たちが続々と集まってきていた。

4. 久しぶりに

もうすぐ初盆なので私は久しぶりに妻の墓を訪れようと思った。

5. なんだか～ように

目が見えなかったので、なんだか自分はもう助からないように思った。

6. 思いがけない

自分が生きながらえているということは、とても思いがけないことだった。

7. 出くわす

川岸で工場から逃げ出した学徒のひとかたまりに出くわした。

8. 見わたす限り

見わたす限り濛々と煙る砂塵の向こうに、うずくまっている避難者の姿が見えてきた。

9. 火の手が回る

火の手が回るのが速く、私は手探りで縁側の方に出て行った。

10. 気持ちがする

映画か舞台の中の光景を見ているような気持ちがした。

11. 生きながらえる

避難者たちはみんな負傷をしていたが、一様に自分たちが生きながらえていることを顧みているようだった。

Futo, KAN-BOKU no soba ni darari to YUTAka na SHI-TAI o NAgeDA-

shite uzukumatte iru CHUU-NEN no FU-JIN no KAO ga atta.

TAMASHII no NUkehateta sono KAO wa, MIte iru uchi ni NANI ka KAN-

SEN shisou ni naru no de atta. Konna KAO ni DEkuwashi-

ta no wa, kore ga HAJImete de atta. Ga, sore yori mo-

tto KI-KAI na KAO ni, sono GO WATASHI wa KAGIRInaku DEkuwasane-

ba naranakatta.

KAWA-GISHI ni DEru yabu no tokoro de, WATASHI wa GAKU-TO no hitoka-

tamari to DE-Atta. KOU-JOU kara NIgeDAshita KANO-JOtachi

wa, ICHI-YOU ni KARUi FU-SHOU o shite ita ga, IMA, ME no MAE ni SHUTSU-

GEN shita DE-KI-GOTO no SHIN-SENsa ni ononokinagara, kaet-

te GEN-KIsou ni shaberiAtte ita. Soko e CHOU-KEI no

SUGATA ga arawareta. *Shatsu* ICHI-MAI de, KATA-TE ni *biiru*BIN

o MOchi, mazu I-JOU nasasou de atta. MUkouGISHI mo

MIwatasu KAGIri, TATE-MONO wa KUZUre, DEN-CHUU no NOKOtte iru hoka,

mou HI no TE ga MAWAtte ita. WATASHI wa SEMAi KAWA-GISHI no MICHI e KOSHI

o Orosu to, shikashi, mou DAI-JOU-BU da to iu KI-MOchi

ga shita. NAGAi AIDA obiyakasarete ita mono ga, tsui

ni KItaru beki mono ga, KIta no datta. Sabasaba shi-

ta KI-MOchi de, WATASHI wa JI-BUN ga Ikinagaraete iru koto

o KAERImita. Kanete, FUTAtsu ni HITOtsu wa TASUkaranai kamo

shirenai to OMOtte ita no da ga, IMA, futo ONORE ga Iki-

te iru koto to, sono IMI ga, hatto WATASHI o HAJIita.

Kono koto o KAkiNOKOsaneba nararanai, to, WATASHI wa KOKORO

ni tsubuyaita. Keredomo, sono toki wa mada, WATASHI wa

kono KUU-SHUU no SHIN-SOU o hotondo SHItte wa inakatta no

de aru.

内容理解: Comprehension Exercises

Answer in Japanese.

1. これは何年にあった話でしょうか。
2. 「私」はどうして妻の墓を訪れようと思ったのでしょうか。
3. 「久しぶりに寝巻きに着替えて眠った」という言葉からどのような生活だったことがわかりますか。
4. 「私」はどうして「ひどく面倒なことになったと思い腹立たしかった」のでしょうか。
5. 「私」は家を出てからどのような光景を見ましたか。
6. 「私」はかねて来たるべきものが来ても必ず助かるだろうと思っていましたか。

練習問題: Exercises

True or False ?

1. 「私」が妻の墓を訪れようと思ったのは、この街にももうすぐ空襲という来るべきものが来るだろうという気がしたからだ。
2. 「私」が一命を拾ったのは前の晩二回も空襲警報を聞いていたからだ。
3. 出会った女子学徒たちが元気そうにしゃべり合っている光景からかえって彼女たちが目の前の出来事におののいていることがよくわかった。
4. この日、すぐこの空襲の真相を知って、「私」はこのことを書き残さねばならないと思った。

Unexpectedly, next to a shrub there was the face of a middle-aged woman, crouched down
with her plump limbs limply thrown out.
While looking at that face, its spirit having fled, I somehow felt
as if I would be infected by it. This was the first time
I had ever seen a face like this. But after that
I had to meet endless numbers of faces more eerie
than that.

Where the thicket comes out on the bank of the river, I ran into a
group of students. These girls, who had all fled from their factory,
were all slightly injured. But now, shaken by the newness of
the events which had unfolded before their eyes, they were, contrary
to expectation, chatting animatedly with one another. There my older brother
appeared. He wore an undershirt, carried a beer bottle in one hand,
and seemed for the most part as if nothing had happened. All one could see
on the opposite bank were the buildings that had crumbled and [some] telephone poles remaining, and other than that
fire was already at work everywhere. I lowered myself and sat down
on the narrow riverbank road and felt that, well, it's safe
now. Something which had been threatening to happen for such a long time,
something which should have come, had finally come. With a sense of
relief I reflected on the fact that I had
survived. From before I had assumed
that the odds that I might die were about fifty-fifty, and now
the unexpected fact that I was alive and its import suddenly startled me.

I must write this down to pass on to others, I
mumbled to myself. But at that time I still knew
almost nothing about the real nature of this air
attack.

語句と語法: Phrases and Usage

あどけない話:

- あどけない: childlike; innocent
- 話・はなし: tale; story
- 智恵子・ちえこ: the name of the poet's mentally-ill wife
- 東京・とうきょう: the city of Tokyo
- 空・そら: sky
- 無い・ない: is not
- という・と言う: (she) says
- ほんと: real [colloquial version of 本当 (ほんとう), with last vowel dropped]
- 見たい・みたい: want to see
- 私・わたし: I
- 驚く・おどろく: to be surprised
- 見る・みる: to look at
- 桜・さくら: cherry trees
- 若葉・わかば: young leaves
- 間に・あいだに: in between
- 在る・ある: to be (there); to exist
- 切(き)っても切れない: "cannot be cut, no matter how one tries"; inseparable, closely associated; constant [modifies むかしなじみ]
- むかしなじみ: an old friend
- きれい・奇麗: pretty; beautiful
- どんより: leaden; overcast
- けむる: "to give off smoke"; to look dim in the mist; be hazy
- 地平・ちへい: the horizon
- ぼかし: shadings or gradations (of color)
- うすもも色(いろ): light pink
- 朝・あさ: morning
- しめり: moistness; water vapor; mist
- 遠く・とおく: far in the distance [noun]
- 見ながら: while looking
- 阿多多羅山・あたたらやま: a group of volcanic mountains in Fukushima Prefecture
- 山・やま: mountain
- 上に・うえに: above
- 毎日・まいにち: everyday
- 出る・でる: to appear; come into view
- 青い・あおい: blue

若葉よ来年は海へゆこう:

- 若葉・わかば: "young leaves"; the name of a grandaughter
- よ: oh [indicates direct address]
- 来年・らいねん: next year
- 海・うみ: ocean; the sea
- ゆこう: let's go [equivalent to 行(い)こう]
- うた・歌: song
- より: (an excerpt) from
- 絵本・えほん: a picture book
- ひらくと: when [I, we, etc.] open (the book)
- ひらける: to open up (to view)
- まだ: (not) yet
- わかる: to know
- になったら: when (next years) comes around
- おもちゃ: toys
- いっぱい・一杯: full (of)
- うつくしい・美しい: beautiful; pretty
- こわれる・壊れる: to be broken [+ やすい = easy (to)]
- ガラス: glass (the substance) [cf. グラス (for drinking)]
- できる・出来る: to be made (of)
- きらきらとする: to sparkle; glitter
- 揺れる・ゆれる: to sway; undulate
- 風琴・ふうきん: an accordian [in full, 手風琴・てふうきん]; an organ
- うたう・歌う: to sing
- あがってくる・上がって来る: to come up
- 貝・かい: shellfish
- たち: indicates a plural number [primarily used in reference to human beings, here it produce a feeling of individuality and intimacy]
- とりまく: to surround; encircle
- 貝(かい)になる: to become a shellfish
- あそぶ・遊ぶ: to play
- そして: then; and then
- ぢいちゃん: how a child might say "grandfather"; grandpa [usually written じいちゃん]
- いっしょに・一緒に: together

あどけない話　高村光太郎

智恵子は東京に空がないという。
ほんとの空が見たいという。
私は驚いて空を見る。
桜若葉の間に在るのは、
切っても切れない
むかしなじみのきれいな空だ。
どんよりけむる地平のぼかしは
うすもも色の朝のしめりだ。
智恵子は遠くを見ながら言う。
阿多多羅山の山の上に
毎日出ている青い空が
智恵子のほんとの空だという。
あどけない空の話である。

若葉よ来年は海へゆこう

「若葉のうた」より　　　　　　　　金子光晴

絵本をひらくと、海がひらける。若葉にはま
　だ、海がわからない。

若葉よ。来年になったら海へゆこう。海はお
　もちゃでいっぱいだ。

うつくしくてこわれやすい、ガラスでできた
　その海は

きらきらとして、揺られながら、風琴のよう
　にうたっている。

海からあがってきたきれいな貝たちが、若葉
　をとりまくと、

若葉も、貝になってあそぶ。

若葉よ。来年になったら海へゆこう。そして、
　ぢいちゃんもいっしょに貝になろう。

Takamura Kōtarō

Takamura Kōtarō (1883–1956) considered himself a sculptor, which may somewhat explain the clarity of his poetic work. His father was also a sculptor. From 1906 he traveled and studied in the United States, England, and France for three years, where at first he felt at home and made many friends. With the passage of time, however, he came to harbor a keen awareness of cultural and racial differences. After returning to Japan, he published his first collection of poetry, *Dōtei* (The Road Ahead, 1914), which is a display of youthful independence. During World War II he adopted a nationalistic stance and wrote poems that reflected that view. Unlike other, mediocre and opportunistic poets, his poetry in this vein is less virulent and has a sincere ring to it, a quality that leads some to judge him less harshly than they might otherwise do. After the war he spent seven years in self-imposed exile, living in a cabin in an outlying rural area. In 1949 he wrote a work that is, in effect, an apologia for his wartime activities.

Takamura Kōtarō is today remembered for his early poems and for his love poems to Chieko, his beloved wife who became mentally ill. The clarity of his style adds to the beauty of his poems and his sincere expression won him a devoted audience.

Kaneko Mitsuharu

Kaneko Mitsuharu (1895–1975) was by nature a skeptic, suspicious of authority. From 1919–21 he spent most of his time in Belgium, where he became very interested in French poetry. In the late 20s, he went back to Europe (to Paris), this time as a married man. After having returned to Japan in 1935, he found, to his great dismay, a militaristic Japan which had allowed its army to commit atrocities, first in Manchuria and later in Nanking (December 1937–Spring 1938). His suspicious nature led him to fervently oppose these militaristic policies. His distaste for the military was so intense, that he helped his son evade military conscription in 1944. He was viewed with great suspicion by the authorities, yet managed to write, in veiled imagery, resistance poetry.

After the war, he reverted to the style of his earlier symbolist period and wrote quieter, perhaps less interesting, works. His verbal attacks against militarism eventually won him the admiration of Japanese audiences.

Adokenai HANASHI   TAKA-MURA KOU-TA-ROU

CHI-E-KO wa TOU-KYOU ni SORA ga nai to iu.

Honto no SORA ga MItai to iu.

WATASHI wa ODOROite SORA o MIru.

SAKURA-WAKA-BA no AIDA ni Aru no wa,

KItte mo KIrenai

mukashi najimi no kirei na SORA da.

Donyori kemuru CHI-HEI no bokashi wa

usumomoIRO no ASA no shimeri da.

CHI-E-KO wa TOOku o MInagara Iu.

A-TA-TA-RA-YAMA no YAMA no UE ni

MAI-NICHI DEte iru AOi SORA ga

CHI-E-KO no honto no SORA da to iu.

Adokenai SORA no HANASHI de aru.

WAKA-BA yo RAI-NEN wa UMI e yukou
"WAKA-BA no uta" yori   KANE-KO MITSU-HARU

E-HON o hiraku to, UMI ga hirakeru. WAKA-BA ni wa ma-
        da, UMI ga wakaranai.

WAKA-BA yo. RAI-NEN ni nattara UMI e yukou. UMI wa o-
        mocha de ippai da.

Utsukushikute kowareyasui, *garasu* de dekita
        sono UMI wa

kirakira to shite, YUrarenagara, FUU-KIN no you
        ni utatte iru.

UMI kara agatte kita kirei na KAItachi ga, WAKA-BA
        o torimaku to,

WAKA-BA mo, KAI ni natte asobu.

WAKA-BA yo. RAI-NEN ni nattara UMI e yukou. Soshite,
        jii-chan mo issho ni KAI ni narou.

JAPANESE POETIC FORM 1

*T*anka or "short poem" is a five-line poem with a syllable pattern of 5-7-5-7-7. It has been the classical vehicle for poetic writing since the seventh century and remains so today. Prior to the twentieth century, poems in *tanka* form were called *waka*. The term *waka* simply meant "poem in Japanese" as opposed to *kanshi*, which meant "poem in Chinese." In the tenth century, the imperial court commissioned *waka* (or *tanka*) poetry, as a result of which this form was for the first time given equal status with *kanshi* (Chinese poetry). For several centuries, *tanka* erudition and writing were an integral part of a person's education. However, with the demise of the imperial court's political power in the 13th century, *tanka* gradually gave way to *renga*.

Haikai no renga, (i.e., *renga* or "linked poetry") had a comic content and became the favorite poetic form of the fifteenth and sixteenth centuries. In the seventeenth century, during the culturally rich Tokugawa shogunate, the 17-syllable *haikai*, also called *haiku*, became the prevalent genre. It should be noted that *haiku* originated as one element of *renga*. Matsuo Bashō (1644–94) was an early master of the form. He taught poetry in Edo (now known as Tokyo) to a circle of young poets. Buson and Issa were later masters of *haiku*, but the genre eventually lost its freshness. Around 1890, Masaoka Shiki revitalized *haiku*, which soon evolved into a popular genre. To this day, *haiku* writing is considered a popular and pleasant pastime. For instance, newspaper columns in the daily press, widely publish *haiku* which are avidly read by a large segment of the population. It can be said that *haiku* is today firmly established as a viable poetic form.

A Childlike Tale — Takamura Kōtarō

Chieko says there is no sky in Tokyo.

She says she wants to see the real sky.

I, surpised, look at the sky.

What exists between the young cherry tree leaves

is my inseparable

old friend the beautiful sky.

The shades of color of the leaden, smoky horizon

have a pink morning dew.

Chieko speaks, looking far away.

On the top of a mount in Atatara-yama

the blue sky that appears everyday

is the real sky, Chieko says.

This is a childish tale of the sky.

"Wakaba, Let's Go to the Sea Next Year"

From *The Song of Wakaba* — Mitsuharu Kaneko

Opening a picture book, the sea comes to view. Wakaba does
    not yet know the sea.

Wakaba, let us go to the sea next year. The sea
    is full of toys.

Beautiful and made of fragile glass,
    that sea

sparkles and sways, singing like
    an accordion.

The pretty shellfish, coming up from the sea,
    surround Wakaba.

Wakaba, too, becomes a shellfish and plays.

Wakaba, let us go to the sea next year. Then,
    let you and Grandpa become shellfish together.

語句と語法: Phrases and Usage

地球へのピクニック:

- 地球・ちきゅう: the earth
- ピクニック: a picnic; outing; excursion
- 愛・あい: love
- について: about; concerning
- より: (an excerpt) from
- 一緒に・いっしょに: together
- なわとび(縄飛び)をする: jump rope
- ～しよう: let's do ~ [many verbs below are conjugated to mean "let's"]
- おにぎり: nigiri; rice balls
- たべる・食べる: to eat
- おまえ・お前: you; used here with affection ("my dear"), but usually used towards inferiors or very informally
- 愛す・あいす: to love [= 愛する]
- 眼・め: eye
- 空・そら: the sky
- 青・あお: blue (of the sky)
- うつす・映る: to reflect
- 背中・せなか: (one's) back
- よもぎ: mugwort or wormwood [a common perenial herb used as a food or dyeing ingredient]
- 緑・みどり: green
- 染まる・そまる: to be dyed; be stained
- 星座・せいざ: stars; constellations
- 名前・なまえ: name
- 覚える・おぼえる: to learn
- すべて・全て: everything; all things
- 遠い・とおい: far; distant
- 夢見る・ゆめみる: to dream (of something)
- 潮干狩り・しおひがり: shellfish hunting; searching for shellfish
- あけがた: dawn
- ひとで: a starfish
- とって来る・取って来る: to go and get
- 朝御飯・あさごはん: breakfast (time)
- 捨てる・すてる: to abandon; discard; throw away
- 夜・よる: night
- ひく・引く: to draw forth; evoke [figurative usage]
- まかせる・任せる: to leave (in the care of); to trust (someone to do something)
- 「ただいま」: "I'm home"
- 言い続ける・いいつづける: to continue to say
- 「おかえりなさい」: "Welcome home/back"
- 繰り返す・くりかえす: to repeat
- 間・あいだ: a period of time; while
- 何度でも・なんどでも: many times; over and over
- 熱い・あつい: hot
- お茶(ちゃ): green tea
- 坐る・すわる: to sit

- しばらくの間(あいだ): for a while; for some time
- 涼しい・すずしい: cool
- 風(かぜ): wind
- 吹く・ふく: to blow

六十二のソネット:

- ソネット: sonnet (a verse in fourteen lines)
- より: (an excerpt) from
- 世界・せかい: the world
- 私(わたし): I
- 愛(あい)する: to love
- むごい: cruel
- 仕方・しかた: way; manner
- また・又: again; as well
- 時(とき)に: sometimes; on occasion
- やさしい・優しい: kind; gentle; tender
- いつまでも: forever
- 孤り: alone; here the character 孤 (cf. 孤独・こどく: solitude; lonely) is used for connotation; usually written 一人 (one person; alone)
- いられる: to be able to be
- 始(はじ)めて: for the first time
- ひとり: single; alone
- ひと・人: person; individual
- 与える・あたえる: to give; grant; confer
- 時(とき)にも: also when
- ただ: only; just
- 物音・ものおと: sounds
- ばかり: only; nothing else but
- 聴く・きく: to listen to
- 単純・たんじゅん: simple
- 悲しみ・かなしみ: sadness
- 喜び・よろこび: joy
- 明らか・あきらか: clear
- いつも: always
- もの: thing; creature
- 空・そら: sky
- 樹・き: a tree
- 自ら・みずから: oneself
- 投げかける・なげかける: to throw; fling
- やがて: by and by; gradually
- 豊かさ・ゆたかさ: wealth; richness
- そのもの: itself
- よぶ: to call
- すると: when that is done; and then
- ふり向く・ふりむく: to turn; look back
- そして: then; and
- いなくなる: to be not (there); to disappear

地球へのピクニック

「愛について」より　　　　谷川俊太郎

ここで一緒になわとびをしよう　ここで
ここで一緒におにぎりをたべよう
ここでおまえを愛そう
おまえの眼は空の青をうつし
おまえの背中はよもぎの緑に染まるだろう
ここで一緒に星座の名前を覚えよう

ここにいてすべての遠いものを夢見よう
ここで潮干狩をしよう
あけがたの空の海から
小さなひとでをとって来よう
朝御飯にはそれを捨て
夜をひくにまかせよう

ここでただいまを言い続けよう
おまえがお帰りなさいをくり返す間
ここへ何度でも帰って来よう
ここで熱いお茶を飲もう
ここで一緒に坐ってしばらくの間
涼しい風に吹かれよう

六十二のソネット　62

「六十二のソネット」より

世界が私を愛してくれるので
（むごい仕方でまた時に
やさしい仕方で）
私はいつまでも孤りでいられる

私に始めてひとりのひとが与えられた時にも
私はただ世界の物音ばかりを聴いていた
私には単純な悲しみと喜びだけが明らかだ
私はいつも世界のものだから

空に樹にひとに
私は自らを投げかける
やがて世界の豊かさそのものとなるために

……私はひとをよぶ
すると世界がふり向く
そして私がいなくなる

Tanikawa Shuntarō

Tanikawa Shuntarō (b. 1931) belonged to a group that founded the *Kai* (Oars) poetry magazine. Too young to have participated in the war, these young poets had no ax to grind and were a happy bunch. Out of this group, Tanikawa Shuntarō emerged as one of the most interesting. With easily accessible language, he tackles philosophical and social issues, partly influenced by Western poets, notably the German poet Rilke. Tanikawa is considered a major poet of the post–World War II period.

CHI-KYUU e no *Pikunikku*
"AI ni tsuite" yori   TANI-KAWA SHUN-TA-ROU

koko de IS-SHO ni nawatobi o shiyou   koko de

koko de IS-SHO ni onigiri o tabeyou

koko de omae o AIsou

omae no ME wa SORA no AO o utsushi

omae no SE-NAKA wa yomogi no MIDORI ni SOmaru darou

koko de IS-SHO ni SEI-ZA no NA-MAE o OBOeyou

koko ni ite subete no TOOi mono o YUME-MIyou

koko de SHIO-HI-GARI o shiyou

akegata no SORA no UMI kara

CHIIsana hitode o totte KOyou

ASA-GO-HAN ni wa sore o SUte

YORU o hiku ni makaseyou

koko de tadaima o IiTSUZUkeyou

omae ga oKAErinasai o kuriKAEsu AIDA

koko e NAN-DO de mo KAEtte KOyou

koko de ATSUi oCHA o NOmou

koko de IS-SHO ni SUWAtte shibaraku no AIDA

SUZUshii KAZE ni FUkareyou

ROKU-JUU-NI no *Sonetto* 62
"ROKU-JUU-NI no *Sonetto*" yori

SE-KAI ga WATASHI o AIshite kureru no de

(mugoi SHI-KATA de mata TOKI ni

yasashii SHI-KATA de)

WATASHI wa itsu made mo HITOri de irareru

WATASHI ni HAJImete hitori no hito ga ATAerareta TOKI ni mo

WATASHI wa tada SE-KAI no MONO-OTO bakari o KIite ita

WATASHI ni wa TAN-JUN na KANAshimi to YOROKObi dake ga AKIraka da

WATASHI wa itsumo SE-KAI no mono da kara

SORA ni KI ni hito ni

WATASHI wa MIZUKAra o NAgekakeru

yagate SE-KAI no YUTAkasa sono mono to naru tame ni

… WATASHI wa hito o yobu

suru to SE-KAI ga furiMUku

soshite WATASHI ga inaku naru

JAPANESE POETIC FORM II

During the Meiji period (1868–1912), serious poetic expression rediscovered the *tanka* form, as well as new forms. Poets were influenced by English and French poetry, especially the romantics and symbolists. They wrote *shintaishi*, New Style Poetry, and translated Western poetry into Japanese. As contacts with the West intensified, the themes shifted from the more static traditional themes of flowers, birds, and the moon to more intense and romantic content. Some poets even wrote about balloons, trains, bicycles, or telegraphy, while others used poetry to express philosophical or other humanistic thoughts. A feeling of unlimited possibilities was unleashed.

Poetry soon reverted to the more concise traditional forms, in particular to *tanka*. In the Meiji era, it was only natural that the imperial court would favor *tanka,* which dates back to the tenth-century Heian period, when tanka was officially adopted by the imperial court. To this day, on the Japanese New Year, there is a gathering around the imperial family at which each participant reads a *tanka* which he/she has composed. Reading tanka in this setting shows the link that exists between today's imperial family and the ancient imperial court where *tanka* was read in a similar manner. This is a reaffirmation of long-held tradition.

Poetry was not confined to *tanka*, for in the turbulent and complex era of the twentieth century poets sought to express various themes through various forms, including free verse.

A Picnic to the Earth

From *Concerning Love*   Tanikawa Shuntarō

Here let us jump rope together, here
Here let us eat onigiri together
Here let me love you
Your eyes reflect the blue of the sky
Your back will be stained by the green of the mugwort
Here let us learn the names of the stars

Being here, let us dream of all things far away
Here let us hunt for shellfish
From the sea of the dawn sky
Let us gather little starfish
At breakfast, let's discard them
and leave them to bring on the night

Here let me continue to say, I'm home
While you repeat, welcome back
Let us return home here many times
Here let us drink hot tea
Here let us sit together and for a while
Be blown upon by the cool breeze

Sixty-two Sonnets 62

From *Sixty-Two Sonnets*

Because the world loves me
(in a cruel way, and sometimes in
a tender way)
I can be alone forever

Even when first accorded an individual
I had only been listening to the sounds of the world
To me only simple sadness and joy are clear
Because I am always a creature of the world

To the sky, to trees, to people
I give myself
By and by to become the richness of the world itself

… I call to someone
And the world turns to look
And I disappear

Acknowledgments and Credits

The copyright holders of the following works have kindly granted permission for their reproduction or use as references in this book.

「メロン」江國香織（新潮文庫『こうばしい日々』新潮社　1995年）

『スピードに生きる』本田宗一郎（実業之日本社　1961年）

新潮文庫『やわらかな心をもつ』広中平祐・小澤征爾（新潮社　1984年）

集英社文庫『夜光時計』津村節子（集英社　1982年）

「怪傑主婦仮面」高橋源一郎（新潮文庫『中吊り小説』新潮社　1994年）

『サラダ記念日』俵万智（河出書房新社　1989年）

『たいのおかしら』「独自の研究」さくらももこ（集英社　1993年）

『ちびまる子ちゃん』三巻「まるちゃん自転車の練習をする」さくらももこ（集英社　1988年）

『ちびまる子ちゃん』三巻「ももこのほのほの劇場『みつあみのころ』」さくらももこ（集英社　1988年）

知的生きかた文庫 『もっともわかりやすい！日本経済入門』日下公人（三笠書房　1994年）

『日本人の周辺』加藤秀俊（講談社　1975年）

"Toward the Recycling Society" Hideaki Koyanagi　邦題「リサイクル社会の構築に向けて」「PACIFIC FRIEND」第24巻第2号（時事画報社　1996年）

『森の365日　宮崎学のフクロウ日記』宮崎学（理論社　1993年）

国語3 『夏の花』原民喜（光村図書出版株式会社　1987年）

「魔法の大金」星新一（新潮文庫『妄想銀行』新潮社　1995年）

株式会社　日本著作権輸出センター

『若葉のうた』金子光晴（勁草書房　1967年）

『愛について』「地球へのピクニック」『六十二のソネット』「六十二のソネット　62」谷川俊太郎（東京創元社　1953年）

This Kind of Woman: Ten Stories by Japanese Women Writers, 1960–1976. Translated and edited by Yukiko Tanaka and Elizabeth Hanson. Copyright 1982 by the Board of Trustees of the Leland Stanford Junior University. All rights reserved.

Photo credits:

Honda Motor Co., Ltd.: photos on page 60
Manabu Miyazaki: photo on page 218
ICRR (Institute for Cosmic Ray Research), The University of Tokyo: photo on page 222

「<ruby>読<rt>よ</rt></ruby>む」<ruby>日本語<rt>にほんご</rt></ruby>
The Japanese Written Word

1998年11月27日　第1刷発行

著　者　グレン・メルチンガー／ヘレン・カシャ
発行者　野間佐和子
発行所　講談社インターナショナル株式会社
　　　　〒112-8652 東京都文京区音羽 1-17-14
　　　　電話：03-3944-6493

印刷所　株式会社　平河工業社
製本所　株式会社　国宝社

INNOVATIVE WORKBOOKS FOR LEARNING JAPANESE KANA & KANJI

HIRAGANA GAMBATTE! *Deleece Batt*
ひらがながんばって！
An entertaining and effective illustrated workbook for younger learners. Clever mnemonic devices make learning the *hiragana* syllabary fun and easy.
Paperback, 112 pages, ISBN 4-7700-1797-9

KATAKANA GAMBATTE! *Deleece Batt*
カタカナがんばって！
This new, interactive workbook teaches *katakana* with *manga*-style art and nearly 100 mini-articles on Japanese society and culture.
Paperback, 112 pages, ISBN 4-7700-1881-9

TALK JAPANESE GAMBATTE! *Kazuhiko Nagatomo*
にほんごがんばって
Covers all the main elements of basic Japanese in twelve culture-based episodes, with interactive games and manga-style artwork.
Text; Paperback , 128 pages, ISBN 4-7700-1932-7 / Tape; 40-minute cassette tape, ISBN 4-7700-1933-5

LET'S LEARN HIRAGANA *Yasuko Kosaka Mitamura*
ひらがな
A well-tested, step-by-step program for individual study of the *hiragana* syllabary.
Paperback, 72 pages, ISBN 0-87011-709-2

LET'S LEARN KATAKANA *Yasuko Kosaka Mitamura*
カタカナ
The companion volume for learning the *katakana* syllabary used for foreign words and new terms.
Paperback, 88 pages, ISBN 0-87011-719-X

LET'S LEARN KANJI *Yasuko Kosaka Mitamura and Joyce Mitamura*
漢字を勉強しましょう
An innovative approach to learning the the basic components of kanji, demonstrating simply how a finite number of parts combine into a wide variety of characters.
Paperback, 272 pages, ISBN 4-7700-2068-6

KANJI FROM THE START *Martin Lam and Kaoru Shimizu*
はじめての漢字ブック
A basic-level reader which teaches *kanji* reading and writing skills in 12 graded lessons. Includes a grammar glossary and index, and Japanese-English and English-Japanese word lists.
Paperback, 372 pages, ISBN 4-7700-1936-X

THE COMPLETE GUIDE TO EVERYDAY KANJI
常用漢字完全ガイド
Yaeko S. Habein and Gerald B. Mathias
An exhaustive guide to the 1,945 most frequently used Sino-Japanese characters in the Japanese language.
Paperback, 344 pages, ISBN 4-7700-1509-7

KODANSHA INTERNATIONAL DICTIONARIES
Easy-to-use dictionaries designed for non-native learners of Japanese.

KODANSHA'S FURIGANA JAPANESE-ENGLISH DICTIONARY
ふりがな和英辞典

The essential dictionary for all students of Japanese.
• Furigana readings added to all kanji   • Comprehensive 16,000-word basic vocabulary
Vinyl flexibinding, 592 pages; ISBN 4-7700-1983-1

KODANSHA'S FURIGANA ENGLISH-JAPANESE DICTIONARY
ふりがな英和辞典

The companion to the essential dictionary for all students of Japanese.
• Furigana readings added to all kanji   • Comprehensive 14,000-word basic vocabulary
Vinyl flexibinding, 728 pages; ISBN 4-7700-2055-4

KODANSHA'S ROMANIZED JAPANESE-ENGLISH DICTIONARY
ローマ字和英辞典

A portable reference written for beginning and intermediate students.
• 16,000-word vocabulary.   • No knowledge of kanji necessary.
Vinyl flexibinding, 688 pages; ISBN 4-7700-1603-4

KODANSHA'S POCKET ROMANIZED JAPANESE-ENGLISH DICTIONARY
ポケット版　ローマ字和英辞典

Compact and convenient, an ideal pocket reference for beginning and intermediate students,
travelers, and business people.
• 10,000-word vocabulary.   • Numerous example sentences.
Paperback, 480 pages; ISBN 4-7700-1800-2

KODANSHA'S COMPACT KANJI GUIDE
常用漢英熟語辞典

A functional character dictionary that is both compact and comprehensive.
• 1,945 essential *joyo kanji*.   • 20,000 common compounds.   • Three indexes for finding kanji.
Vinyl flexibinding, 928 pages; ISBN 4-7700-1553-4

KODANSHA'S POCKET KANJI GUIDE
ポケット版　教育漢英熟語辞典

A handy, pocket-sized character dictionary.
• 1,006 *shin-kyoiku kanji*.   • 10,000 common compounds.   • Stroke order for individual characters.
Paperback, 576 pages; ISBN 4-7700-1801-0

EFFECTIVE JAPANESE USAGE GUIDE
日本語学習使い分け辞典

A concise, bilingual dictionary which clarifies the usage of frequently confused words and phrases.
• Explanations of 708 synonymous terms.   • Numerous example sentences.
Paperback, 768 pages; ISBN 4-7700-1919-X

THE MODERN ENGLISH-NIHONGO DICTIONARY
日本語学習英日辞典

The first truly bilingual dictionary designed exclusively for non-native learners of Japanese.
• Over 6,000 headwords   • Both standard Japanese with *furigana* and romanized orthography.
• Sample sentences provided for most entries   • Numerous explanatory notes and kanji guides.
Vinyl flexibinding, 1200 pages; ISBN 4-7700-2148-8